ALL NEW
SQUARE FOOT
GARDENING

3RD EDITION
FULLY UPDATED

COOL
SPRINGS
PRESS

ALL NEW
SQUARE FOOT
GARDENING

3RD EDITION
FULLY UPDATED

- MORE PROJECTS
- NEW SOLUTIONS
- GROW VEGETABLES ANYWHERE

MEL BARTHOLOMEW
WITH THE SQUARE FOOT GARDENING FOUNDATION

Brimming with creative inspiration, how-to projects, and useful information to enrich your everyday life, Quarto Knows is a favorite destination for those pursuing their interests and passions. Visit our site and dig deeper with our books into your area of interest: Quarto Creates, Quarto Cooks, Quarto Homes, Quarto Lives, Quarto Drives, Quarto Explores, Quarto Gifts, or Quarto Kids.

© 2018 Quarto Publishing Group USA Inc.

First Published in 2018 by Cool Springs Press, an imprint of The Quarto Group, 100 Cummings Center, Suite 265-D, Beverly, MA 01915, USA.
T (978) 282-9590 F (978) 283-2742 QuartoKnows.com

Cool Springs Press titles are also available at discount for retail, wholesale, promotional, and bulk purchase. For details, contact the Special Sales Manager by email at specialsales@quarto.com or by mail at The Quarto Group, Attn: Special Sales Manager, 100 Cummings Center, Suite 265-D, Beverly, MA 01915, USA.

10 9 8 7

ISBN: 978-0-7603-6285-3

Library of Congress Cataloging-in-Publication Data

Names: Bartholomew, Mel, author.
Title: All new square foot gardening : more projects, new solutions, grow
    vegetables anywhere / Mel Bartholomew with the Square Foot Gardening
    Foundation.
Description: 3rd edition, fully updated. | Minneapolis, Minnesota : Cool
    Springs Press, 2018. | Includes index.
Identifiers: LCCN 2018022926 | ISBN 9780760362853 (pb)
Subjects: LCSH: Vegetable gardening. | Square foot gardening.
Classification: LCC SB321 .B284 2018 | DDC 635--dc23
LC record available at https://lccn.loc.gov/2018022926

Acquiring Editor: Mark Johanson
Project Manager: Alyssa Bluhm
Art Director: Brad Springer
Layout: Amy Sly
New Photography: Paul Markert
Edition Editor: Bryan Trandem

Printed in China

DEDICATION

The Square Foot Gardening Foundation believes that everyone should enjoy fresh harvested produce without the exhaustive work. Gardening should be fun, simple, and easy to understand and create. We dedicate this book to all the Square Foot Gardening fans who over the years have moved this amazing method from the fringe into the mainstream, and to the foundation teachers and volunteers who have done so much to teach the method across America—and now across the world.

And we of course dedicate our most recent effort to Mel Bartholomew himself. His memory guides our every gardening effort and he remains an inspiration to us all.

In Mel's words, "Happy gardening, friends."

CONTENTS

FOREWORD

"End world hunger."

That's the mission of the Square Foot Gardening Foundation, articulated by Mel Bartholomew, the inventor of Square Foot Gardening and founder of the Square Foot Gardening Foundation. It's a tall order, but one we're already tackling, one square foot at a time.

As the Foundation enters our third decade in operation, we're continuing to spread Mel's original message of growing more food in less space with less waste (of time, materials, and money). Here's how we're doing it, at home and abroad, and how you can join us!

SFG AT HOME

Biting into a ripe, juicy tomato and tasting the flavor bursting on your tongue. The delight of pulling a carrot up and seeing its fat root ready for eating. Snipping lettuce leaves for a fresh spring salad. Knowing you have enough peppers to feed your family, sweet potatoes to store over the winter, and herbs to make your soups and stews flavorful. Not wondering whether you'll have to feed your family packaged food filled with preservatives. Motivation for growing your own depends on your situation. For some, it's all about flavor. For others, it's a matter of food security and regaining control of where your next meal is coming from, or knowing that you'll *have* a next meal.

Individuals interested in Square Foot Gardening can find certified instructors via our website to help them get started with gardening. We've debuted a new Square Foot Gardening Foundation website, www.squarefootgardening.org, and are working on quarterly newsletters to get home gardeners excited and connect them with the resources they need to get growing, including books, classes, and materials.

Our long-term goals include establishing Square Foot Gardening Foundation Learning Centers. These learning centers will encompass demonstration gardens, hands-on creations of Square Foot Gardens, and classes and workshops to help people learn about the environment, composting, pollinators, and a host of other sustainable practices.

In the meantime, we're working with organizations such as PlantPure Communities, which advocates a whole-food, plant-based lifestyle to help in reducing and preventing disease. We believe people will gravitate more and more towards a plant-based diet, and we're doing what we can to support that. Mel believed that making it easy to grow vegetables means:

- Less cooking (eating more salads)
- Less fuel (no trucks bringing your vegetables to you)
- Eating fresh
- No waste (composting your veggie scraps)

- Less trash
- Less water used
- Less groundwater pollution
- No fertilizers
- No plastic waste

All great reasons to grow your own!

SFG IN OUR COMMUNITIES

We believe Square Foot Gardening can bridge gaps between young and old, urban and rural, and individuals from different backgrounds. We envision Square Foot Gardens not only in classrooms, but also outside of houses of worship, as community gardens, at libraries, shelters, and assisted living communities. We plan to focus on tabletop gardening for those who use a wheelchair—especially our veterans.

Science tells us that people are happier when they spend time outside, and Square Foot Gardening is the perfect way for new gardeners to get their hands in the soil and see tangible results straight out of the gate. Biting into a radish straight from the garden or snacking on snap peas fresh from the vine creates an instant connection to our earth and virtually guarantees a new gardener is hooked for life. Cultivating more gardeners will benefit all of us, particularly when those gardeners are children, the stewards of our environment and our future.

To connect with kids, we're revising K-12 curricula to bring Square Foot Gardening into every classroom and homeschool arena in the United States. Wouldn't it be wonderful to help inner-city schools bring Square Foot Gardening to their rooftops and urban community gardens, and bring food security to their communities?

The Square Foot Gardening Foundation is already working with our Certified Instructors in YMCAs in New Jersey. They have put together a successful summer camp program that is serving as a pilot program that will soon expand. We would love to expand to other states and groups, such as the Boy and Girl Scouts of America.

SFG INTERNATIONAL INITIATIVES

Food security is not just an issue in our own homes, it is something people struggle with the world over. We have proof that Square Foot Gardening can help people in impoverished countries feed themselves while teaching about the environment and nutrition. This type of gardening empowers citizens (especially women) to provide for their families and their communities. Through international organizations, including Farm4Real and Cultiva International, Square Foot Gardening is changing people's lives. We're so excited to grow our resources and funding to help support those efforts.

From South Africa to Haiti to Guatemala, certified instructors, humanitarian organizations, and individuals are making a difference with Square Foot Gardening. A big part of founder Mel's original vision was to teach people how to take care of themselves through gardening, and we're continuing to build on that.

CHANGING THE WORLD ONE SQUARE FOOT AT A TIME

We're delighted to introduce the newest book in the Square Foot Gardening family. In *All New Square Foot Gardening, 3rd Edition*, you will not find any major or even significant changes to the method Mel developed and perfected over the years. Because, frankly, it did not need improving. But we believe we have made some extremely helpful changes to the way the method is presented, making it much easier for readers to navigate through the steps and create an efficient plan for putting the Square Foot approach into action. And we have included some very helpful information about new products and clever solutions, along with some fabulous new illustrations and photographs. The result, we think, is a book that takes a proven method and cuts a new path that gets you directly to the information you need to understand it.

We hope this new edition will encourage you to grow your own vegetables at home, share your love of gardening with your community groups, and inspire new Square Foot Gardeners.

We look forward to meeting you as we travel around to see Square Foot Gardening in action in the United States and overseas. Come say hi on social media and visit our website, www.squarefootgardening.org.

Happy gardening!

Laura & Steve Bartholomew
The Square Foot Gardening Foundation

A Square Foot Garden is not only efficient but a treat for the eyes.

INTRODUCTION

Mel Bartholomew began developing his method of gardening relatively late in life, after he retired in the mid-1970s from his first career as an engineer. It was born to some degree out of Mel's pointed disagreement with the most traditional gardening methods that didn't make practical sense to him. There's irony to the fact that this man who made growing "in a box" so famous developed his methods by thinking entirely "outside the box" when it came to rebelling against conventional wisdom. It is perhaps this attitude of the stubborn revolutionary that makes the Square Foot Gardening method so very popular to this day.

When Mel began gardening in about 1975, it was simply a hobby for a newly retired fellow to pursue, a chance to get out in the fresh air and mingle with other hobbyists. At that time, of course, vegetable gardening was a rather utilitarian activity in which large rectangular plots of ground were churned up, fertilized, planted in long rows spaced about 3 feet apart, and regularly watered. And weeded. And weeded. And weeded.

Mel's analytical mind, bolstered by a common-sense attitude, soon picked up on many limitations to traditional gardening methods—reasons why the activity was neither as enjoyable nor as productive as it might be. Among the questions he asked:

- Why do gardeners grow in rows spaced 3 feet apart? That space is nothing more than room for weeds to grow.

- Why do gardeners always grow more food than they can possibly eat? Almost every gardener wastes food by growing too much.

- Why do vegetable gardeners plant such long rows? It takes up too much space.

- Why do they fertilize so much? It is costly and inefficient.

- Why is it necessary to weed constantly? All that work spoils the fun.

Over the next few years, Mel systematically found solutions to all these problems and more. And as his method was perfected, more and more people wanted to learn how he did it. Mel soon was in full swing in his second career as a community activist, lecturer, and author, promoting efficient and enjoyable methods of vegetable gardening.

The insights Mel developed would revolutionize gardening forever:

Vegetables can be tightly spaced. Vegetables can be planted mere inches apart and still can grow quite productively, and you can get far more produce in a limited space than people realize. A lot of produce can be grown in a very small space. In fact, a single 4 × 4-foot raised bed subdivided into 16 squares using dividers can grow a lot of the produce a normal family needs. Simple succession planting—introducing a new crop when the previous crop is done—allows a single 4 × 4 Square Foot Garden to make a huge dent in your grocery bill.

Weeding is not necessary. The reason weeds grow so rampantly is usually because too much fertilizer is applied—and because it is often dumped on ground that is not even planted with vegetables. Instead of churning up a huge garden bed and tilling in massive amounts of fertilizer that then stimulates weeds, Mel saw that confining vegetables to a 4 × 4 Square Foot Garden filled with controlled growing mix can eliminate most weeds and make it extremely easy and quick to pull them when they do appear.

Garden "dirt" is not a very good medium for growing produce. It contains too many weed seeds and not enough natural nutrients. You can create your own growing medium that is far better for growing vegetables than ordinary garden soil. "Mel's Mix" was born out of experimentation to find the perfect growing medium.

Traditional gardening methods are wasteful. You can grow better produce in less garden space, planting fewer seeds, using less fertilizer, watering less often, and with almost no weeding necessary. Rather than planting scads of seeds over long rows, then thinning out the seedlings once they started crowding each other, Mel recognized that very careful planting of seeds right from the start could eliminate a great deal of work and could make a single pack of seeds last for several growing seasons.

Similarly, Mel saw that careful application of water where it was needed in a small, carefully planted Square Foot Garden was infinitely more efficient than dumping untold gallons over an enormous vegetable garden covering most of your yard.

ADVANTAGE TO BEGINNERS

Although the so-called experts were slow to embrace the Square Foot Gardening method, novices quickly learned that it was both much easier and more productive than traditional gardening methods. That, of course, makes it a lot more fun too. Mel's vision of Square Foot Gardening has now been around for 40-plus years, yet it remains as revolutionary today as it was when he first created it. There are still some "experts" who look down upon doing anything

the easy, fun way, but there are also millions of real-life gardeners who enthusiastically practice Square Foot Gardening in exactly the way that Mel would want. We humbly smile and listen to experts trumpet the virtues of row gardening, while harvesting enormous quantities of delicious vegetables to feed our families and friends.

Have a look at some of the very clever ways in which everyday gardeners have used the Square Foot Gardening method.

SQUARE FOOT GARDENING IN PRACTICE

↑ Don't discount the sheer appeal of a Square Foot Garden as a landscape feature. The various shades and colors are nourishing in many ways.

→ This stacked pyramid garden is perfect in an urban space. Ordinary concrete block is used to edge the garden, with the voids in the blocks used for additional planting.

→ When gardening with kids, downsizing to a smaller box (2 × 2 or 3 × 3) will make it easier for the little ones to tend their garden.

↓ The small size and high density of a Square Foot Garden makes it the perfect method for family gardening with kids of all ages. Raised beds are also ideal for seniors, for whom accessibility can be a challenge in a traditional single-row garden.

↑ Truth be told, a Square Foot Garden need not be "square" at all, provided the area of the grid squares is about the same. This gardener has created a visually striking pyramid box with triangular planting spaces.

← A raised bed like this one can be fitted with a grid to make a perfect Square Foot Garden for a gardener in a wheelchair.

In this major Square Foot Gardening setup, the gardener has adapted the classic square box into narrower 3 × 7 shapes to take advantage of the space. Each box is equipped with a standard conduit trellis frame, some with traditional nylon netting, others with simple strands of vertical twine.

A serious Square Foot Gardening practice can easily be integrated into an ordinary suburban landscape as part of the decorative border to the yard. Here, the owner has built a series of classic 4 × 4 boxes, plus two narrow boxes to take advantage of a space near the privacy fence.

This garden is being built with convenient raised-bed kits made of PVC plastic with corner connectors.

In this rural setting, a gardener has created a major operation using nothing but Square Foot Gardening boxes, each equipped with a classic conduit trellis.

Equipped with a trellis, a Square Foot Garden can support climbing vegetables and make a strong vertical statement as an element of the landscape design.

A YEAR OF SQUARE FOOT GARDENING PRODUCE

On the following page, you'll see all the produce you can grow in one Square Foot Garden in a moderate climate with a regular growing season. If you live in the South, you might get even more food than this. Our 16 grid squares are planted as follows.

This Square Foot Gardening setup is a standard 4 × 4 box. The back side is mounted with a classic conduit-and-net trellis. It was planted with maximum diversity in mind, with one different type of vegetable in each grid:

(1) pole beans, 8 seeds/plants

(2) climbing peas, 8 seeds/plants

(3) cucumber, 2 plants

(4) musk melon, 1 plant

(5) tomato, 1 plant

(6) green pepper, 1 plant

(7) eggplant, 1 plant

(8) potato, 1 plant

(9) head cabbage, 1 plant

(10) broccoli, 1 plant

(11) cauliflower, 1 plant

(12) curly kale, 1 plant

(13) leaf lettuce, 4 plants

(14) onions, 16 sets

(15) radishes, 16 seeds/plants

(16) leaf spinach, 9 seeds/plants

Some of these vegetables bore fruit only one time, while others were constant producers, and a couple of the squares were replanted for second harvest at midseason.

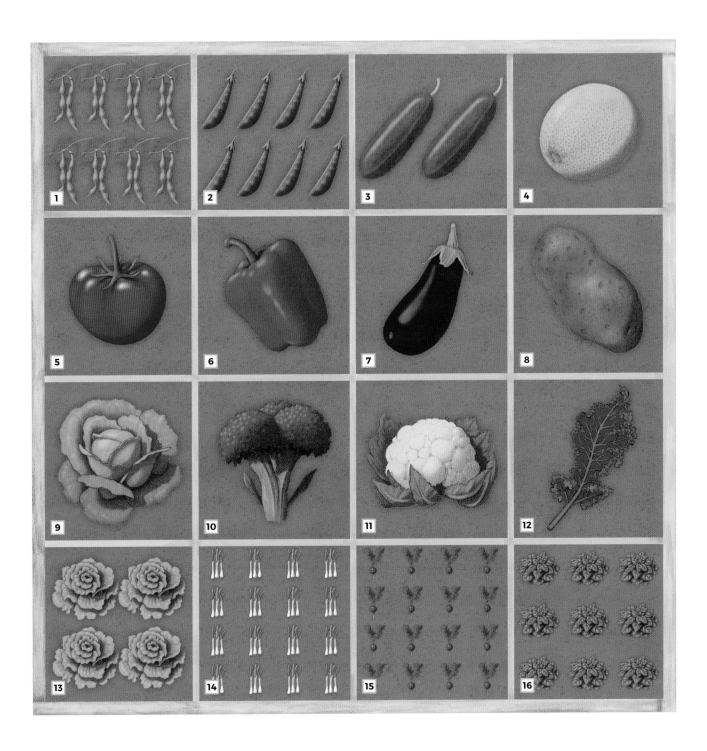

THE HARVEST FROM ONE 4 × 4 SQUARE FOOT GARDEN IN A SINGLE GROWING SEASON

- 2 gallons green beans
- 2 gallons peas
- 18 cucumbers
- 4 muskmelons or cantaloupes
- 18 tomatoes
- 12 green peppers
- 10 eggplants
- 8 potatoes
- 1-3 heads cabbage
- 1-4 heads broccoli
- 1-4 heads cauliflower
- 4 gallons kale
- 8 shocks lettuce
- 16 onions
- 48 radishes
- 2 gallons spinach

SQUARE FOOT GARDENING

IN MEL'S WORDS

It all started in 1975 after my retirement from my engineering consulting business in New Jersey. To celebrate, I moved my family to a waterfront home on the North Shore of Long Island. After a year of rebuilding the house and another year of landscaping and improving the grounds, I decided to take up gardening as a hobby. My first step was to attend a lecture on composting given by a local environmental group. It was a warm spring day in April—a great time to be out in the garden. A small group milled around at the advertised meeting point, but no instructor ever showed up. So, rather than disband, I suggested to the group that we each share our knowledge with each other and tell what little we knew about composting. We had a wonderful time and actually learned a little bit from each other. As we prepared to leave, someone asked me, "Can we do this again next week?" And I said, "Sure, why not?" Thus began my new career of teaching gardening while I was still a novice myself.

The next step was organizing a community garden for this same environmental group. I found some land and convinced the town to cut down all the weeds and fence it in. A local farmer delivered two truckloads of well-rotted manure, and, after the ground was all fertilized and plowed up, we laid out plots and aisles and opened for business. All the spaces were quickly taken by people in the community, and everyone started with great enthusiasm. Because most of the participants were novices who didn't have a garden at home, they were enthusiastic about obtaining instruction and insights on gardening.

So, I initiated a Saturday-morning gardening workshop and presented information on a different subject each week while everyone sat around on bales of hay, listening. I was teaching basic single-row gardening because that's all anyone knew back then. The local county agricultural agent helped out and everything went well until about midsummer. It was about then that our once-enthusiastic gardeners stopped coming out to the garden. However, the weeds kept coming—and growing! Pretty soon the place was overgrown and looked a mess.

I was discouraged and thought I had better do some research to figure out why we had failed, so I visited many backyard gardens. What I found was a big space way out in the farthest corner of the yard, about as close to the neighbor's property line as possible. In most cases, these individual gardens were also filled with overgrown weeds. The first red flag went up in my mind, indicating that there was something wrong with traditional single-row gardening. I thought about all the conventional gardening practices we'd been taught and began to question the efficiency of each. Gardening shouldn't be a lot of hard work. Gardening should be fun! There was something wrong here.

This led to further questions. Why do the planting instructions on packages of seeds direct the gardener to pour out an entire packet along a row, only to have you later go back and tear out 95 percent of the seeds you planted once they sprout? Why use up an entire packet of seeds for every row you plant? Isn't that rather wasteful? Why would they instruct us to plant that way? Who's in charge here, anyway?

Row gardening is the traditional way, but it is wasteful, inefficient, and a whole lot of back-breaking work—everything that Square Foot Gardening is not.

I soon realized that I had a lot of questions with very few answers, so I traveled all over the country seeking out the best experts: agricultural college professors, county agricultural agents, garden writers, radio and TV gardening personalities, gardening publishers, book writers, garden clubs—all those who were supposedly knowledgeable in the field of gardening. I sought answers to all the gardening questions I had, but, no matter where I traveled throughout the country, from Maine to California, I kept receiving the same answer. Can you imagine what that answer was? It soon became apparent that the only reason traditional single-row gardening methods continued to exist was "Because that's the way we've always done it!" Right then and there I said, "I'm going to invent a better way to garden."

CHAPTER

2

THE 10 BASICS AND 8 STEPS OF SQUARE FOOT GARDENING

Mel Bartholomew was something of a rebel, an engineer turned garden revolutionary who challenged many aspects of conventional gardening wisdom and, over time, developed some core innovations that formed the basis of the Square Foot Gardening Method. He also continued to innovate throughout his life. The original Square Foot Gardening method became *All New Square Foot Gardening*, which became the second edition of *All New Square Foot Gardening*, and today—with the information gleaned from hundreds of instructors and many thousands of home gardeners—the innovation continues with this third edition.

A Square Foot Garden can grow an impressive number of plants.

Among the core innovations that make today's Square Foot Gardening methods so very different from traditional gardening methods are the following. You can think of these as the 10 principles of Square Foot Gardening:

1. Plant densely. Don't waste space. You can grow a *lot* of produce in much less space that you dreamed possible. A huge row garden just isn't necessary—placing a few Square Foot Garden beds in a relatively small space can be more productive than a large row garden that occupies a good portion of your yard.

2. Grow up. The greatest productivity comes by growing *up*, not out. A variety of easy-to-build trellis structures allow vining vegetables to use the vertical plane rather than sprawling out and taking up space, as they do in a traditional row garden.

3. Mel's Mix, not garden soil. You don't need garden soil at all to grow great vegetables. You not only *don't need* it but

shouldn't use it. The best results come if you make your own growing medium—the fabulous formula Mel Bartholomew created, which we call Mel's Mix.

Mel's Mix is the key to the productivity for which Square Foot Gardening is famous.

A Square Foot Garden will be easier to tend and harvest if you position it close to your home. It is also easier to admire if it is closer to the home.

4. Garden close to your home. Gardens are more efficient when planted close to your house, not in a distant plot. It's human nature to pay attention to what is close by hand, and Square Foot Gardens need to be close to your house when you can admire them and tend them easily, rather than carrying tools out to a distant garden and lugging produce back to the house.

With Mel's Mix, a planting box just 6 inches deep is enough to grow great herbs and vegetables.

Individual boxes planted about 3 feet apart make for a very efficient and productive vegetable garden that won't gobble up your entire yard.

Most of the nutrients needed by a Square Foot Garden are provided by the rich compost that is one component of Mel's Mix.

5. Grow shallow. Raised beds don't have to be large and deep: a mere 6 inches of growing medium is all it takes for most crops. Gone are the days of laboriously digging and double-digging a row garden to mix in soil amendments to improve the soil.

6. Fertilizer is not needed. Mel's Mix includes a rich mixture of different composts, and in its first year provides all the nutrients that plants need.

7. Keep aisles between boxes narrow. Rather than long rows, a vegetable garden is most efficient planted in small boxes with aisles set about 3 feet apart. The traditional practice of planting long rows with wide, empty spaces between them just creates more ground in which weeds can grow. There is no reason to take up a huge amount of your yard for your garden.

It's not necessary to randomly scatter seeds, then thin them to the desired spacing once they sprout. If you plant seeds carefully to the final spacing you want, a single seed pack can last several growing seasons.

8. Be stingy with seeds. Rather than planting lots of seeds, then thinning them out to the desired spacing, you can plant very carefully to make maximum use of a seed packet. Mel was very big on economy and efficiency, and he found ways to make a single packet of seeds last for two or more growing seasons by being very careful with planting.

9. Plant in squares. Planting in carefully arranged 1-foot squares is the most efficient way to plant—simplifying both

A grid defines a Square Foot Garden, making it easy to plant and visualize your harvest.

planting and care and maximizing yield. Mel viewed this as one of the very important basics of his method. The grids are key to planting efficiently and rotating in new crops when the first crop has produced its bounty. And by planting with diversity—many different types of plants intermingled in a single box—you eliminate many of the disease problems that can plague a traditional garden.

As early crops ripen and are harvested, that square can be replaced with new plantings of the same crop or with different vegetables.

10. Rotate crops. Rotation planting gets the maximum yield from your garden. The yield from a single 4 × 4-foot SFG will surprise you, and the reason is that those many of the squares can be planted at least twice in a gardening season—either with two successive crops of the same vegetable or swapping out a new crop for late-season produce.

In practice, these 10 principles of Square Foot Gardening become the core of an eight-step process by which you can garden with remarkable efficiency. The first steps can be done well before the growing season starts—and don't we all like to dream and plan during the late-winter and early-spring months, when we are just itching to get out in the garden again?

STEP 1: PLANNING YOUR GARDEN

In Chapter 3, you'll learn how to plan your boxes to provide the amount of produce you're likely to need. Mel Bartholomew agonized when he saw waste of any kind—land, water, or seeds—but nothing made him more frustrated than to see perfectly good produce wasted because there was too much of it to eat. So, a very important part of Square Foot Gardening is determining exactly how many vegetables to plant, which then dictates how many Square Foot Garden boxes you need. A single Square Foot Garden square can hold as few as one plant, for large vegetables such a cabbage, or as many as 16 for small vegetables, such

as radishes or carrots. Some larger plants may require more than one square. A single square can also be doubled up to grow two vegetables in two separate rotation plantings in some cases. For example, spinach is typically an early-season vegetable, and its square can be replanted with a fall crop after the early spinach finished its run.

By the time this planning step is done, you'll have a pretty good idea of just how many garden squares you'll need to grow the produce you want. The winter months are a good time to start thinking about this, because you may want to order seeds well in advance of the growing season.

STEP 2: LAYING OUT A SQUARE FOOT GARDEN

In Chapter 4, you'll get the information you need to plan the shape and configuration of your Square Foot Garden boxes and map out where they will be located in your yard or on your patio. Understanding sunlight patterns and the size and shape of available spaces will help you determine what shape your boxes need to take and where they should be positioned. The shape of your yard may be conducive to the classic 4 × 4-foot garden boxes, or maybe you have narrow spaces along a fence that are better suited to 2 × 8-foot boxes.

This step will also give you a sense of where to position trellises within your square foot boxes, because you want to configure and position the boxes so that plants growing vertically on trellises don't cast shade on other plants in the box. In most climates, this means the trellises will be positioned on the north side of the garden boxes as they sit in your yard. Issues such as accessibility and access to water can also play a part in where you position your boxes.

This is another planning stage that you can do in the late winter or early spring. By the time this layout step is done, you'll be ready to build your Square Foot Garden boxes.

STEP 3: BUILDING BOXES AND GRIDS

Square Foot Gardening can be considered a form of raised-bed gardening, but it is raised-bed gardening with a notable difference. Because of the special growing medium used, a Square Foot Garden bed can be a mere 6 inches deep and still grow fabulous vegetables. Chapter 5 provides instructions for not only the basic 4 × 4-foot box that is 6 inches deep but also a variety of other box shapes and sizes, including an easy-to-build table-height Square Foot Garden that is ideal for older gardeners who may have trouble stooping down to tend a ground-level box. Also included are instructions for the all-important grids that make a Square Foot Garden different from a run-of-the-mill raised bed. These grids are crucial to keeping your Square Foot Garden organized for planting and harvesting, and without a grid, a Square Foot Garden is just . . . well, it's just *not* a Square Foot Garden.

The standard 4 × 4 classic Square Foot Garden box built from 1 × 6 lumber is very lightweight and easily moved, so some people who are eager to get to physical activity can choose to build their boxes in a garage or workshop long before the weather warms and then move them into place once the weather is suitable. They can also be built right on the spot where the boxes will be positioned, but it's important to have this work done by the time planting time rolls around, because you don't want to waste a moment of the growing season.

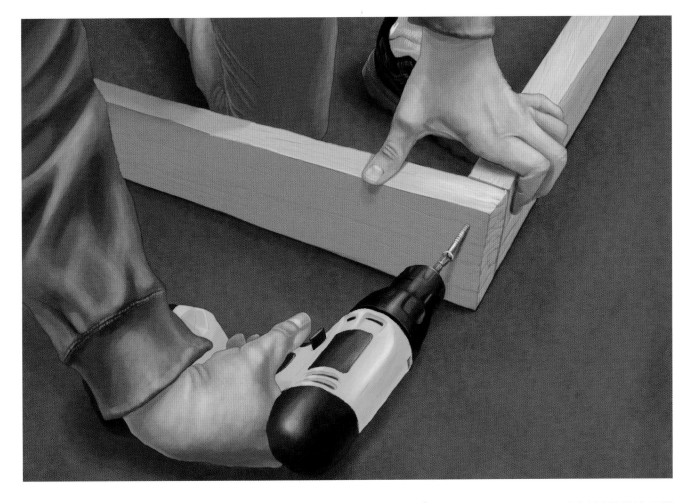

STEP 4: BUILDING BOX ACCESSORIES

A plain, ordinary box with grid is just fine, of course, but getting maximum productivity and convenience out of your Square Foot Garden may mean that you'll want to add trellises, protective covers, or other accessories. After completing work on the boxes themselves, now's the time to consider the add-ons you might want. Mel was quite forceful in his belief that all vining crops—even things like melons and pumpkins—should be grown vertically when planted in a Square Foot Garden, and many years of experience have borne this out. Chapter 6 gives you instructions for the classic Square Foot Garden trellis, but also included are step-by-step instructions for trellis variations; protective structures to guard your garden against wind, cold, or animal pests; an archway to span the aisle between Square Foot Garden boxes; and a plant-support netting structure.

This too is a step that gardeners can do before the growing season begins. Having your accessories ready to go as soon as the weather is warm enough to fill your square foot boxes with growing medium will let you take full advantage of the entire growing season.

STEP 5: CREATING MEL'S MIX GROWING MEDIUM

One of the most important steps in the entire Square Foot Gardening process is creating a special growing medium to provide the porousness, water-retention properties, and nutrients plants require. This now-classic mixture is widely known as Mel's Mix, and Chapter 7 explains why it is so important. This simple but remarkable combination of organic peat moss, coarse vermiculite, and a blend of compost varieties, all mixed together in equal proportions, is the very best of growing mediums. It is free of weeds; it is free of pathogens, such as fungi, bacteria, and viruses; and it provides perfect nutritional support for nearly all plants.

Field tests have shown that one batch of Mel's Mix can continue in use for nearly 10 years before it needs to be replaced, provided you replenish the compost as it breaks down and is consumed by plants. Chapter 7 both explains the magic of this mixture and shows you how to create it—and it provides some options for gardeners who may have trouble finding some of the ingredients.

STEP 6: PLANTING YOUR GARDEN

Chapter 8 provides all the details of the oh-so-efficient planting practices used in Square Foot Gardening. This is a method in which no seeds are wasted and Mel's Mix is so nutritious that transplant seedlings almost never fail to thrive. Most startling to people who have not gardened by this method before is just how fast their vegetables sprout and shoot upward to their adult sizes. Also unique to this method of gardening is the very tight spacing of plants—another thing that's made possible by Mel's Mix. This growing medium is so friable and loose that plants can thrive even when spaced very close together. Finally, the Square Foot Garden method intermingles different species in adjacent grid squares, and this diversity means that disease problems rarely devastate an entire garden, the way they can in a traditional row garden.

Planting is not a one-and-done proposition with a Square Foot Garden. Getting maximum efficiency out of a Square Foot Garden means that as one crop ripens and is harvested, you'll immediately replant another. In favorable climates, some gardeners can get three, or even four, plantings in a long growing season.

 IN MEL'S WORDS

I have fun when teaching a class or seminar by asking, "How many seeds do you think are in a packet of leaf lettuce?" Some guess 50, 100, or 200, and some even venture a guess as high as 500 seeds. I then astound them by saying that I once opened a packet and counted them, and I found that there were well over 1,000 seeds! Why plant hundreds of seeds in one long row and then turn around when they sprout and thin them out to one plant for every 6 inches? It's all a terrible waste of seeds and time and work—all useless, unnecessary work. If you're growing lettuce, for example, and the seed packet says to thin plants to 6 inches apart in the row, how far away does the next row really need to be? The answer, of course, is 6 inches—not 3 feet!

STEP 7: MAINTAINING YOUR GARDEN

In Chapter 9 you'll learn all about the efficient techniques for watering and weeding your Square Foot Garden, as well as inspecting it and tending to any pest problems and diseases caused by fungal agents, bacteria, or viruses. If you are familiar with traditional row gardening, though, you'll be pleasantly surprised by just how easy it is to maintain a Square Foot Garden. Mel's Mix growing medium holds water much better than garden soil, making watering chores a breeze, but for even more convenience we've provided you with two options for creating your own very efficient automatic watering systems for your garden boxes. Weeding is equally easy with a Square Foot Garden, because the Mel's Mix you start with has no weed seeds in it, and later invaders that arrive on the wind are easily removed after they sprout by simply pulling them from the loose growing medium.

Make no bones about it: Mel Bartholomew and we at the Square Foot Gardening Foundation promote a fully organic, green method of gardening—one that strongly frowns on the use of chemicals and pesticides. Where treatment is necessary, we recommend you use organic solutions at every opportunity. Fortunately, Square Foot Gardens are typically very healthy places that diseases rarely visit.

STEP 8: HARVESTING

As your crops ripen, it will be time to harvest them, the topic of Chapter 10. Given the nature of the diverse planting pattern we use with the Square Foot Gardening method, this pleasure occurs all through the garden season, as cool-season leaf vegetables, such as leaf lettuce, spinach, and herbs, may ripen faster than they do in a conventional garden. Fruit crops such as tomatoes and peppers will be ready to harvest by midsummer when growing in the perfect growing medium of Mel's Mix, and the harvest reaches a pinnacle in fall, when vine crops, such as winter squash and melons, ripen on the vine as they grow up the trellis on the back of your Square Foot Garden. Key to the enormous productivity a Square Foot Garden provides in a very small space is the practice of replanting each square as it is harvested. In some cases, this means planting the same crop a second time—a second crop of leaf lettuce, for example. In other cases, you might swap out the square for an entirely different crop.

In the final measure, harvesting a Square Foot Garden is really not much different from harvesting a traditional garden—except for the fact that it's easier, it's more fun, and it provides a lot more produce in a smaller space. Which means, actually, that it's quite a lot different after all.

IN MEL'S WORDS

The 10 Commandments of Square Foot Gardening

I. Thou shalt not waste space with a large row garden.

II. Thou shalt not use or dig up your existing soil.

III. Thou shalt not use a hoe, shovel, or rototiller.

IV. Thou shalt not waste seeds by planting, then thinning.

V. Thou shalt not remove your Square Foot Garden "grid."

VI. Thou shalt not use any fertilizer, insecticides, or pesticides.

VII. Thou shalt not plant more than you can harvest or take care of.

VIII. Thou shalt not waste water by hosing, sprinkling, or heavy irrigation.

IX. Thou shalt not fail to grow all your vine crops on a vertical support.

X. Thou shalt not fail to replant each square as it is harvested.

3

PLANNING YOUR SQUARE FOOT GARDEN

As you get ready to be a Square Foot Gardener, there are two important planning stages you need to complete. First, you need to decide which vegetables to plant, and how many of them. This will help you figure out how many squares you need and how many boxes are necessary to accommodate them. This first part of the planning process is the subject of this chapter.

The second planning stage is to decide what shape your Square Foot Garden boxes need to be, and where they should be positioned within your yard. The second half of the planning process will be covered in Chapter 4, "Laying Out Your Square Foot Garden."

Choosing the vegetables you want to grow is the first step in planning a Square Foot Garden.

HOW MUCH IS ENOUGH?

Figuring out just how many squares and how many Square Foot Garden boxes you need is difficult for beginners, because Square Foot Gardening is such a productive method of gardening that it's common for newcomers to plant far more produce than they can use—even if they have friends and neighbors who can make use of the excess. It's further complicated by the fact that everyone is different in terms of their consumption of vegetables. Here are some basic rules of thumb, though, to guide your decisions.

If you're figuring a SFG for an adult, remember that:

- One 4 × 4 Square Foot Garden box (16 square feet) will supply enough produce to make a salad for one adult every day of the growing season.

- Add a second 4 × 4 box and you'll supply the daily supper vegetables for that person for each day of the growing season.

- Adding a third 4 × 4 box will supply that person with extra vegetables to be used for preserving, special crops, showing off, or giving away.

So, each adult needs one, two, or three boxes with 16 squares each, depending on how much produce they can use. In other words, 16 square feet, 32 square feet, or 48 square feet.

If you're figuring a SFG for a child, remember that:

- One 3 × 3 Square Foot Garden box (9 square feet) will supply enough produce to make a salad for one child every day of the growing season.

- Adding a second 3 × 3 box will supply supper vegetables for that child every day.

- Just one more 3 × 3 box will supply the child with extra of everything for show-and-tell or science projects at school, special crops, showing off, or giving away.

So, each child needs one, two, or three small boxes of 3 × 3, depending on how much they will eat. In square feet, that's 9, 18, or 27 square feet of grid space.

A SQUARE FOOT GARDEN FOR A TYPICAL FAMILY

Any way you look at it, a Square Foot Garden is considerably more efficient than a traditional garden. According to homeowner surveys, the average conventional row garden measures 20 feet wide by 35 feet long—700 square feet. To grow the same amount of produce, a Square Foot Garden requires about 20 percent of that space. And not only do get you get this space savings, but a Square Foot Garden requires a fraction of the work, a fraction of the water, and a fraction of the fencing and other supplies required by a traditional row garden.

IN MEL'S WORDS

I think the easiest way for most gardeners to plan out their crops is to just draw a big square with a grid of 16 squares inside to represent each Square Foot Garden box. Then all you do is label the squares with what you want to grow in them. To start out, work in pencil because you may need to adjust your plans. This gives you the chance to play with different combinations of plantings and ensure what we call "selective separations"—growing the same crops in different boxes so that anything affecting one square won't easily spread and affect another crop nearby. It's wise to label the squares with the number of plants per square foot, so you can get a sense of how full the overall Square Foot Garden box will be. You can also graph out different versions of the same box to show the transition plantings as you will move through the seasons. (Some people even color-code the squares!) Keep an eye out for the basics, such as putting taller plants on the north side of the box. Put plants that require a lot of attention, grooming, or harvesting (such as bush beans) near the outside and low-maintenance plants (such as radishes and carrots, which you can plant and pull) in the inside squares.

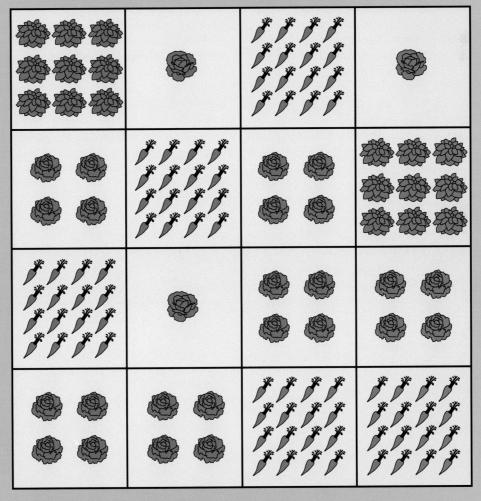

Once you lay out your Square Foot Garden box with crops, it's easy to see just how much bounty one box can provide.

HOW MANY VEGETABLES IN EACH SQUARE?

Figuring how many total squares you need is one thing, but there is also the issue of planning what vegetables will go into those squares, and how many squares will be devoted to each type of vegetable. Part of this determination is a matter of personal preference, of course—if you don't like brussels sprouts, then you won't plant any of them. But it is also a matter of knowing the density at which each vegetable can be planted and whether the time required to ripen those vegetables will allow for you to plant the square more than once in a growing season. The appendix information on page 258 will give you full information on seed-to-harvest times and on how closely the seeds or transplants can be planted, but for now it's important to know that in Square Foot Gardening we divide different vegetables into four classes: Extra Large, Large, Medium, and Small. Your planting density will depend on what class the vegetable falls into. Extra Large vegetables generally can be planted only one per square (or sometimes even one plant for two grid squares); Large vegetables are planted four per square; Medium vegetables are planted nine per square; and Small vegetables are planted sixteen per square.

WHICH VEGETABLES IN WHICH SQUARES?

The Square Foot Gardening method is built on three premises that affect how you organize the vegetables within the grids of the Square Foot Garden box.

First, Square Foot Gardening makes use of the vertical dimension whenever possible. So, when you are growing climbing, vining plants—such as pole beans, cucumbers, squash, melons, or even tomatoes—these should always be planted on a row of outside squares where you can install a trellis made of conduit and nylon netting.

Second, efficient Square Foot Gardening requires that you "recycle" each square as its vegetable is harvested,

HOW MANY SQUARES?

Here is a convenient worksheet to help you figure out exactly how many squares you need. You can use this chart to calculate the number of full boxes or individual squares needed for each member of the family.

NUMBER OF BOXES OR SQUARES	SALAD	SUPPER	EXTRA	TOTAL
Parents				
Grandparents				
Brother				
Sister				
Pets				
Other				
			Total Squares	

replanting it for a second harvest. Some vegetables, of course, continue to produce throughout the growing season and will occupy their squares for the entire season. But for those that ripen and are then harvested within a short window, such as beets or spinach, make sure to plant them in grids that will be accessible for replanting—don't bury them in the middle squares where it will be more difficult to replant.

Finally, the Square Foot Gardening method recommends that you create deliberate diversity in your garden by not planting adjoining grid squares with the same vegetables. Although this isn't true of all vegetables, many are susceptible to species-specific diseases, and if you plant three or four adjoining grid squares with the same or related species, there is a chance that they will all be affected. This is especially true of vegetables in the nightshade family, such as tomatoes, eggplant, and peppers. While many gardeners plant several types of these vegetables, it is better practice to keep them as far apart as possible so as to avoid the possible transmission of diseases specific to them. You may like tomatoes well enough to want three or four plants, but if possible, plant them in different square foot beds. This holds true pretty universally—avoid planting the same vegetable in adjoining squares.

NONVEGETABLE SQUARE FOOT GARDENS?

Once you become a true square foot enthusiast, you might want to consider a purely ornamental garden. The Square Foot Garden is an excellent method for growing beautiful flower gardens if you are a fan of cutting flowers and flower arranging. Few gardening methods work better for annual flowers or bulbs.

Also, as a general rule of thumb you should try to organize your plants within the grids so that tall plants will not overshadow shorter ones. Where feasible, this will mean that your vertical trellis plants and tall species, such as tomatoes, are best placed on the northern side of the box, with intermediate plants occupying the center grids and smaller plants toward the front, facing south. (The rules are, of course, different in the Southern Hemisphere, where the north side gets the most sun exposure.)

MAPPING YOUR SQUARES

There is a lot of information to consider when planning your Square Foot Garden, complicated by the fact that this style of gardening is so productive. Mel Bartholomew was very concerned about not wasting produce, and we at the Square Foot Gardening Foundation are the same way. An easy way to plan your Square Foot Garden boxes is to map them out to ensure that you don't end up with more produce than you can possibly use. Below, you'll find a sample mapping chart, along with a blank template you can use to sketch out the produce that's likely to result from your garden. Remember that many vegetables ripen in a short enough time that will allow you to plant a square at least a second time, and perhaps even a third time if you live in a climate zone with a very long growing season. It will be something of a guess to estimate how many fruits will be produced by repeat-bearing vegetables, such as tomatoes or peppers, but just remember that this garden will be more productive than any you have planted before. Of course, if your Square Foot Garden box is a different size with a different number of squares than the standard version, you can easily adapt this map for different variations.

FIRST HARVEST FROM EACH SQUARE: CLASSIC SFG

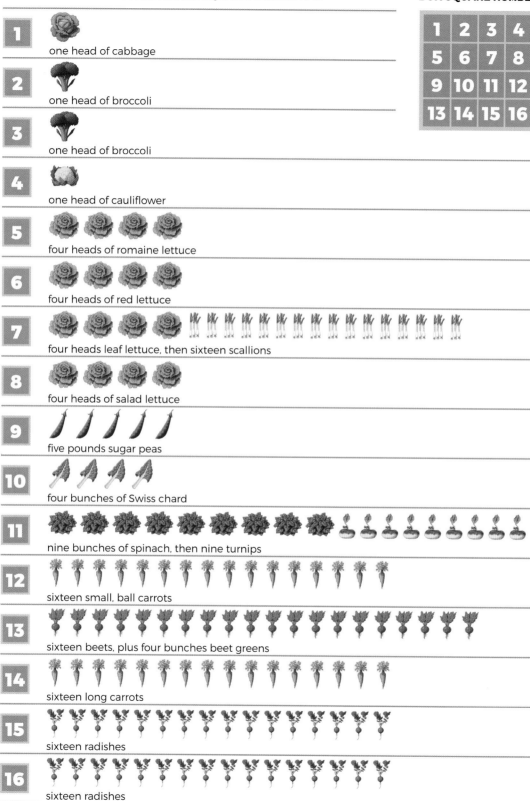

1 one head of cabbage

2 one head of broccoli

3 one head of broccoli

4 one head of cauliflower

5 four heads of romaine lettuce

6 four heads of red lettuce

7 four heads leaf lettuce, then sixteen scallions

8 four heads of salad lettuce

9 five pounds sugar peas

10 four bunches of Swiss chard

11 nine bunches of spinach, then nine turnips

12 sixteen small, ball carrots

13 sixteen beets, plus four bunches beet greens

14 sixteen long carrots

15 sixteen radishes

16 sixteen radishes

BOX SQUARE NUMBER

1	2	3	4
5	6	7	8
9	10	11	12
13	14	15	16

FIRST HARVEST FROM EACH SQUARE: YOUR SFG

BOX SQUARE NUMBER

1	2	3	4
5	6	7	8
9	10	11	12
13	14	15	16

1

2

3

4

5

6

7

8

9

10

11

12

13

14

15

16

The Square Foot Gardening method is ideal for flower gardens too.

START SMALL

Even if you've determined that three or more full-sized 4 × 4 Square Foot Garden boxes are appropriate for your needs, many Square Foot Gardening instructors have recommended that you start small, using a three-phase approach. You don't have to build and plant all your boxes all at once. Instead, if you build and plant one-third of your ultimate goal to start with—in the spring season, for example—you can then observe how much you harvest and get a sense about whether your overall estimate is correct.

Then, in the second phase you can build boxes to house the next one-third of your grid squares and use them for

summer planting. By the time you have fully integrated a second or third box into your routine, you'll likely have a pretty good idea of just how many square foot boxes and how many squares are really necessary to give you the produce you can efficiently use. If you wish, you can add another box or two for fall planting, or you can now start planning for the next spring season and even more garden boxes if they make sense.

If you have more square foot boxes than you are using—perhaps your kids have now gone off to college or you are downsizing for some other reason—spare boxes make great gifts for friends and neighbors. Or, if your boxes are of different sizes, they can be stacked pyramid style to offer another option.

SAMPLE GARDEN DESIGNS

The following sample Square Foot Garden maps will give you a place to start as you plan your own square foot vegetable garden. Although we've presented these as classic 4 × 4-foot boxes, remember that you can configure your own garden in whatever shape you like as long as it still has 1 × 1-foot squares. In most of these maps, the top row is fitted with a trellis, and this is intended to be the northern edge of the garden.

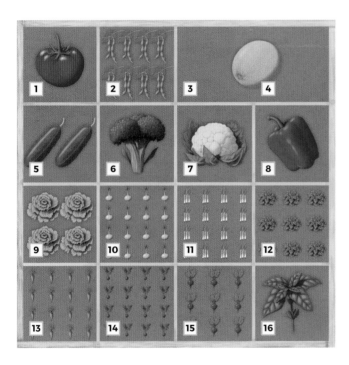

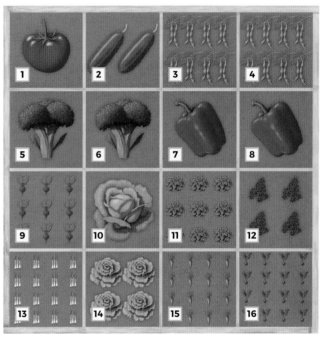

#1 A BASIC SAMPLER GARDEN

Here is a basic, well-rounded garden that provides the most common vegetables that most people enjoy. If there are some you don't care for, you can of course swap them out for others.

> The basic vegetable garden is planted with these vegetables, reading from top left: (1) Beefsteak tomato × 1; (2) Pole bean × 8; (3) (4) Cantaloupe × 1; (5) Cucumber × 2; (6) Broccoli × 1; (7) Cauliflower × 1; (8) Green pepper × 1; (9) Lettuce × 4; (10) White onion × 16; (11) Green onion × 16; (12) Spinach × 9; (13) Carrot × 16; (14) Radish × 16; (15) Beet × 9; (16) Basil × 1.

#2 EASY-TO-GROW GARDEN

If you have concerns about the color of your thumb and prefer to try simple vegetables to start with, here is a garden filled with very easy vegetables.

> The easy vegetable garden is planted with these vegetables, reading from top left: (1) Tomato × 1; (2) Cucumber × 2; (3) Pole bean × 8; (4) Pole bean × 8; (5) Broccoli × 1; (6) Broccoli × 1; (7) Green pepper × 1; (8) Green pepper × 1; (9) Beet × 9; (10) Cabbage × 1; (11) Spinach × 9; (12) Parsley × 4; (13) Green onion × 16; (14) Leaf lettuce × 4; (15) Carrots × 16; (16) Radishes × 16.

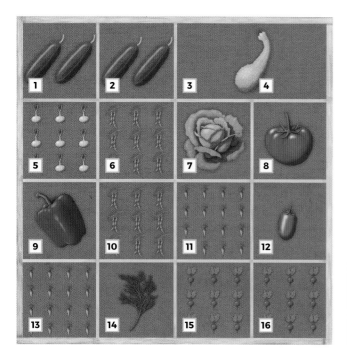

#3 CANNING GARDEN

Consider a garden like this one if you like to can vegetables to put away for the winter or to give away as gifts. All the vegetables in this garden are suitable for canning or pickling. Note that tomatoes will need a trellis or other form of vertical support and should be placed on the north side of your garden so as not to block out the light.

> The canning garden is planted with these vegetables, reading from top left: (1) Large cucumber × 2; (2) Large cucumber × 2; (3) (4) Summer squash × 1; (5) White globe onion × 9; (6) Bush bean × 9; (7) Cabbage × 1; (8) Large tomato × 1; (9) Sweet pepper × 1; (10) Bush bean × 9; (11) Carrot × 16; (12) Plum tomato × 1; (13) Carrot × 16; (14) Dill × 1; (15) Beet × 9; (16) Beet × 9.

#4 CULINARY HERB GARDEN

Consider a garden like this one if you enjoy cooking with herbs or drying them for craft use. Note that some squares contain two different herbs. This garden does not require a trellis. With judicious pruning, rosemary and lavender can be grown in one grid square. Lemongrass should be grown as an annual.

> The culinary herb garden is planted with these vegetables, reading from top left: (1) Italian parsley × 1; (2) Sweet marjoram × 1; (3) Common chives × 8 and garlic chives × 8; (4) Lemon thyme × 1 and lime thyme × 1; (5) English thyme × 1 and French thyme × 1; (6) Lemongrass × 1; (7) Blue rosemary × 1; (8) Lemon verbena × 1; (9) Fernleaf dill × 1; (10) Provence lavender × 2; (11) Sage × 1; (12) Tarragon × 1; (13) Lemon basil × 1; (14) Large-leaf basil × 4; (15) Sweet fennel × 1; (16) Italian oregano × 1.

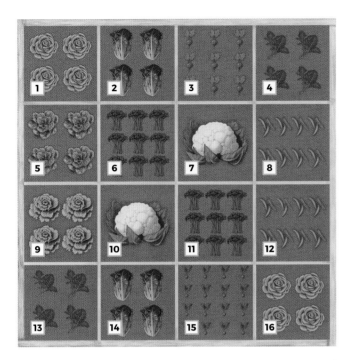

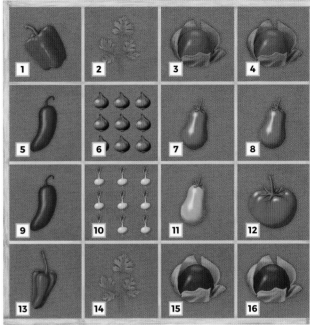

#5 SALAD GARDEN

Here is a basic Square Foot Garden for salad lovers. This garden does not require a trellis.

> **The salad garden is planted with these vegetables, reading from top left: (1) Bibb lettuce × 4; (2) Red romaine lettuce × 4; (3) Beet × 9; (4) Arugula × 4; (5) Freckled lettuce × 4; (6) Broccoli rabe × 9; (7) Cauliflower × 1; (8) Sugar snap peas × 8; (9) Leaf lettuce × 4; (10) Cauliflower × 1; (11) Broccoli rabe × 9; (12) Sugar snap peas × 8; (13) Arugula × 4; (14) Red romaine lettuce × 4; (15) Radishes × 16; (16) Bibb lettuce × 4.**

#6 SALSA GARDEN

Here's a perfect garden collection if you like to make large batches of delicious salsa. If you have trouble finding any of these varieties, you can substitute others. They key to good salsa is using a variety of peppers and tomatoes. Note that, again, tomatoes will need a vertical support in this garden and should be grown on the north side to avoid shading the other plants.

> **The salsa garden is planted with these vegetables, reading from top left: (1) Red bell pepper × 1; (2) Cilantro × 1; (3) Green tomatillo × 1; (4) Green tomatillo × 1; (5) Jalapeno pepper × 1; (6) Purple onion × 9; (7) Pear tomato × 1; (8) Pear tomato × 1; (9) Jalapeno pepper × 1; (10) White onion × 9; (11) Yellow pear tomato × 1; (12) Beefsteak tomato × 1; (13) Ancho pepper × 1; (14) Cilantro × 1; (15) Purple tomatillo × 1; (16) Purple tomatillo × 1.**

CHOOSING VEGETABLES FOR HEALTH

Vegetables are delicious, of course, but a primary reason for eating lots of them is the benefits for your health. All vegetables are healthful, but the following is a hall of fame for the very best vegetables for health—the most healthful of the healthful.

BROCCOLI

Broccoli is a great source of fiber, with a unique combination of vitamins A and K (thought to promote production of essential vitamin D, which is usually produced through exposure to sunlight). The vegetable has excellent allergy-fighting compounds.

KALE

Kale is a "superfood" nutritional powerhouse. Low calories, no fat, more iron than beef—what's not to love? Kale offers abundant vitamin K—a cancer-prevention nutrient—and vitamins A and C. It is rich in antioxidants and anti-inflammatory compounds and has been proven to reduce cholesterol.

BRUSSELS SPROUTS

When it comes to glucosinolates, you can't top brussels sprouts. Glucosinolates are phytonutrients that set the stage for cancer prevention in our bodies and our cells.

TOMATOES

Aside from abundant vitamin C, tomatoes have significant levels of an antioxidant called lycopene. A disease fighter, lycopene may help maintain bone health, and it works with other compounds to fight heart disease.

SUMMER SQUASH

Summer squash boasts strong antioxidants, including carotenoids, lutein, zeaxanthin, and others. Certain compounds in summer squash may play a role in diabetes prevention. The skin is rich in nutrients, so prepare the squash with the skin left on.

BEETS

Beets contain special phytonutrients called betalains—antioxidants, anti-inflammatories, and detoxifiers. The greens are even more nutritious, containing whopping amounts of lutein, a compound associated with eye health.

COLLARD GREENS

Collard greens are chock-full of folate, calcium, vitamins K and C, and beta carotene. The cooked greens also help lower cholesterol.

CARROTS

Carrots grown in season are likely to be the most nutritious. Ripe carrots are best known for their high levels of carotenoids, but they also may play a role in preventing cardiovascular disease.

The most critical element for a good Square Foot Garden: a spot with plenty of sun.

CHAPTER 4

LAYING OUT YOUR SQUARE FOOT GARDEN

In Chapter 3, you learned about how to determine the types of vegetables to plant and came away with a good estimate of how many squares will be needed to grow that produce. Now comes the second part of that planning process: figuring out where in your yard is best for your Square Foot Gardens, what shape and size to build your boxes, and how to arrange the boxes within the yard.

YARD LOCATION

Square Foot Gardening is a good deal more flexible than traditional gardening. A traditional row garden takes up a fairly large amount of space—so much that it can occupy most of a moderate-sized backyard. But because Square Foot Garden boxes are relatively small, they can fit into almost any space that has the requisite conditions. And you don't need to space them close together; any small patch of yard that gets enough sunlight will suffice for a Square Foot Garden box with the proper size and shape for the space.

There are several conditions to look for when determining where in your yard to position a Square Foot Garden bed:

- Place it close to the house for convenience.

- Pick an area that receives 6 to 8 hours of sunlight each day.

- Keep away from trees and shrubs where shade can interfere, or where protruding roots can be a problem.

- Avoid low-lying areas where water may pool after a rain.

- Don't worry about soil conditions, because your Square Foot Gardens will use their own special Mel's Mix growing medium.

- Consider access to water sources.

Let's look at these issues one at a time.

CLOSE TO THE HOUSE

Square Foot Gardens can be positioned just about anywhere, but when suitable spots near the house are available, grab the opportunity. If your Square Foot Garden is close to the house or to attached features, such as a deck or patio, you'll be able to keep an eye on it and admire it more often. Having the boxes near sidewalks or other traffic paths also makes it easier to tend them and will simplify things when harvesting the produce.

Ideally, your Square Foot Garden boxes should be clearly visible from inside the house. Consider what rooms you use the most, and if suitable garden spots are available within view of those rooms, make use of them. Keeping an eye on things is not only for your pleasure but for the protection of the garden. If it's close, you'll be able to spot problems like feeding deer or neighborhood pets before they can wreak havoc on your garden.

IN MEL'S WORDS

Remember that the Square Foot Garden way is to treat your plants just like you treat your children or grandchildren, and you know you would be glancing out the window at them. I believe that every plant out there is constantly seeking your attention by saying, "Look at me, look at my new blossom, look how big I'm getting." Isn't that just like children? Placement of your Square Foot Garden opens up so many doors to the way you care for, enjoy, appreciate, and harvest it. Plus, you'll show it off more often and get the whole family involved. It's even possible to split up your garden and place some of your boxes in different locations for perhaps a different visual effect or a different purpose.

SUFFICIENT SUNLIGHT

Perhaps the most important element of Square Foot Garden location is sunlight. Although some vegetables are slightly less hungry for sunlight than others, as a class of growing plants, food-producing species all need a good amount of direct sunlight in order to thrive. How much a particular plant needs depends on what type it is. Generally speaking, plants with large flowers or those that produce fruit or vegetables need a lot of sunlight—8 hours per day or more. We think of these types of vegetables as "summer crops" or "warm-weather" plants, and they include many common favorites: tomatoes, beans, peppers, squash, and cucumbers.

When scouting your yard for places with proper sunlight, remember that sunlight exposure changes through the year as seasons change. The sun is lower in the sky and less direct in early spring and late fall than it is during midsummer. Not only is the sun less direct, but there are fewer hours of it in spring and fall as well. But although midsummer days are long and the sun is direct, heavy, dense leaf canopies can create deep shade that isn't present in the spring time when the trees are just beginning to leaf out.

If you happen to have a yard with no areas that receive 8 hours or more of sunlight, it's still possible to grow a garden in a yard with 4 to 6 hours of sunlight, but you'll have to limit your selection. Plants that produce large vegetables are almost impossible to grow in shade. Instead, plant vegetables that are normally eaten for the leaves, such as kale, leaf lettuce, and spinach, and those grown for their roots, such as beets, carrots, turnips, and potatoes. Very dense shade from morning to night will make it very hard to grow much of anything, though. In such situations, professional removal of a tree or two may be the only option if you're determined to have a vegetable garden.

It's also possible to have too much sun. A yard with full direct sunlight from dawn to dusk will usually be too much for cool-weather and leafy crops. Especially in dry southern climates, too much sun can be a serious problem. One advantage of a Square Foot Garden, though, is that its small size makes it possible to take advantage of the smallest amount of shade, such as the morning or afternoon shadow cast by a house or garage. It's also fairly easy to cover a Square Foot Garden with a canopy of shade cloth to protect it from too much sun.

STAY AWAY FROM TREES AND SHRUBS

There are two reasons why it's wise to position your Square Foot Garden beds well away from trees and shrubs. First, all shrubs and even small trees will cast some shade, and in almost every climate, your garden will thrive better if it gets as much sun as possible. Second, trees and shrubs have an uncanny way of detecting where there is moisture and nutrients, and they very likely will reach out and send roots up into your square foot boxes if they can reach them. The only way to defend against that situation is to cover the bottoms of your boxes with plywood or raise them up off the ground. The raised Square Foot Garden box described on page 78 is one way to keep tree and shrub roots from finding your garden. You can raise the box up by simply putting a brick or concrete block under the corners and one in the middle—the concrete post piers sold for building freestanding decks work great for this purpose—or see page 82 for instructions to build a more elegant elevated Square Foot Garden. By raising the box up off the ground, even slightly, trees and shrubs won't sense the ideal conditions of your

Choose a location where there is plenty of sunshine and access is easy.

Square Foot Garden and send out their roots on search-and-destroy missions.

Keep in mind that shrubs can be equally guilty when it comes to infiltrating roots and casting shade—maybe even worse, because most shrubs by nature are shallow-rooted plants that seek out moisture near the surface. And keep in mind that a tree or shrub will grow, and that what is now a sunny spot in your yard may be a shady one in another season or two.

AVOID LOW-LYING AREAS

Roots need moisture, but they also need air. In low-lying areas where rainwater pools, your Square Foot Garden may get saturated with water, and the plant roots can easily drown when their air supply is choked off. Although the ingredients of Mel's Mix drain well, they also hold moisture very well, and if the bottom of the box sits in a puddle for too long, the roots may rot and the plant may drown. Puddles can also shorten the life of the wooden sides of your garden boxes, and standing water can turn the aisles between the boxes into a muddy quagmire, which can really spoil the fun of gardening.

If your yard is so boggy that there's really no choice, you might consider raising up the area where you position your Square Foot Garden by adding some sand, creating a slight island on which to place your box. And again, you can also raise the garden box off the ground entirely by supporting it on bricks or piers, or by building an elevated Square Foot Garden.

BAD SOIL? NO WORRIES

When planning a standard row garden, it's quite critical to evaluate the soil to make sure it will support crops. The process can be time consuming as you take samples, wait for the results, then laboriously dig up the soil and add whatever nutrients are recommended by the soil test. Not so with Square Foot Gardening. You can even place your Square Foot Garden on a concrete or brick patio, for that matter, because you'll be creating your own "soil" by making up a batch of Mel's Mix growing medium.

AVAILABLE WATER

Square Foot Gardens don't require much water, and simply keeping a 5-gallon bucket of water near each box can be all you really need in most climates. The water in the bucket will warm up in the sun, and a cupful of water per square is completely sufficient. Still, you will need to keep those bucket reservoirs full, and if you have several Square Foot Garden boxes, positioning them where you can easily replenish the water supply will simplify your work. Look for places where there is easy access to a hose spigot or rain barrel, and ideally a spot where you won't have to carry water very far or where a modest length of garden hose will suffice. If you are installing a commercial drip-watering system (page 172) or a DIY watering grid (page 174), access to a hose spigot is even more important.

To summarize, then, the ideal spots for Square Foot Garden boxes will be places relatively close to the house or easy-access pathways, where there is plenty of sunlight and no trees or shrubs to mess things up with their roots, and where the ground is high enough that rain water doesn't puddle. The next step is to map out your yard and pinpoint the areas that fit the bill.

HOW TO MAP YOUR YARD

If you want to be truly precise about positioning your Square Foot Gardening boxes, make a series of maps of your yard to identify areas where the ideal conditions are found. It will take several maps, though, because the sunlight patterns change throughout the day. You can do this mapping on ordinary paper or, if you want to be more precise, use graph paper and make your drawings to exact scale. If you do this, though, you'll also need a long tape measure to take measurements of your yard features in order to draw to a precise scale.

MORNING

On paper, sketch out your yard and the important features, including the house and other buildings, trees and shrubs, fences, and walkways. Observe your yard in the early morning, and use pencil to shade areas where features cast shadows. Note the location of hose spigots and rain barrels, if you have them. Make additional illustrations showing shade patterns at midmorning, early afternoon, and late afternoon (opposite).

MIDMORNING

MID-AFTERNOON

LATE AFTERNOON

SHADE PATTERNS

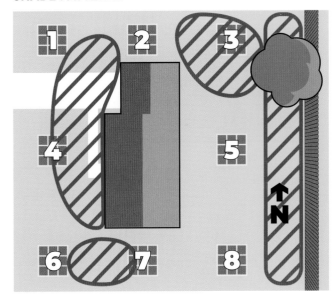

SIZE AND SHAPE OF SQUARE FOOT BOXES

With an idea of how many total squares you need to grow the produce you want, and a yard map that identifies the areas best suited for garden boxes, you can now determine how many boxes to build and what shape they should be.

The traditional Square Foot Garden box is a 4 × 4-foot box divided into 16 grid squares. Three such boxes would give you 48 squares for planting. But it's entirely possible that your yard might not really be suitable for three boxes of this size. Perhaps you only have a narrow swath of space next to a fence on the north side of your property that provides the suitable conditions. Here, the best way to get your 48 grid squares might be three boxes that are each 2 × 8 feet in size.

There are endless configurations you can use—the important thing is to build boxes with just enough (not too few and not too many) squares to provide the produce you need, without waste. One important note, though: don't build individual boxes that are too big. The classic 4 × 4 box is a classic because it is the ideal size for each access to the plants inside. If you build a box that is 5 or 6 feet across, you would indeed have a lot of squares, but you would also find it very hard to tend the plants and harvest the produce in the center of the box. So, keep your square garden boxes no more than 4 feet across.

If you make long, narrow boxes, such as when you need to fit in a garden near a fence, make it no more than two squares deep. You won't have access from all sides of the garden from this configuration, and reaching to the back of a 4-foot-wide box is very difficult. Long gardens are best sized at 2 or 3 feet wide.

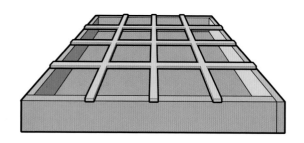

The classic 4 × 4 is the standard for good reason: it has lots of planting squares and is easily accessible from all sides.

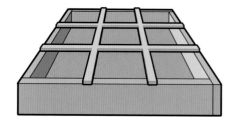

The 3 × 3 box is a good configuration where space is limited, and perfect for a kid's version of a Square Foot Garden.

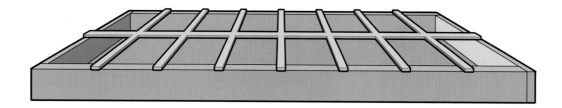

Do you have a long, narrow space? Consider a box that's 2' wide and 6', 8', 10', or even 12' long. A shape like this can be great for placing along a fence. The box shouldn't be more than 3' wide if you'll only be able to access it from one of the long sides.

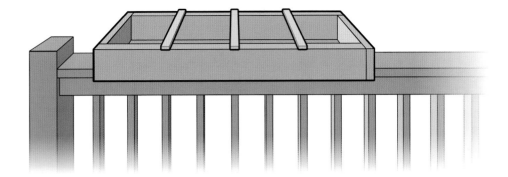

Not all Square Foot Gardens are in the yard itself. Page 87 will give you instructions for a long, narrow Square Foot Garden box that can fit on a deck railing.

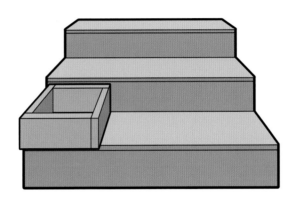

Where space is really limited, square foot boxes can be very, very small. This 1' square box can be positioned on stairway steps or wherever there is a sunny corner.

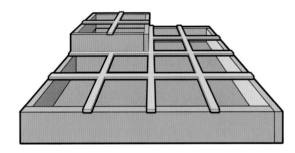

It is sometimes helpful to add a vertical dimension with a pyramid garden box. This configuration has a 4 × 4 base layer with a 2 × 2 layer positioned on top. Because there is extra growing depth on the top tier, it might work well for deep-rooted vegetables, such as potatoes. The extra height also makes a pyramid garden more visually interesting as a landscape feature.

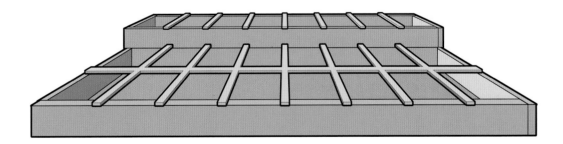

Another vertical adaptation is a tiered garden, in which the base layer is 3' or 4' wide, with the upper tier 1' wide. Such a tiered configuration might serve as a "hedge" to mark space boundaries in your yard.

POSITIONING THE SQUARE FOOT GARDEN BOXES

The planning stage is pretty close to done. It's really now just a matter of noting on your yard map the locations of all your planned Square Foot Garden boxes.

AISLES

Mel Bartholomew strongly believed that adjacent Square Foot Garden boxes should be no closer than 3 feet apart, and this has time and again proved to be a pretty ideal spacing. A group of classic 4 × 4-foot boxes with 3-foot aisles between them conserves overall yard space but provides enough space to comfortably move between the boxes and kneel when you need to.

 ## IN MEL'S WORDS

The whole idea of Square Foot Gardening is to walk around your garden boxes and reach in to tend your plants. This way, the soil never gets packed down, and you eliminate having to dig it up to loosen it again. So, how wide should your aisles be? It depends a lot on how much room you have and what kind of look you want for your garden. If you're going to have many boxes—remember, we suggest you begin using only a small number because you can always add more later—you may want to have, for example, a center aisle that is 4 feet wide so you can easily get in with a garden cart or wheelbarrow, or so several people can walk down the aisle at once. (Hey, how about a garden party or a wedding?)

   I would suggest you make aisles no narrower than 3 feet; 2-foot-wide aisles will seem crowded once plants grow and some cascade over the sides of the boxes, which can shrink them down to 18 or even 12 inches. Because a SFG takes up so little room, why crowd all your boxes together? The more spacious your all-new SFG is, the more time you are likely to spend there enjoying it.

GARDENING WITH LIMITATIONS

Over the years, the popularity of the Square Foot Gardening method has grown so rapidly that our certified instructors frequently find themselves adapting the method to the needs of special situations and special needs gardeners. Not every yard is the ideal flat and sunny surface—some are sloped, some are shaded, and some are oddly shaped. Gardeners also come in many different forms, from the very young to the very old, with a range of physical abilities. But regardless of the specific conditions in your yard, or what type of gardener you may be, the beauty of the Square Foot Gardening method is that it can accommodate everyone.

NO YARD

Sometimes a property may have limited space for a garden. If you're in a no-yard situation, think creatively and look to the spaces closer to your front or back door. For instance, patios, decks, and balconies almost always have room for a small garden—the corner of a patio or balcony could accommodate several 2 × 2-foot boxes. These could be stacked up creatively at different heights to form a very attractive corner garden that would use less space than a 4 × 4-foot area. The boxes can be placed on low tables of different heights or on something like milk crates or cinder blocks in order to give each one a different height. Even in very small spaces, the vertical dimension can be used. Attach nylon netting to a frame anchored to a building, fence, or patio wall to expand your small garden.

   In small townhomes, condominiums, or rental units, take advantage of balcony or deck spaces. For example, you could install 6- to 12-inch-wide boxes on the floor or bolted to the top of the railing on both sides to create a garden wall.

   When creating deck gardens in an apartment or condominium, be sure to consider the people below you and how you're going to water the garden. Your garden may not be a problem when it rains, but when it is sunny and bright and your garden water drips down on the neighbors while they are at their barbecue below, they may not look favorably upon you or your garden.

   There are several things you can do about this situation. First of all, because Mel's Mix holds water so well, it's highly unlikely you will overwater, which will prevent a lot of dripping or excess water leakage. Just in case, though, you can always choose not to drill drain holes at consistent intervals over the entire bottom of your SFG but only a couple in one corner. Then, slightly slope the box towards this one corner and put a decorative vase or other container underneath to catch any drips that may leak out.

WOODED YARD

If you have a heavily wooded yard, your choices are admittedly limited. One solution is to locate several small boxes around the property wherever you find a spot that gets the required amount of sunlight. Some boxes can even be built small enough to be repositioned as the sun moves throughout the day and seasons. If you have a southern exposure with enough sunlight, consider a long double-decker box against the house. If you are really determined, it might be time to consider having a tree or two removed by professionals. Letting a bit of sunlight into a very shady yard will help lawn grass as well as give you a spot for Square Foot Gardening.

GARDENS FOR EXPERIENCED PEOPLE

Of all methods for gardening, the square foot approach may well be the one best suited for mature gardeners. As we get older, it may become harder to do certain things, many of which are required for traditional gardening. Square foot gardening has the advantages of small space, simple hand tools, and raised boxes—all ideal for older people and those with physical limitations. Gardening is excellent therapy for conditions like arthritis, and Square Foot Gardening allows for movement but is not so demanding as to cause pain. An aging gardener may need help with building the box and making up the initial batch of Mel's Mix, but once that's done, he or she can garden independently and enjoy all the benefits of a garden.

Wheelchair, sit-down, or standup gardening is a real possibility, either by building the elevated square foot box described on page 82 or simply by building a garden box with a plywood bottom and supporting it on pillars of stacked bricks or concrete blocks, or even on sawhorses, if you provide for center support.

You can put various sizes of boxes on patios, near the pool, the back door, or any pleasant area around the house that is easy for an older person to attend to their garden. No heavy tools are required—it is just a matter of going to your garden and tending it with the minimal amount

IN MEL'S WORDS

One of the greatest bonds that I have found between grandparents and grandchildren is formed during a gardening project, even if the visit is short. Give your grandchild a garden or just a square, let him write his name on the grid, encourage her to plant her garden, and you may find your grandchildren will keep in touch more often just to find out how the garden is growing. This, of course, can work just the opposite way when the grandparent visits the child's home and they plant a garden there. And, of course, there will be great anticipation for the next visit and what has happened in the garden. Selecting plants for children is quite simple; plants should be easy to grow, fast growing for quick results, and something that will produce an exciting result.

of effort. There is no weeding, and because a Square Foot Garden starts with a perfect soil mix, there is never any heavy digging.

COMMUNITY GARDENS

With Square Foot Gardening, it is possible to have pocket gardens anywhere in the community, even right in the center of an urban area. The compact size of a Square Foot Garden means that community gardening is possible without an entire empty lot to do it in. It is now possible to take just a corner of that lot or any other small space—perhaps even in an existing city park—and have a very small community Square Foot Garden. Each person can have from one 4 × 4-foot box up to an area of perhaps 12 × 12, which would enable them to have four or more boxes.

One of the best things about using Square Foot Gardening in a community program is that because it is never overrun by weeds, it doesn't become eyesore by the middle of the summer. This means it is much easier to operate and get public and official approval. Even a slab of concrete in front of an abandoned store can become a vibrant location for a community garden populated by Square Foot Garden boxes.

Community gardens do require a set of guidelines for what participants can and cannot grow to ensure they don't interfere with a neighbor's garden. These guidelines should also cover the hours of operation, use of water, and maintenance of the gardens. The use of pesticides and fertilizer is always a big concern with community gardens, but that issue can be totally eliminated with Square Foot Gardening. If you are involved in the planning and layout of a community Square Foot Garden, consider including several tables where people who use wheelchairs can access a garden plot. Also, several benches and some shade are always good features to include.

IN MEL'S WORDS

Square Foot Gardens have gone a lot of places over the years. They've been placed on wheels—we know of a veterans' hospital where a Square Foot Garden was built on a gurney and wheeled from the roof down the service elevator so it could be taken to bedridden patients. The SFG Foundation has taught blind gardeners; I designed a SFG for the Helen Keller Institute on Long Island, where blind students learned gardening. We have also taught at the school for the deaf in Salt Lake City, Utah. Other worthwhile places we have installed SFGs are in prisons and troubled-youth facilities. Building a small portable garden (in sizes from 2 × 2 up to 4 × 4 with a plywood bottom added) allows people to participate who otherwise might not have been able to garden.

One thing I've learned from teaching Square Foot Gardening over the last 30 years is that kids love to garden. They are so excited about growing plants. From the beginning, it was obvious that Square Foot Gardening was perfect for teaching arithmetic and all kinds of math and that, in fact, anything in the scientific field is easily taught using gardening as the vehicle. But then I began to see that a teacher could readily relate all subjects to gardening.

We have worked with all age groups from preschool through high school using gardening as a teaching tool. Suddenly learning begins to have some type of meaning in students' lives, and they can see the value of the subjects they have been learning in the past.

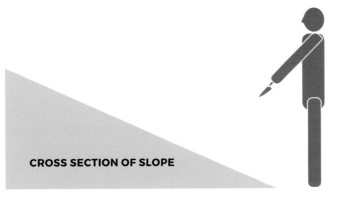

CROSS SECTION OF SLOPE

1. The "cut and fill" technique is an effective way to install an SFG box on a sloping yard. First, decide exactly where you want to install the box.

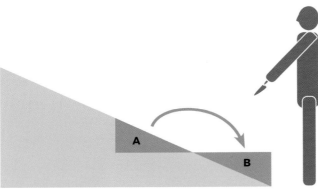

2. The beauty of this method is that the minimum amount of earth is moved around. A section is dug out (A) and then placed at the foot of the slope to create a base (B).

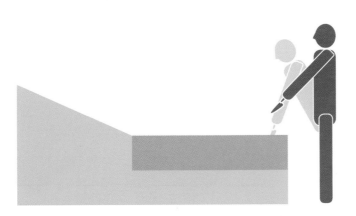

3. The ground is leveled off and you can now place a box frame there, line it and fill it with Mel's Mix.

STEEPLY SLOPED YARD

If you have only a hillside or steep slope that meets the requirements for a Square Foot Garden, you don't necessarily need to give up, especially if the hillside faces south. Although extreme slopes are difficult to work with, you may well find that you can build boxes that fit the lay of the land.

In order to have a level garden so soil and water don't run off, you'll need to cut a terrace into the slope in order to create a flat spot just big enough to make a small garden area. A classic 4-foot-wide box may be not practical on a steep slope, but a 3 × 3-foot box may well work. Gentler slopes may still be suitable for a 4 × 4-foot box.

To get a level spot, you just cut into the hill and move the soil downhill to form the flat area for the box. But think ahead about water availability, and also about the time it will take to dig out the hillside. On steep slopes, accessibility may be a problem, and even if you get the garden installed, the challenges of tending it may make it impractical.

BUILDING BOXES AND GRIDS

As outdoor building projects go, building Square Foot Gardens and accessorizing them is about as easy as it gets. The classic Square Foot Garden is essentially just a shallow raised bed made from ordinary 1 × 6 or 2 × 6 lumber, available at any big-box home center, lumberyard or even your local hardware store. The ends are joined together with deck screws—these are called butt joints—and the box is then positioned on a sheet of landscape fabric in the yard. Into the box goes a filling of Mel's Mix growing medium, and then narrow slats or lath are laid across the top of the box to form a grid of 1-foot-wide squares, which will guide your planting process. If you want, you can accessorize your Square Foot Garden with trellises, fences, or covers, but this isn't always necessary.

A variety of masonry and stone products can be used to build a Square Foot Garden box. Because these materials are heavy, you don't even need to mortar them together—they can simply be stacked freehand to make a functional garden box.

Building a basic Square Foot Garden, or even a custom one, is well within the skill level of just about anyone—which is likely why this is one of the favorite gardening methods of all time. The advantages of the classic 4 × 4-foot box with 1-foot-wide grid squares are both profound and obvious:

- A Square Foot Garden is neat and tidy. Carefully arranged, this is a type of vegetable garden that is very attractive to look at, unlike many traditional vegetable gardens with their sprawling layouts.

- A box garden greatly simplifies gardening chores. Weeding, watering, and harvesting are very simple with access around all four sides of a neatly contained garden.

- A shallow box confines and holds Mel's Mix—the special growing medium that is so crucial to the success of a Square Foot Garden.

- The box structure makes it easy to accessorize with trellises and other add-ons. Wire, pipes, or wooden stakes can be easily screwed to the wooden walls of the box or driven into the surrounding ground. Either way, the traditional SFG box is only 4 feet square so your accessories will remain secure.

- The grid structure makes it easy to plan and plant your garden for maximum yield, and it simplifies the process of replanting that is integral to maximizing the Square Foot Garden method.

BOX BASICS

The classic 4 × 4-foot square box has now been adapted in several ways—both by Mel over the years and by the many Square Foot Gardening instructors and home gardeners who have developed variations to the idea—but many of the basic principles have remained the same since the beginning.

MATERIALS

Square Foot Garden boxes can be made from a variety of lumber types and other materials.

Natural lumber. The traditional building material for a Square Foot Garden is standard dimensional lumber in 1 × 6 or 2 × 6 dimensions. One of the better choices is cedar, which has natural resistance to rot and insect damage.

In other outdoor applications, such as decks or fences, a standard choice is pressure-treated lumber, which is treated with chemicals to keep it from rotting. Although the chemicals used in such lumber are now of a different composition that is much less toxic than what was used in the past and no longer contains arsenic, many purists (including those of us at the Square Foot Gardening Foundation) still caution against using pressure-treated lumber for any structure that will be used to grow edibles. There is debate over whether or not these chemicals actually leach into the soil and are taken up by the roots of vegetables, but it's best not to take a chance on foods your family will be eating.

If you have trouble finding cedar or cypress lumber, or find it too expensive, ordinary pine or fir can be used to build a Square Foot Garden—just be aware that it will decay faster than a garden built with cedar. Pine lumber is quite cheap, though, so building new boxes after a few years is not a big expense.

Composites and plastics. The synthetic lumbers that first came into use for decking and fences also make good materials for building a Square Foot Garden. Many forms of plastic are available, but we find that the best choice is true composite lumber—which consists of recycled plastics bonded to wood byproducts, such as sawdust. Composites have better rigidity than older plastics and will hold up better over time. One complication of composites is that screwing the ends together doesn't form the same kind of secure joints you get when screwing wood. If you build with composites, you should expect to reinforce the corners with some kind of metal brackets or metal connectors.

Stone, brick, and block. You can construct a very functional and attractive Square Foot Garden from natural stone, concrete foundation block, or cast cement block, such as that used to build retaining walls. A Square Foot Garden, after all, is basically four small retaining walls joined to form a square, so any material that works for a standard retaining wall will also work for a Square Foot Garden.

Other materials. Home gardeners have made functional Square Foot Gardens from many materials. Logs and tree branches can be used to form the walls of the raised bed, giving it a rustic look. Gardeners have also experimented with straw bales, leftover rubber tires, and concrete blocks. The key here is to use a material to which grid slats can be successfully attached or anchored if you live in a windy area. Without the grid, your garden is not a Square Foot Garden at all, just another raised bed.

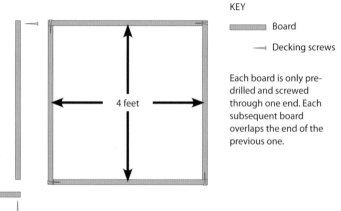

In a standard Square Foot Garden, the joints are staggered so that the inside dimensions remain exactly 4' in both directions. Drill pilot holes first, then drive 1½" deck screws (for 1× lumber) or 3" screws (for 2× lumber). Use three screws for each joint.

4 feet

Each board is only pre-drilled and screwed through one end. Each subsequent board overlaps the end of the previous one.

IN MEL'S WORDS

My idea of the best kind of lumber is free lumber. Go to any construction site, tell the foreman you are building a Square Foot Garden, and ask if they have any scrap wood. Chances are they will be throwing out just what you need. They may even cut it for you if you ask nicely. Then your box is free.

If you're starting with used lumber and it already has paint on it, you must make sure that it's not old paint, especially if it's peeling or crumbling; some older paints include lead, which is toxic. You don't want that in your garden. I also don't recommend using pretreated timbers or lumber in your garden because it also can leach chemicals.

JOINERY METHODS

In the classic 4 × 4 Square Foot Garden, each side is 4 feet long, and the corner butt joints are arranged to maintain the exact same dimensions on each side. On a wooden box, the ends of the side boards can be simple butt joints, with screws driven through the ends of one piece and into the end grain of another piece. Generally, you should use three screws at each corner, or four screws if you're building a deeper box.

Some gardeners prefer to reinforce the corners of the square-foot box with angle irons or another type of metal connector attached to the inside of the box. This reduces the chances of the corners cracking and breaking out. If you reinforce the joints, make sure to used double-dipped galvanized hardware that won't corrode.

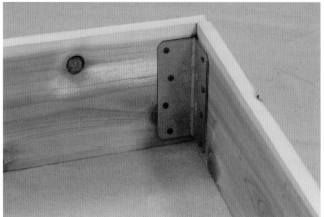

A double-dipped galvanized bracket can be used to reinforce corners. This can greatly lengthen the lifespan of a Square Foot Garden box.

A 3 × 3' box with nine squares (right) is ideal for a Square Foot Garden box for children. The standard 4 × 4' box (left) may be too large for them to easily access the inner grids. Children are captivated by the SFG method, so why not give them their own Square Foot Garden box?

BOX SHAPES

Gardeners, including Mel himself, quickly adapted the classic 4 × 4 Square Foot Garden box to other circumstances and spaces. Some people, for example, found that a narrower 1 × 8-foot box made makes a great size for planting flush alongside a fence. And several 2 × 8-foot boxes positioned with 2 or 3 feet between them is efficient for certain types of yards.

Today, you can find Square Foot Gardens in L shapes, built as long, narrow boxes to sit on deck railings, stacked "top-hat" style, and in many other shapes. What doesn't change, though, is that the bed, no matter what size or shape, needs to be divided into 1-foot-wide grid squares for effective planting and harvesting. And be aware that a long, narrow box will lose moisture a little faster than a square box.

Tall individual boxes with 1-foot-square bases can be great for positioning on steps. They are ideal for vegetables such as sweet potatoes or carrots that have deep roots.

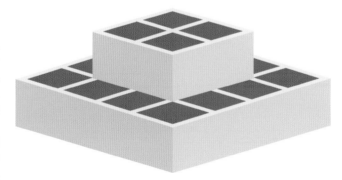

A top-hat Square Foot Garden is just a smaller garden placed on top of a larger one. The grids in the top box will enjoy greater depth, ideal for some larger root vegetables.

Small but tall boxes work well on steps for vegetables that have deeper roots.

BOX DEPTH

One of the big revelations of the Square Foot Gardening method is that you don't need to double-dig a massive garden bed to a depth of 18 inches in order to have a productive garden. Instead, you can get great results with a simple 6-inch-deep box if it's filled with the right growing medium.

But instructors and gardeners have found that there are some circumstances where including a few deeper boxes is helpful. Root vegetables like potatoes, carrots, and leeks can benefit from more space to grow. Toward this end, you can add a type of box sometimes called a top-hat or pyramid box, in which a smaller Square Foot Garden box is placed on top of a larger one, providing both greater depth for vegetables in the top box and visual interest for your yard.

Sometimes the impulse for building a deeper box is purely ornamental. A Square Foot Garden can be a very

Drainage holes are essential if you build your Square Foot Garden box with a plywood bottom.

BOX BOTTOMS?

In most instances, your Square Foot Garden can simply rest on a sheet of landscape fabric, which will prevent weeds from growing up through the box while still allowing moisture to drain down into the ground. If you choose, though, you can instead build your box with a plywood bottom. This is necessary if the box is resting on uneven ground, or if you are positioning it on a deck or patio. It will give the box greater strength.

If you build a bottom, use exterior ¾-inch-thick sheathing-grade plywood, and cut it to the exact size of the outer perimeter of your box. Turn the four-sided frame upside down, position the plywood over the bottom of the frame, then attach it with 1½-inch deck screws. Drill ¼-inch drainage holes spaced every foot.

FINISHING A BOX

Most people leave their Square Foot Garden boxes unfinished to weather naturally. A wood finish is really not necessary if you have built your box from cedar or another weather-resistant lumber. But if you want to lengthen the life of your box or want the decorative benefit of a finish, you can use linseed oil, paint, or a stain to color the edges and outside faces of the box sides. Traditionally we don't recommend that you paint or stain the inside face, though, to avoid the possibility of chemicals leaching into the roots of your vegetables. However, new generations of wood coatings are being developed with toxicity levels that are much lower, so feel free to investigate the option with your paint and stain retailer if it is important to you to coat the inside surfaces.

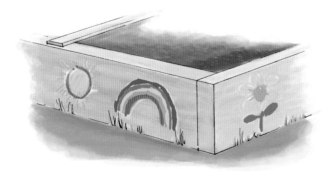

Painting a Square Foot Garden box is a good task for getting kids excited about gardening.

attractive garden feature, and some gardeners may want to elevate it just to highlight its beauty, especially if it's built with attractive materials, such as natural stone. If you do this, remember that most vegetables only need a 6-inch layer of Mel's Mix growing medium. Don't waste money by filling a deep box completely with this mix—instead, fill the bottom of the garden with ordinary sand or even dirt to save money; BUT only do this if you separate the sand or dirt from the Mel's Mix with a layer of landscape cloth.

HOW TO BUILD A BASIC SQUARE FOOT GARDEN BOX

Here is the classic Square Foot Garden box that made this method famous: a simple 4 × 4-foot cedar planting box with butted end joints resting on a sheet of landscape fabric. It's best to build this on a flat surface, like a driveway or the floor of your garage, to ensure that it goes together flat and square.

MATERIALS

The materials you'll need include:

- 1 × 6" × 4' (or 2 × 6" × 4') cedar lumber (4)
- Drill and bits
- 1½" or 3" deck screws
- 4 × 4' landscape fabric
- Staple gun (optional)
- Mel's Mix growing medium (see Chapter 7)
- Spade
- Eye and ear protection
- Work gloves

PREPARATION

ASSEMBLY

1, 2 Stack the four side boards for the box as shown here, step fashion. Outline the butt joint on the end of each board as reference for drilling pilot holes. Drill three pilot holes in the end of each board, using a drill and 1/8" bit. Slide each board back as you finish to access the next board.

3, 4 Position the side pieces in a square so that the pilot holes are aligned with the end grain of the adjoining board. One end of each board should overlap another board. Drive three deck screws into each joint to secure it.

5, 6 Move the box frame to the desired location, then insert landscape fabric to fit from edge to edge. If you wish, you can staple the cloth to the bottom edge of the frame.

7, 8 Add Mel's Mix to cover the bottom of the box, then add water until the Mel's Mix is thoroughly wet. It may take a while for the peat moss to become saturated, so be patient. Repeat in gradual stages (at least three times) until the box is full. You're now ready to add the grid and plant your garden.

HOW TO BUILD A PREFAB SQUARE FOOT GARDEN KIT

A variety of commercial kits are available that make it even easier to build a Square Foot Garden. Some kits use preformed plastic lumber, such as the kind commonly used on deck railings and railings. The one demonstrated here comes with corner brackets and metal corner hardware. Most kits can be stacked if you need to increase box height; all you will need to add here is the top grid (page 90).

MATERIALS

The materials you'll need include:

- Prefab Square Foot Garden kit
- Drill with driver bits
- Landscape fabric to match kit dimensions
- Mel's Mix growing medium (see Chapter 7)
- Spade
- Hammer
- Eye and ear protection
- Work gloves

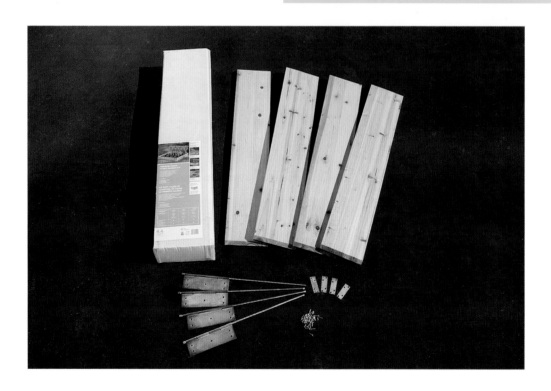

ASSEMBLY

On a flat surface, assemble the panels and corner brackets (or hinge brackets), using the kit's enclosed hardware. Follow the kit instructions and make sure all corners are square.

Begin filling the box with Mel's Mix. Check the box to make sure it is level as you fill, then drive in the corner stakes to anchor the box in the ground. If you wish for deeper box, add an additional kit and use metal connectors to join the side panels, following the manufacturer's directions.

Position the box on the site, making sure the angle is optimal for sun exposure. When satisfied, cut around the edges of the Square Foot Garden box with a spade, then move the box and slice off the sod in the garden area. Put a layer of landscape fabric down over the excavation, then reposition the Square Foot Garden box over the fabric.

HOW TO BUILD AN ELEVATED SQUARE FOOT GARDEN

Gardeners with physical limitations may want to raise a Square Foot Garden to a comfortable height near hip or waist level or even higher. An elevated garden can also be a great way to avoid damage from rabbits and other hungry creatures. This design provides a classic 4 × 4-foot Square Foot Garden that will sit 36 inches above the ground. You can easily adapt the design to a box of a different size (such as 2 × 4 feet) or build it to a different height by changing the length of the legs.

MATERIALS

The materials you'll need include:

- ¼ × 1½" × 8' cedar lattices (3)
- 2 × 10" × 8' cedar lumber (2)
- 2 × 6" × 12' cedar lumber (1)
- 2 × 4" × 12' cedar lumber (1)
- 1 × 4" × 8' cedar lumber (2)
- 2 × 2 × 36" cedar balusters (4)
- 2½" galvanized deck screws
- 1⅝" galvanized deck screws
- ¾" exterior-grade plywood, 49½ × 46½"
- 4 × 4" cedar post caps (4)
- Mel's Mix (see Chapter 7)
- #10×1" zinc-plated bolts with nuts (9)
- Sealer or wood finish (optional)
- Saw
- Drill with bits
- Landscape fabric
- Scissors
- Staple gun
- Eye and ear protection
- Work gloves

PREPARATION

Cut the 2 × 10 lumber and the lattice into four 4' lengths. These pieces will form the sides and the grid pieces. To form the leg pieces, cut the 2 × 6 and 2 × 4 boards each into four 36"-long lengths. (Note: these are the legs of the Square Foot Garden; if you want a taller garden, you can use longer legs.) For the top plate, cut the 1 × 4 into 4' lengths.

Drill three ³⁄₁₆" pilot holes near the end of each 2 × 10 board. Drill five ³⁄₁₆" pilot holes spaced evenly along the balusters.

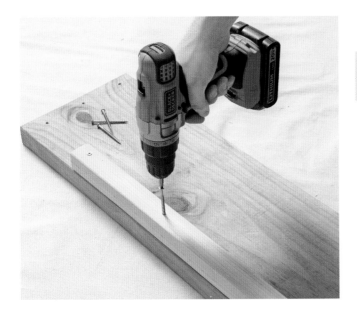

Center one baluster along the bottom edge of each 2 × 10 side, and secure it with 2½" deck screws driven through the pilot holes and into the 2 × 10. The balusters will form the cleats that will support the bottom of the box.

ASSEMBLY

Assemble the box by joining the 2 × 10 sides at the corners, joining the pieces by driving 2½" deck screws through the pilot holes and into the end grain of the adjoining side.

To build each leg, position a 2 × 6 board over a 2 × 4 board with the edges aligned, then drill ³⁄₁₆" pilot holes and attach the pieces together with 2½" deck screws. Drive at least five screws along the length of the leg. Repeat to complete all four legs.

Turn the box right-side up, then insert the plywood bottom into the box so the edges rest on the cleats. Drive 1⅝" screws along the edges of the bottom to secure it to the side cleats. Drill ¼" holes, spaced every 6", through the bottom of the box for drainage.

Measure and cut the 1 × 4 top plates to fit over the box sides, flush along the inside edges. The top plates should overhang to the outside of the box. Leave corner gaps for the cap pieces. Attach by drilling ³⁄₁₆" pilot holes and driving 1⅝" screws down through the top plates and into the box sides.

Drill pilot holes and attach corner caps to cover the exposed corners of the raised bed. If you wish, a sealer or finish can be applied at this time.

Cut and staple a piece of landscape fabric into the bottom of the planter so that the edges extend up the sides. Fold the corners, bed-sheet style, and secure with staples. Position the box at the desired location in the yard, then fill it with Mel's Mix.

Position the grid pieces on a flat surface, propping them up on scrap wood. Arrange the pieces so the spaces are 1' squares, then drill ¼" holes down through each intersection. Secure each intersecting joint with a bolt, washer, and nut. The grid now can be collapsed for storage, if needed.

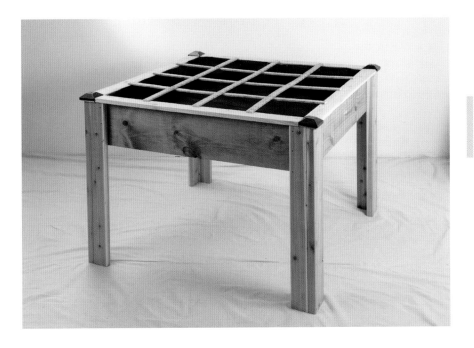

Position the grid on top of the square-foot box and if you live in a windy area secure it in place by drilling ³⁄₁₆" pilot holes and driving 1⅝" screws. Plant your garden (see Chapter 8).

ALTERNATE SQUARE FOOT GARDEN DESIGNS

Ever since the Square Foot Garden method was first created, gardeners and Square Foot Gardening instructors have experimented—as did Mel Bartholomew himself—with new shapes and configurations that would allow this method to be adapted to various unique needs of different garden sites. Here are some of the variations that are frequently used.

TOP-HAT SQUARE FOOT GARDEN

This very popular variation is also commonly called a pyramid design. The essence is simply a standard 4 × 4 Square Foot Garden box onto which is stacked a smaller box with a smaller number of squares. The merit here is twofold: First, the second tier can provide extra-deep growing space ideal for potatoes or other deep-root vegetables that benefit from this. Second, it increases the visual appeal of the garden by adding a vertical design element to the landscape. A well-tended Square Foot Garden is a very attractive garden, and increasing its height makes it even more attractive in the yard. Vegetables with a cascading habit can be planted in the top layer, or it can be used for those with an extremely upright growing habit, keeping them up and out of the way of lower plants.

In the top-hat design, the second tier is often positioned exactly in the center of the lower box, providing uniform access from all sides, but it can also be placed to one side or flush in the corner of the lower tier. This can work well if, for example, you want vine crops to cascade down the tall side where the two tiers share an edge.

When building this design, first complete the bottom box first and fill it with growing medium. Then, figure out the size and shape of the upper tier, designing it so that it will still allow for perfect 1-foot growing squares on both levels. For example, on a 4 × 4 box, a top tier that is 2 × 2 and centered within the lower tier will allow for four grids in the top tier and twelve grids on the bottom level, positioned around the upper tier. Fill the top tier with growing medium, then build and install the grids in the normal fashion.

L-SHAPED SQUARE FOOT GARDEN

In some situations, an L-shaped Square Foot Garden bed is most practical, such on a patio or deck or in a small yard. The easiest way to do this is by simply butting two rectangular square foot beds together. Two 3 × 8-foot or 2 × 8-foot beds butted together in one corner make an excellent Square Foot Garden. Keeping the overall dimensions of the garden such that both legs are 8 feet long can simplify construction because you can rely on stock 8-foot-long lumber. Built as two separate gardens, this design will let you rearrange the Square Foot Garden if you want.

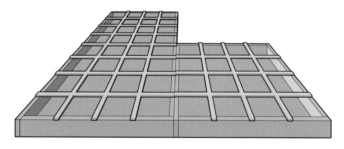

Option 1: Butt two boxes together.

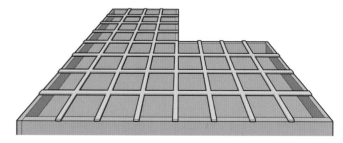

Option 2: Build a single box with irregular shape.

You can also build an L-box as a permanent garden with a shared side where the two legs of the L meet. This design uses slightly less lumber but isn't portable in the same way as if you build it from two separate boxes.

With L-shaped gardens, it's best to keep the width a little narrower, because access to the center area where the two legs meet will require an inconveniently long reach if the legs are a full 4 feet wide.

LONG AND NARROW SQUARE FOOT GARDENS

Square foot gardens that are quite narrow—1 or 2 feet—may be perfect for some applications, such as running around the perimeter of a patio or alongside the fence in a small yard where you want to maximize lawn space. If you are building on a patio surface it is best to build the box with a plywood bottom to give it better stability.

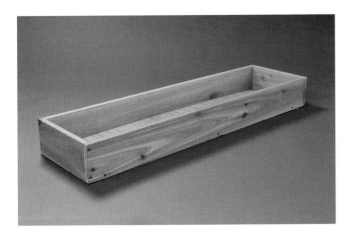

SQUARE FOOT GARDEN RAILING BOXES

The best location for square-foot planting in some homes might be on the railings of a deck. The essence of this kind of garden is a box 1 foot wide and 4 feet (or 6 or 8 feet) long that can be bolted or screwed down securely to the top of the railing. This is really only practical where you have railings that are flat and sturdy enough to carry the weight. Railing Square Foot Gardens can be extremely attractive when trailing vegetable vines cascade over the sides. Build railing boxes with plywood bottoms that can be screwed or bolted securely to a flat railing.

Theoretically, it is possible to hang a Square Foot Garden off the face of a sturdy railing using the kind of metal hangers available at home-improvement stores. However, a true Square Foot Garden needs 1-foot-square planting grids, which means these boxes will carry a fair amount of weight. It's recommended to rest a railing box on top of the railing wherever possible.

It's also not recommended to use railing boxes except on the first story, where they can't do a lot of damage if they fall. If you are trying to garden on the second story or higher, it's best to rest the box on the deck or balcony itself.

EXTRA-DEEP SQUARE FOOT GARDENS

If you use your Square Foot Garden for growing potatoes or some other edible that sends down deep roots, the standard 6-inch-deep box may not be quite enough. If other dimensional lumber (normally available in sizes up to 12-inch widths) won't suffice, you can create deeper sides to your Square Foot Garden by stacking two layers of side boards. Holding two layers together at the corners is done by using pieces of 4 × 4 or 2 × 4 in the corners as cleats with which to attach both layers of side boards.

Short interior posts serve as cleats for attaching the sides of double-layer garden boxes.

An alternative way to join the corners of a Square Foot Garden box made from composite lumber.

Among materials you can use for the sides of a Square Foot Garden box are:

- Repurposed decking boards
- Cedar siding pieces
- Oak or pine floorboards
- Insert leaves from dining tables

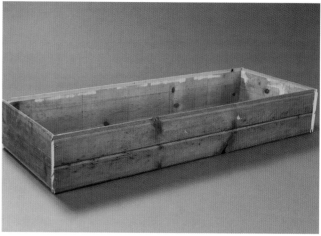

This Square Foot Garden box was built with reclaimed planks of wall paneling.

COMPOSITE-LUMBER SQUARE FOOT GARDENS

Composite lumber of the same type commonly used as surface planks for decks makes a very good material for Square Foot Garden boxes. But because this material does not have the same holding power when screwed into the end grain, it's best to reinforce the inside corners of these boxes with either metal connectors attached with short ½" screws or interior cleats made from short lengths of 2 × 4 or 4 × 4 lumber. Because composite lumber is made from recycled plastics and wood byproducts, it's a material that very much appeals to the inherent efficiency and "green" mentality that is part of our Square Foot Gardening lifestyle.

RECLAIMED LUMBER SQUARE FOOT GARDENS

Reclaimed lumber of all sorts can be used to make a Square Foot Garden bed, and in the right environment, materials that look very rustic and worn can make their own statement in the landscape. A landscape that makes use of repurposed and upcycled materials sends a message of self-sufficiency and environmental consciousness.

The sky is pretty much the limit, in other words. Just about any leftover wood pieces of sufficient length can be recut and put to use to build Square Foot Garden boxes.

STONE OR CONCRETE-BLOCK SQUARE FOOT GARDENS

A variety of stone materials, both newly purchased and reused, can be used to build the walls of a Square Foot Garden. Retaining-wall block, ordinary foundation block, paver brick, and even stacked pieces of sidewalk slab can create very stable walls for your Square Foot Garden. The only trick here is in finding a way to anchor grid material on top of the box walls, but this is usually easily accomplished with a bit of ingenuity. Masonry nails or construction adhesive, for example, can easily secure the ends of the grid to the stone or concrete sides.

IN MEL'S WORDS

Want a garden all winter? Well, who wouldn't, really? Of course, you're probably asking yourself, "How the heck can I garden through the sleet, snow, and freezing temperatures?" Good question, and I've got just the answer for you. If you love gardening and like a bit of a challenge, this may be just the thing for you: build a greenhouse structure! Yes, I know full-blown greenhouses are expensive. But you can start small—maybe with one that's expandable. It doesn't have to be glass; you can make the panels out of thick plastic that will work almost as well.

Take advantage of the sun by making sure one long wall of the greenhouse faces south. Line the wall with tanks or jugs of water, and they will suck up warmth during the day and release it at night, keeping your plants warm and cozy during the chilly evenings without a lot of supplemental heat.

You can build a greenhouse against a garage wall or house foundation wall, which might aid in keeping it warm. One year in Long Island, New York, moving into a new house, I found a way to take advantage of natural heating: I dug down 3 feet and built my greenhouse into the ground. That did two things. First, it limited the amount of glass I needed to use (I built a brick foundation). Second, it helped keep the temperature higher in the winter and cooler in the summer just like a cave in the ground.

All right, let's suppose you can't afford a greenhouse, even a makeshift one. You can build the SFG version of a 3 × 6-foot cold frame, as I did one winter. Rather than build the usual wooden sloping sides and go to the trouble of cutting plywood at an angle, I dug down about 1 foot and created a sloped bed that faced the sun. I created a berm all the way around with the soil I removed. Then, I put a couple inches of sand in the bottom and laid a heating coil (you can find these at home centers and hardware stores) along the bottom and ran it up to a plug and a thermostat. I ran an extension cord out from the garage to the plug, then made a watertight connection for the plug. I kept the temperature between 50°F and 60°F, which conserved electricity but still kept the plants warm. I covered the wires with a little more sand and laid down a weed fabric, 4 inches of compost, and 4 inches of Mel's Mix. So, I had 8 inches of growing soil.

I laid out my squares, put down a grid, and started planting. Around the hole in the ground, I installed a bottomless 3 × 6-foot box made from 2 × 6 lumber, two stories high. It lay right on the sloping bottom so the sides as well as the bottom were sloping toward the southern winter sun.

Of course, you need a top over the cold frame, so I laid a large storm window frame across the wood sides. It kept the plants toasty, and I could easily remove it to water, tend, and harvest my crops or to let a little heat out if things were too hot.

GRID BASICS

The box is, of course, essential to a Square Foot Garden, but all on its own it is really nothing more than a raised garden bed. This raised bed transforms into an official Square Foot Garden when you add the planting grid on top. This is what makes it possible to achieve such amazing yield results, as the 1-foot grid squares, 16 of them in the standard 4 × 4-foot box, allow for very careful planting of seeds and separation of plants for maximum productivity.

HOW TO BUILD A TRADITIONAL SQUARE FOOT GARDEN GRID

The most traditional and basic of grids is created from lengths of ordinary lattice slats or plaster lathe material cut to fit across the Square Foot Garden box, then secured at the intersections with small bolts. It is a very easy thing to do.

IN MEL'S WORDS

Grids need to remain in place during the entire growing season. Remember, you're harvesting and replanting each square throughout the season. Besides that, you want to make sure everyone notices you have an authentic Square Foot Garden.

MATERIALS
Tools and materials you will need include:

- Saw
- ¼ × 1½ × 50" cedar slats (6)
- Drill with ¼" twist bit
- ¼ × 1" bolts with washers and nuts (9)
- 1" exterior screws (12)

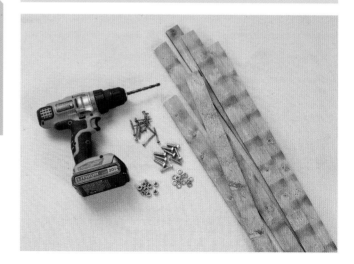

ASSEMBLY

1 Cut slat pieces to length, then position them across the top of the Square Foot Garden box so that they form grid squares that are 1 × 1' in size. Drill ¼" holes at the intersections of the lattice pieces.

2 Next, secure a bolt into each hole and secure it with a washer and nut.

3 Drill ⅛" pilot holes at the ends of each lattice piece, down into the box sides.

4 Secure the lattice strips to the box with screws driven down through the holes.

5 At the end of the season, you can detach the grid from the box by removing the end screws, then collapse the grid, accordion style, to store it for winter.

6 With grid attached, your Square Foot Garden is ready for planting.

5

6

ALTERNATIVE GRID MATERIALS

Cedar lattice slats will be quite resistant to weathering, but all manner of things to form the grid, provided they don't rot away immediately. Here is an ideal place to practice your ingenuity and upcycling skills. For example, if you have old lumber lying around, such as old decking boards, you can rip ¼-inch-thick strips off the boards to make your own cedar lattice strips for Square Foot Garden grids. Although this can also be done with a circular saw or jigsaw, it is much easier to set up a table saw to rip thin strips.

Wood Lathe

Rip-Cut Lumber

Metal Re-Bar

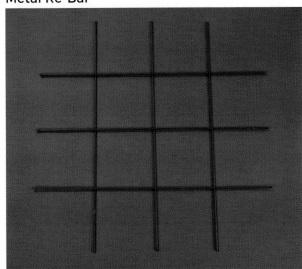

PVC Tubing

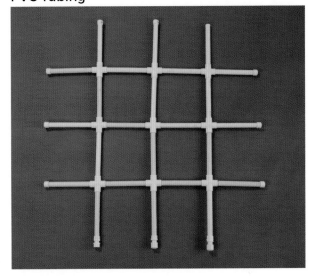

Some examples of alternative materials you can use for the Square Foot Garden grid include wood lathe, bamboo or plastic plant stakes wired together, or leftover pieces of plastic plumbing pipes joined together with cross-fittings. Just about any long, narrow items you have around the house or garage could be upcycled to form a grid.

CHAPTER

SQUARE FOOT GARDEN EXTRAS

I f the essence of a Square Foot Garden is a simple raised bed filled with the special Mel's Mix growing medium and divided into 1-foot-square planting grids, the truly fulfilled Square Foot Garden is one that features the important add-ons that let you take full advantage of the SFG magic and make it more productive, more convenient, and more secure.

A basic box and grid are all you really need, but adding trellises and other extras can make your SFG experience even more rewarding.

GARDENING VERTICALLY

Perhaps most important of all the extras you can bring to a Square Foot Garden is the use of the vertical dimension. Mel Bartholomew himself said this was the innovation that really moved Square Foot Gardening into another realm—Square Foot Gardening was the first technique that demonstrated that many traditional ground-vine vegetables actually love to grow vertically. Plants grown vertically get more air circulation and sun, and getting them off the ground removes them from close contact with many of the pests, fungi, and diseases that can plague them at ground level. And there is the aesthetic issue: a Square Foot Garden with the back edge formed by a green wall of healthy, twining plants is just a beautiful thing to behold.

Over the years, many people have tried different materials for the netting on vertical trellises, but the nylon mesh with large squares that Mel felt to be the best . . . well, it simply is the best. The large squares allow you to readily weave vines and growing fruit back and forth through the squares, and nylon is sturdy enough to support all but the very largest pumpkins. Most other materials that we've experimented with just haven't worked as well. Plastic mesh isn't strong enough, and most wood trellises that are simply stapled together aren't strong enough either, although you might have luck with a homemade wood trellis assembled with sturdy joints (we'll show you that variation later). One suitable alternative is steel fence mesh with large grids, attached to a sturdy wooden framework anchored to the Square Foot Garden box (we'll show you that variation too).

Many newcomers to Square Foot Gardening are surprised to realize just how many vegetables can be grown upward. Not only do tomatoes and other upright vegetables benefit from vertical supports added to a Square Foot Garden, but even many vegetables traditionally grown as ground vines can quite easily be grown upward on a trellis structure attached to a Square Foot Garden bed. At

one display garden in Utah, the Square Foot Gardening Foundation demonstrated how 35-pound pumpkins could happily grow 7 feet in the air. Here are just some of the vegetables that are well suited to growing upwards:

- Tomatoes
- Pole beans
- Cucumbers
- Melons
- Pumpkins
- Squash (summer and winter)

IN MEL'S WORDS

Here's a quick flashback to 1976, when this retired engineer took up gardening. I developed Square Foot Gardening, but as I looked at tomato plants growing in pots on decks and in single-row gardens, I knew my work wasn't complete. Not only are tomatoes America's favorite vegetable to grow, but they also take up the most room and cause quite an unsightly mess by the end of the season if they are allowed to sprawl all over the ground. There are also the complaints of slugs getting in and ruining all the tomatoes as well as gardeners stepping all over the vines and crushing them when trying to harvest the fruit. The whole idea of growing tomatoes this way seems very counterproductive. At the time, the only cages available were too short and too weak to solve the problem.

I said, "This is no way to treat a tomato. We can't let it lie down and sprawl all over the ground. It should be allowed to stand up straight and tall so that it can be proud of itself and a benefit and credit to the community."

Six months later, my vertical frame was designed, tested, and put into operation. It was an all-American design made from rigid German steel conduit and Japanese twine. It was so strong that it held up through rain, sleet, snow, and heavy September storms when the tomato plant filled the entire frame and was loaded with red, ripe tomatoes.

After growing tomatoes this unique and attractive way for several years, I began thinking about the other vine crops that spread all over the garden. Could they be grown the same way? First, I tried pole beans (a no-brainer), then cucumbers and peas. Then even winter and summer squash. They all worked and grew well, and they looked just great growing on a vertical frame. And I was so pleased with the results of growing vine crops this new way that I said, "This is a good thing," and included the method in my first book on Square Foot Gardening.

The merits of growing vertically in a Square Foot Garden can be described by the classic Why, How, Where, and When list:

WHY Should You Grow Vertically?

- It is spectacular—a visual treat for the eyes.
- It saves space—no additional garden beds are necessary; everything you need can be grown in in a Square Foot Garden box.
- Vining crops grow more successfully—separated from contact with the ground, fungal problems and rot are less likely.
- It is less expensive than you imagine—it only requires ordinary building materials.
- Vertical structures properly built will last for years.

HOW Do You Grow Vertically?

- Build a sturdy frame and attach it to your Square Foot Garden box.
- Use a nylon mesh or other fill material that provides support and space for vines to grow through.

WHERE Do You Grow Vertically?

- Along the north edge of your Square Foot Garden box.
- Next to any fence or building wall.

WHEN Do You Grow Vertically?

- Anytime before vine crops start sprawling over the ground.

HOW TO BUILD A CLASSIC SQUARE FOOT GARDEN TRELLIS

Mel developed the classic trellis for a 4 × 4-foot Square Foot Garden box after years of experimentation, and it remains perhaps the best way for supporting vertical crops—ridiculously simple, easy, and inexpensive.

For the vertical supports, ordinary electrical conduit has proven to be an inexpensive and very sturdy material to use. It never rots away, and it is strong enough to bear up under the winds that can buffet a trellis once it is filled with growing vines. The bottom ends of the frame are fit over lengths of ordinary concrete rebar driven deep into the ground at the corners of the Square Foot Garden box. For the top corners of the trellis, convenient elbows or sweep fittings can be attached to make the transitions from the vertical poles to the horizontal crossmember.

These project directions provide for a 5-foot-tall trellis that spans one side of a 4 × 4-foot planting box. The materials can easily be adapted for a taller trellis or to fit a Square Foot Garden box that is a different size.

Positioning the Trellis

When deciding where to place the vertical frame for a trellis, keep in mind that you don't want the vines to shade the rest of the garden.

For this reason, it's best to place the trellis on the north side of the box. If you want more vertical crops, you can make double- or triple-sized boxes, then orient them running east–west so there is a long line of planting grids along the north. Or, you can make a specialty Square Foot Garden box that holds only vertical crops—such as a 2 × 12-foot box that stands adjacent to a fence or wall. To hide the sparse bottoms of the vines, you can add ornamental flowers or low-growing crops to the front grids.

There are many types of trellises you can use on a Square Foot Garden, but the old standard—nylon netting attached to a framework of metal conduit—remains one of the best.

Any number of vining crops can be grown up this deceivingly strong trellis made from metal conduit and nylon netting.

Anchoring the Trellis

Firmly anchoring the vertical supports of the trellis is critical. The trellis should run all the way to the ground along one side of the Square Foot Garden box, with the ends fitted over lengths of ½-inch-diameter rebar driven into the ground before the conduit frame in installed. For extra reinforcement, you can also anchor the bottom of the trellis frame to the wooden box itself using galvanized pipe straps.

Extra-Strong Frames for Heavy Crops

If you plan to grow extra-heavy vine crops, such as watermelons, squash, or pumpkins, replace the rebar support posts with steel fence posts driven into the ground—short, 3-foot-tall posts will work just fine. After the fence posts are driven, you can attach the conduit with pipe clamps. With this construction, a trellis frame is strong enough to hold almost any weight at any height.

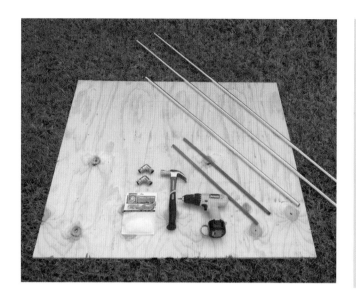

MATERIALS

The materials you'll need include:

- 90° conduit elbow fittings (2)
- 4' length of ½" steel electrical conduit (1)
- ½" steel rebar, 18" long (2)
- Hammer
- ½" steel electrical conduit, 5' long (2)
- Drill driver
- Trellis netting
- Scissors or knife
- Eye and ear protection
- Work gloves

ASSEMBLY

1

2

1 Attach an elbow fitting to each end of the 4'-long conduit crossbar. Lay the crossbar across the side of the Square Foot Garden box where the trellis will be installed. Drive a length of rebar into the ground at the point corresponding to the end socket on the crossbar, using a hammer. Drive each rebar about halfway into the ground. (If building an extra-strong frame, use fence posts instead of rebar.)

2 Attach the top crossbar to the uprights by sliding the sockets of the elbows over the pipes, then securing the screws tightly.

3

3 Slide the 5'-long conduit pipes over the rebar. (Or use pipe clamps to attach the pipes to fence posts.)

COMPLETION

4 Spread out the netting on a flat surface, making sure there are no snarls. Tie the netting onto the two top corners. Cut the netting at each connection along the top bar, leaving one long strand. Loop each strand over the top of the frame and tie it in a knot. Make sure to keep each strand the same length to ensure the net isn't crooked.

5 This double-wide Square Foot Garden fitted with two conduit-and-nylon trellises is growing pole beans and tomato plants supported by the trellises, joined by sage and squash. The harvest will be amazing.

6 Cut the connections down each side and repeat the tying process by securing each strand to the vertical pipe. Try to keep the length of the loops uniform to avoid making the netting crooked.

HOW TO BUILD A WIRE FENCE TRELLIS

This slight variation on the conduit and nylon net trellis uses a frame of 2 × 4 lumber with an interior "net" made of welded steel wire fencing material. Most fencing products sold in home-improvement centers use a 2 × 4-inch grid, and while this will be fine to use for trellis material if you are growing pole beans, cucumbers, or other small crops, if you're planning to grow squash or pumpkins up your trellis, you'll want to seek out a fencing material with larger grids, such as 4 × 4. The 2 × 4-inch-grid fencing (often sold as "rabbit guard") won't be large enough to allow larger vines to weave freely.

The edges of the fencing are secured to the wood frame with ordinary fence staples. This project is sized to provide a 5-foot-tall trellis for a standard 4 × 4 Square Foot Garden box. If your box is a different size, adjust the measurements of the frame and fencing accordingly.

MATERIALS
The materials you'll need include:

- Level
- 2 × 4 lumber, 5½' long (2)
- 2 × 4 lumber, 4' long (1)
- 1½" deck screws
- Drill driver
- Galvanized mending plates (4)
- Hot-dipped galvanized fencing, 4 × 5'
- Wire cutters
- Fencing staples
- Saw
- Eye and ear protection
- Work gloves

ASSEMBLY

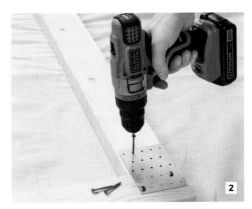

1 Temporarily attach the two 2 × 4 uprights to the corners of the box on the outside face, using screws. Use a level to make sure they are perfectly plumb. Position the single 4' crossmember between the uprights and mark it for cutting.

2 Lay the frame pieces on a work surface and join the crossmember to the uprights using mending plates and screws. Using mending plates on both sides of each joint.

3 Cut a piece of wire fencing to fit the trellis frame, using wire cutters. The fencing can run slightly short at the bottom, where the uprights will be screwed to the garden box.

4 Attach the fencing piece to the trellis frame with fencing staples driven every 8".

5 Add growing medium (Mel's Mix) to cover the bottom of the box, then water. Repeat in gradual stages (at least three times) until the box is full. You're now ready to add the grid and plant your garden.

6 Your trellis is complete. The grid squares adjacent to the trellis will be perfect for growing vining crops, such as beans, cucumbers, or melons.

BUILDING AN A-FRAME TRELLIS

A straight trellis along one edge of a Square Foot Garden box isn't always the most practical solution to the need to grow upward. Large tomatoes, for example, need support from all sides. This adjustable A-frame trellis, with a frame built from 1 × 4 lumber and two metal hinges, meets that need. It can be installed in a variety of ways—with the legs in two adjacent rows of box grids or with the legs in the first and third row to provide plenty of growing space beneath.

The face of the trellis frame can be covered with either the nylon netting used in the classic Square Foot Garden trellis (see page 98) or the welded wire fencing used in the trellis variation (page 102). Or, as we've chosen to do in our demonstration, you can install wooden crossmembers running up both sides, ladder fashion, which makes for a sturdy support structure for large tomato plants.

In our example, the A-frame trellis is sized to fit exactly inside a classic 4 × 4 Square Foot Garden box. For a different-sized box, this design is easy to adapt by changing the sizes of the parts.

MATERIALS
The materials you'll need include:

- Tape measure
- Saw
- 1 × 4 cedar lumber, 6' long (4)
- 1 × 4 cedar lumber 4' long (4)
- 1¼" deck screws
- Drill driver
- 2 galvanized hinges with hardware
- 1 × 2 cedar lumber, 4' long (10)

ASSEMBLY

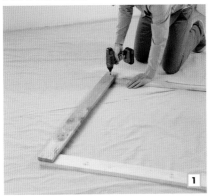

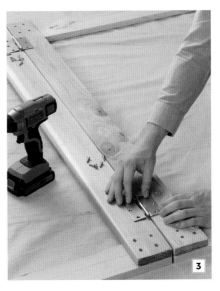

1 Lay out the 6'-long leg pieces on a flat surface, such as a driveway. Arrange them in pairs, end to end, with the legs spaced 4' apart. Now cut four pieces of 1 × 4 to 4' lengths for cross-rails. Lay one pair of cross-rails across the top of each pair of legs, flush with the end. Make sure the legs are exactly parallel, then secure the top cross the rails with 1¼" deck screws driven down through the rails and into the legs.

2 Position the bottom cross-rails across each pair of legs, the top edge of the rails 1' above the bottom of the legs. Check to make sure the leg pairs are square, then attach the bottom rails with deck screws.

3 Butt the top of the leg pairs together, then place the two hinges across the top rails, just inside the legs. Secure the hinges to the top rails with the included hardware screws.

ATTACHING THE TRELLIS

4 Place the trellis frame on the flat surface. Measure and cut 1 × 2 cedar trellis bars to match the length between the outer edges of the legs (4' in our project). Test-fit the trellis bars across the pairs of legs. On our example with 66" legs, there will be one trellis bar spaced every 10", beginning at the top edge of the bottom rail. If your dimensions are different, space the trellis bars accordingly. Test fit all five bars on each leg frame before attaching any of them.

5 Once satisfied with the layout, secure the trellis bars with 1¼" deck screws driven through the bars and into the legs.

6 Position the A-frame trellis in the Square Foot Garden box as desired. In our example, we are embedding the legs in the first and third rows, which will leave the center squares open, ideal for planting large tomato plants.

PROTECTING YOUR SQUARE FOOT GARDEN

A Square Foot Garden is so productive that it will be very, very attractive to a variety of insect and animal pests, including rabbits, raccoons, and birds. Neighborhood kids may also be tempted to pick your strawberries or gulp down your cherry tomatoes. While we encourage you to let kids eat your produce (with the supervision and the approval of their parents, of course), your gardens need to be protected from most of the other types of pests. In addition, your garden may need occasional protection from the elements and from weather extremes: low temps, harsh sun, strong winds, or hail and heavy rain. Here are some projects that will help offer protection for your Square Foot Gardens.

HOW TO BUILD A WIRE CAGE

A simple cage made from chicken wire (also called poultry netting) that covers your entire Square Foot Garden box is a simple yet effective way to protect it from rabbits, rodents, and other pests. A well-constructed cage can also keep out dogs and cats. Chicken wire works quite well for this purpose and can be cut with pliers or wire cutters. The ends are sharp, so be sure to wear gloves. Chicken wire comes in 3-, 4-, 5-, or 6-foot-wide rolls with 1-inch or 2-inch openings. The 1-inch size is a little harder to work with but is much stronger. Some hardware or farm-supply stores may be able to sell exactly the amount you need off of large spool rolls in the stores—otherwise, you'll need to buy a full roll.

The cage is light enough you can simply lift it off and put it back on for harvesting or tending your garden. Make sure to build your wire cage to fit the mature size of the plants you're growing—once plants start growing through the openings in the cage, it will be very hard to get the cage on and off. A full cage needs a wooden-frame bottom for support but will fit nicely over the garden box.

The cage bottom is built with simple 1 × 2 pine lumber, 4 feet long, assembled in a square with deck screws driven into the corners. Then, you'll cut and shape chicken wire to the 4 × 4 frame to whatever height you want. The chicken wire is stapled to the wood frame with ⅜-inch staples. Because the ends of chicken wire are sharp, you may want to cover the points with duct tape to prevent scratches when you are moving the cover. You can also attach the wire to the inside of the 1 × 2 frame, where the sharp points won't scratch you.

Some gardeners find that it's helpful to have several cages made up ahead of time—one at 6 inches or so, another at 12 inches, another at 18 inches, and so forth. This allows you to swap them out as your garden grows upward.

You can also temporarily attach protective cloth or plastic sheeting to the cage to protect your garden from cold snaps, or to shield it from harsh sun or wind at times when young seedlings are most susceptible. These covers can be clipped to the cage with ordinary clothespins or spring clamps. Shade cloth, landscape fabric, or plastic sheeting can be used to cover your cage, depending on what your needs are.

MATERIALS

The materials you'll need include:

- 1 × 2 pine boards, 4' long (4)
- Drill with driver bit and ³⁄₁₆" twist bit
- 2" deck screws
- Roll of chicken wire
- Wire cutters
- Stapler with heavy-duty ⅜" staples (optional)
- Plastic zip ties
- Duct tape (optional)
- Eye and ear protection
- Work gloves

ASSEMBLY

1 Drill two ³⁄₁₆" pilot holes in one end of each 1 × 2 board.

2 Arrange the sides of the cage frame in a square, and join the pieces together by driving deck screws through the pilot holes and into the end grain of the adjoining piece.

3 Roll out the chicken wire and cut it to length, with the sides high enough to cover your mature plants. Depending on the height you want, a single piece of chicken wire might be sufficient to wrap and attach upright around the entire frame. Or, you may be able to cut two long pieces and attach them to opposite sides of the frame. The number of pieces you need will be determined by the size of your frame and the width of your chicken-wire roll.

4 Lay the frame onto the length of chicken wire and use it as a template to bend the wire sharply to form corners for the cage.

5 Position the chicken wire around the wooden frame and secure it to the frame with heavy-duty staples or zip ties.

6 Use zip ties to secure the open areas and to add a top panel for the cage, if necessary. If there are sharp wire tips exposed, use small tabs of duct tape to cover them.

7 When in use, the cage can easily be lifted on or off the square-foot box for maintenance of the garden or to harvest.

 IN MEL'S WORDS

If tunnelers are a problem in your neck of the woods, you can take extra precautions to protect all your delicious plants. As you can imagine, voles and gophers like to dig through nice, soft dirt—but they really don't like their paws to come into contact with sharp metal edges. That's why the best deterrent is a wire product called hardware cloth, available at your local hardware of home-building store. It comes in a roll; buy by the foot only what you need. Place it under your box to block these vermin.

ARCHED TRELLIS OVER TWO BOXES

Here is a unique way to take vertical advantage of not only the Square Foot Garden boxes themselves but also the space over the walkway between two boxes. This project is suitable if you have two or more Square Foot Garden boxes positioned with aisles 2 to 4 feet wide.

This design calls for ordinary ½-inch steel concrete reinforcement bar (rebar)—the type with the raised ribs running along the length. It is readily available at home-improvement centers in lengths up to 20 feet, which will be plenty for your purposes. If you cannot find rebar of sufficient length at your local building centers, you can also wire together shorter lengths in order to make the ribs for the archway.

To build the archway, you will bend long sections of rebar to arch over the walkway between two Square Foot Garden boxes, planting the ends of the rebar in the sides of the boxes. These lengths of rebar will form ribs, over which you will attach welded-steel fencing. If you prefer, you can use a nylon netting instead of the fencing.

Our design aims at an archway that is 6 feet high at the center, allowing ample room to walk beneath it. The length of the rebar ribs, then, will depend on the width of the aisle between your boxes:

> 2-foot-wide aisles: 14-foot-long rebar ribs
> 3-foot-wide aisles: 15-foot-long rebar ribs
> 4-foot-wide aisles: 16-foot-long rebar ribs

If you will be covering your archway trellis with nylon netting, you might want to add some extra reinforcement bars, one at the top ridge of the trellis and one each on each side, at about 4 feet or so above the ground. If you are using welded fencing, this reinforcement isn't necessary.

Our demonstration uses classic 4 × 4-foot boxes and an archway with three ribs. For bigger boxes, you may want to add one or more additional ribs. Normally, it's recommended that a trellis be placed on the north side of a Square Foot Garden box, but in this case, we recommend that the archway runs north–south on boxes that are squared up to compass directions. This will minimize the amount of shade cast on the plants and ensure that no vegetables are shaded for too much of the day.

Not only does this archway provide extra growing space for vegetables, but it will be very attractive addition to your garden as the growing season progresses and climbing plants create an inviting, shaded walkway between the Square Foot Garden boxes.

MATERIALS
The materials you'll need include:

- ½" steel rebar, 15' long (3)
- Hacksaw or jigsaw with metal-cutting blade (if needed)
- Pipe clamps with screws (12)
- Roll of welded steel fencing, 4' wide
- Tape measure
- Wire ties
- Wire cutters
- Torpedo level
- Eye and ear protection
- Work gloves

MATERIALS AND TOOLS

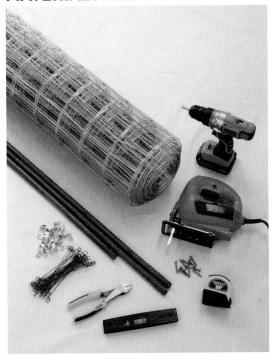

PREPARATION

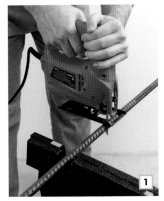

1 If necessary, cut the lengths of rebar to the proper length using a hacksaw or jigsaw with metal cutting blade. With the assistance of a helper, bend the rebar into a U shape with the space between the legs equal to the width of the aisle between your boxes. Bend slowly to avoid creating a sharp crimp. You may want to use a large tree or heavy stake driven into the ground as a pivot point around which to bend the bars.

2 Insert the first rib at the front corners of the Square Foot Garden boxes, driving the ends of the rib down into the soil, if possible. Make sure the legs are perfectly plumb by checking with a level. Secure the rib to the boxes with pipe clamps and screws. Repeat for the other ribs, making sure the middle rib is exactly centered between the outside ribs.

ASSEMBLY

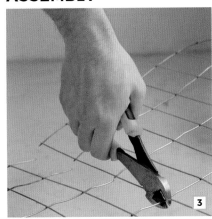

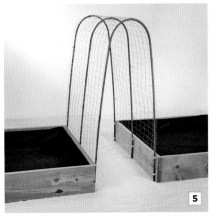

3 Unroll the welded-wire fencing and flatten it out. Use a tape measure to measure the arch of the ribs, from the top of the box on one side to the top of the box on the other side. Use wire cutters to cut the fencing to this length.

4 Lift the length of wire fencing over the top of the ribs and bend it down on the ends to meet the bottom of the arched ribs. Use wire ties to secure the fencing to the ribs. Check frequently to make sure the ribs remain straight as you work from the peak of the archway down to the bottom on both sides. Again, a helper makes this work easier.

5 When planting your Square Foot Garden boxes, use the grids closest to the archway for the vining, climbing plants. Climbing vegetables such as cucumbers, pole beans, or even melons can be trained up the archway, with the center aisle space offering convenient access for harvesting the hanging produce.

DECORATIVE ARCHWAYS

Instead of an arched trellis for growing produce, you can also build a purely decorative archway between boxes using copper plumbing pipes joined together with T-fittings and elbows. Any number of "looks" are possible, limited only by your imagination. A Square Foot Garden is attractive as well as productive, so turn it into a landscape design element with an ornamental archway over the aisles. Decorative archways are also readily available at garden centers.

HOW TO BUILD A PROTECTIVE DOME

A very simple but functional dome support can be made with pieces of ordinary ½-inch PVC plumbing pipe arched from corner to corner of your Square Foot Garden box and secured in the center. This dome framework can support any type of cover. In the early spring, it can be covered with clear plastics to retain heat from the sun; in the late spring, it can be covered with cheesecloth to keep out egg-laying insects; and in the summer, it can be covered with shade cloth to provide shade for young, tender plants. In the fall, it can also protect late crops.

MATERIALS
The materials you will need include:

- ½" PVC pipe, 10' long (2)
- Zip tie
- Plastic sheeting or other covering of your choice

1, 2 Bend two lengths of PVC pipe from corner to corner in the Square Foot Garden box, inserting the ends deep into the ground. The bent pipes should form a tent-like frame over the box.

3 Secure the dome frame at the intersection of the bent pipes using a plastic zip tie.

4 Cover the dome frame with the covering of your choice. Thick, durable plastic sheeting as shown here can protect your plants form many things, including harmful weather and animal and insect pests.

IN MEL'S WORDS

Everyone loves corn—especially chipmunks, squirrels, and raccoons!

To keep them out and your harvest in, try this foolproof secret. Put one steel fence post in each corner of your 4 × 4 garden. Use tall metal 5- or 6-foot fence posts, and then, when the corn reaches 4 feet, run chicken wire with 1-inch openings around the outside, forming four walls. Next, add one more piece across the top at a height of about 4 feet.

This will keep the critters out of the corn and prevent the crows from eating the seeds and seedlings when first planted. Then, as the corn grows, it will grow right through the top of the wire, which will support the tall corn stalks when the wind blows—at the same time, keeping the raccoons and chipmunks from getting in before the corn can be harvested. You can easily tie the horizontal top wire with temporary bows so that you can undo a few and still reach in. Because it is chicken wire, make sure you wear a long-sleeved shirt when you reach in so you don't get scratched. You'll be able to water easily either by hand or using a long-handled wand and shut-off valve on the end of your hose.

BUILDING A COVERED-WAGON SUPPORT

In this variation of the protective dome project, the ribs of the covering arch in pairs on opposite sides of the Square Foot Garden box rather than meeting in the center. This provides slightly more interior space for larger plants, and it allows the ends to remain open so that plenty of air circulates even while overhead protection is offered. It is also somewhat easier to use when you want to cover and uncover your garden.

It requires the same two 10-foot-long PVC pipes as the dome support but adds a short 4-foot-long ridge-strut pipe running between the arches. Tying the intersection doesn't work in this design, so you will have to drill holes in the center of the arches and in each end of the ridge strut to hold zip ties that will connect the ridge strut to the arches.

If you don't want a frame this high, you can cut the PVC pipes down to 6 or 8 feet to make a much lower wagon top. But don't go any lower than this, because the pipes need to be at least 6 feet long order to bend into an arch shape.

As you'll soon learn, this shape makes it easy to throw a blanket over the entire 4 × 4 Square Foot Garden box on those cold nights.

MATERIALS
The materials you'll need include:

- Tape measure
- ½" PVC pipe, 10' long (2)
- ½" PVC pipe, 4' long (1)
- Drill and twist bits
- Zip ties
- Eye and ear protection
- Work gloves

ASSEMBLY

1 Locate the centers of the two 10'-long PVC pipes.

2 Drill holes through the pipes at these marked points.

3 Place the pipes along opposite sides of the Square Foot Garden box, arching the ends into the ground in the corners.

4 Drill holes in the ends of the 4'-long PVC pipe, then use zip ties to secure it to the middle of the arched pipes, forming a ridge strut at the top of the arch.

HOW TO BUILD A CROP CAGE

This modular cage features a series of panels built with 2 × 2 frames and covered with nylon-mesh bird screening. You can build four side panels if you wish to protect your garden on all four sides from small animals or add a fifth top panel to protect your garden from insects feeding birds from above. The nylon mesh will stop most casual animals from entering your garden, but if your pests are particularly prone to gnawing in an effort to get at your vegetables, you can cover the side panels with chicken wire, which rodents won't be tempted to chew.

The individual frames are intended to be temporarily clamped or screwed together so that they can be quickly removed when you need to tend your garden. For extra sturdiness against the wind, the side panels can be screwed to the base of your Square Foot Garden box.

MATERIALS
The materials you'll need include:

- 2 × 2 pine lumber
- Tape measure
- Saw
- 2½" deck screws
- L-brackets (4 for each cage panel)
- Nylon mesh
- Stapler with heavy-duty staples
- Utility knife
- Spring clamps or C-clamps (optional)
- Eye and ear protection
- Work gloves

ASSEMBLY

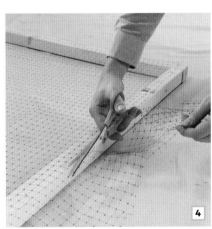

1 Measure one side of your Square Foot Garden box to determine the width of the side panels on the crop cage. Cut top and bottom frame pieces to this length. Cut two side frame pieces to whatever height you choose for your cage—ours is built to 4'.

2 Assemble a square frame by laying the top, bottom, and sides in a square on a flat surface and securing the joints with 2½" deck screws. Make sure the top and bottom overlap the side pieces.

3 Reinforce the joints of the frame pieces with L-brackets screwed to the frame.

4 Unroll the nylon mesh and stretch it over the face of the frame. Use a stapler to secure the mesh to the 2 × 2 frame. After attaching, use a utility knife to trim the edges to size. Repeat this process for the other side frame.

5 The back and front panels will be slightly wider than the side panels because they will overlap the side panels. Measure the back and front of the Square Foot Garden box and add 3" to accommodate the frames on the side panels. Cut frame members and assemble the panels for the front and back of the cage.

6 Assemble the cage panels around the Square Foot Garden box and secure the corners with clamps or screws. If you are creating a top panel, measure the opening and build a top panel to fit over the cage. The crop cage can stay in place protecting your garden most of the time, because you can water your crops right through the mesh. When you need to tend your garden or harvest vegetables, one or more panels can be temporarily removed. At the end of the season, the panels can be stored flat in your garage or shed.

ACCESSORIES FOR YOUR SQUARE FOOT GARDEN

Another group of SFG add-ons includes a variety of accessories that make Square Foot Gardening more efficient and more convenient. These include solutions for supporting plants that may grow tall but are not really suitable for trellis growth; ways to cover the walkways between Square Foot Garden beds; a simple composter for recycling old plant material; and a cold frame for giving your young, tender plants a head start in the spring.

PLANT SUPPORTS

In a traditional garden, tall, heavy plants such as peppers, eggplants, and giant marigolds are supported against toppling by individual staking, either with single poles or with some kind of cage. But in a Square Foot Garden, the easiest way to support the branches of these plants is to make a permanent cage covering the entire garden box, through which the plants can grow. The cage's height depends on the mature height of the plants you are growing, and it can be sized to cover the entire 16-square grid in a classic 4 × 4-foot box or adapted to cover just a few squares in the box.

The cage can be self-supporting with sides that stick into to the soil—like the commercial cages widely available. Or, if you are making a support for the entire box, it is very easy to put of stake of some type—either wood or metal—into each corner, then suspend the wires or netting between those four corners.

Nylon netting is actually a very good choice, because it is soft and cushiony and won't cut the plants when they rub against it in the wind. It has large openings you can reach into and through which the plants can easily grow.

The corner posts for this kind of large plant support must be very strong and firmly planted so that the horizontal wire or netting won't sag. The posts can be constructed of wood and driven into the ground or attached to the sides of the box with wood screws. Or, you can use metal pipes, metal fence posts, or lengths of rebar driven into the ground at the corners of the box. Smooth posts may have some advantages, as the netting can be slid up the poles as the plants grow taller.

HOW TO INSTALL A FULL-BOX PLANT-SUPPORT NET

This is a very simple, easy-to-build plant support that requires only a 4 × 4 piece of nylon netting and four posts. For tools, you need only a hammer and, if necessary, a saw suitable for cutting the metal posts to length. In our demonstration, we are using metal conduit for the corners, but lengths of steel rebar would also work.

MATERIALS

The materials you'll need include:

- Metal conduit (4 pieces)
- Saw (if needed)
- Pipe clamps (optional)
- Nylon netting
- Scissors
- Duct tape or zip ties
- Mallet or hammer
- Eye and ear protection
- Work gloves

ASSEMBLY

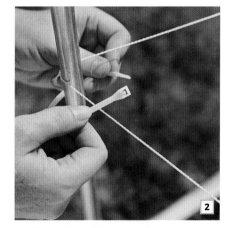

1 Cut four metal bars to the length you want for the corner posts. Ideally, the posts will need to be driven at least 1' down into the soil, so oversize the posts by at least 1'. If you wish, you can secure the posts in the corners with pipe clamps driven into the sides of the box.

2, 3 Cut a piece of nylon netting to 4 × 4' and slide it down over the corner posts. Secure it in place with pieces of duct tape. (If you are using lengths of rebar with ridges, zip ties can be used to secure the netting.) Once the plants start growing, their stems will hold the netting in place, causing it to become self-supporting.

4 Nylon netting stretched between four corner posts provides a plant support covering the entire Square Foot Garden box. With long enough posts, a second layer of netting could be added as the plants grow taller.

IN MEL'S WORDS

And now a word about composters . . .

A composting operation can be as simple as a pile of leaves, weeds, and kitchen scraps. Mother Nature does it all the time—go to any forest or field, and you'll see she gets the job done without any structures. But people are different. We like to conserve space and keep things in their place. This means we usually want to build a container or enclosure for our compost materials, which also speeds up the operation by creating bulk, allowing the pile to heat up and decompose faster.

What can we buy or build? There are many compost containers on the market, mostly made from plastic. All work well and are attractive and reasonably priced. There are composters that tumble or turn, speeding up the process, but they cost more—and, worst of all, you still have to turn them. It's fun at first, but it gets old very fast.

MAKE YOUR OWN

We need a structure that will hold a pile of material in either a round or a square shape. Wire fencing works well for round and even square structures if you use four fence posts. Make wire cylinders at least 3 to 4 feet in diameter. The exact length of fencing you'll need isn't critical, but if you want a 3-foot-diameter composter, buy 10 feet of fencing. If you want a 4-foot-diameter composter, buy 15 feet of fencing and have enough for a door.

And if you don't like round composters, buy four 6-foot-long steel fence posts, drive them in each corner of your composter location, bend the wire around those, and you'll have a square composter, much more suited to Square Foot Gardening. Find the best location for your composter and fill as explained in Chapter 5. When full or ready to turn, just lift up the wire cylinder, place it next to the pile, and use a garden fork to fill the cylinder in its new location—you've just turned the pile!

WITH A GATE

Another idea is to make an enclosure with an opening, so it's easier to get into to mix and water or even turn. Start by driving two steel fence posts in the ground at your selected location; place them about 3 or 4 feet apart. Then attach your wire fencing to these posts. Two options are available for you: with and without a gate. If you want a gate, it will cost you an extra 3 or 4 feet of fencing. No big deal, and it will look nicer and be neater when the enclosure starts filling up. You still tie or wire the fencing to both fence posts; one becomes the hinge, the other the door latch.

Make the latch S-hook from wire or buy this type of hook at the store. You can have one compost bin, two together, or even three, depending on how large your operation is.

WEEKLY BINS

Just like the wire enclosures, you can have one, two, or up to six bins all together for Monday through Saturday. (Don't forget we rest on Sunday!) When and why would you need more than one? When you get serious about composting, you may be able to get enough material to fill up one every week. Then, for mixing (as explained in Chapter 5), you just move material from a full bin into an empty one right next to it. The nice thing about a series is you only need three pallets for each additional bin.

Composting is essential to a Square Foot Gardening lifestyle, so if you don't already have one, now's the time to start a compost pile or bin.

I could include directions for other materials to use, such as bricks or cement blocks, landscape timbers, or logs, but no one is going to build a composter out of those materials. They would be too expensive and inefficient. They may look good in books but not in our system because they are just not practical.

Of course, no one says you have to have an enclosure, but if you're a Square Foot Gardener and you have nice square boxes for all of your garden, why would you want just a pile for your composter?

HOW TO BUILD A SIMPLE WIRE COMPOSTER

A compost bin can be an elaborate affair with wooden sides made of high-quality cedar or redwood, but you can create a perfectly serviceable composter from five metal fencing posts, a piece of 4-foot-wide welded-metal fencing about 8 to 10 feet long, and a dozen or so 1 × 4 pine boards. With this composter, it's very easy to add materials and turn your compost regularly.

This design is from Joel Karsten, author of *Straw Bale Gardens Complete*.

MATERIALS

The materials you'll need include:

- Metal fence posts, 4' long (5)
- Hammer or mallet
- Spool of wire
- Wire cutters
- 1 × 4 pine lumber, 4' to 6' long (12)
- 4' wide wire fencing, 8' to 10' long
- Eye and ear protection
- Work gloves

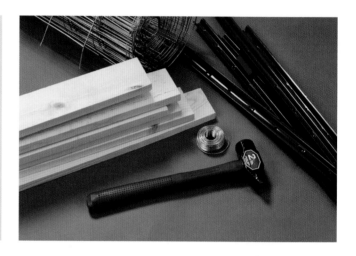

ASSEMBLY

1 Begin by driving in two metal posts, spaced about 1" apart, using a hammer or mallet. Secure the tops of the posts together with wire, maintaining the spacing. Slip one 1 × 4 board between the posts.

At the other end of the board, drive two more posts to sandwich in the 1 × 4, and again wire the posts together at the top.

Wrap wire fencing in a half loop around the back of the bin and attach it to the rear posts with wire. If the metal posts have tabs, you can use these to grip the fencing wire. Along the back side of fencing hoop, drive another stake near the center of the hoop and secure the post and fencing together with wire.

2 When you use your composter, just fill it from the top, adding boards as the level of materials rises. When you need to turn and mix your compost, you can simply remove the boards for access.

AISLES

When gardening with several Square Foot Garden boxes, most people simply place the boxes on the lawn and leave the aisles between boxes as growing grass. There's nothing wrong with this—it creates a natural look and is easy enough to maintain through regular mowing and edge-trimming. But if you don't want grass in the aisles, you can lay down a mulch, such as wood chips, shredded wood, or gravel.

Attach an elbow fitting to each end of the 4'-long conduit crossbar. Lay the crossbar across the side of the Square Foot Garden box where the trellis will be installed. Drive a length of rebar into the ground at the point corresponding to the end socket on the crossbar, using a hammer. Drive each rebar about halfway into the ground. (If building an extra-strong frame, use fence posts instead of rebar.)

MULCHING THE AISLES

For best results, strip away lawn grass and weeds from the aisles, then put down a layer of landscape fabric, which is readily available in 3-, 4-, and 5-foot rolls. Don't use sheets of plastic, because it won't allow water to drain through it.

For the surface mulch, there are many materials you can use: shredded wood, bark chips, gravel, pine needles, straw, or leaf mulch. A 1- to 2-inch layer is usually enough—just enough to cover the landscape fabric. If you use organic mulches, they will eventually break down and decompose. It's best to scoop them up and add them to your compost heap yearly, then lay down a new layer of mulch. If you just add new mulch over the old, weeds will eventually take hold in the thickening layer.

OTHER AISLE OPTIONS

You can also create walkways between the boxes using wood planks, concrete pavers, or repurposed clay bricks. Take out any weeds and lay down landscape fabric first. Bricks and pavers can be used to create some very interesting patterns. A final idea: use artificial grass or indoor/outdoor patio carpeting to cover the aisles between Square Foot Garden boxes.

IN MEL'S WORDS

In my PBS TV garden, we had a small 15 × 15' area with several boxes and plain dirt aisles. I spent 5 minutes every week running an action hoe over the soil to cut off any new weeds, and it looked pretty nice. But then, some of the people in one of the classes I was giving wanted to know how to lay brick, so I thought this would be fun to teach as well as improving the garden. So, without moving the boxes, we laid down many layers of newspaper. Next, we added a 1-inch layer of sand and then started laying bricks right on that sand base. No mortar of cement is needed—just fill in the tight joints with loose sand. When we got to the existing 4 × 4 garden boxes, we just went right around them. It went well, and in one afternoon it was all done. What an improvement—wow! We added some patio furniture, and this area became a favorite spot to sit and enjoy the yard and garden. We also began to notice more of a certain kind of visitor to the garden: the birds and bees and butterflies and so many more insects. And all for the price of a few bricks (well, a small truckload actually) and a little sand.

Frost-resistant bricks or pavers make smart paths. Place them on a sand bed and tap each brick down as shown so it is even and level with the others.

Making Mel's Mix can be a family affair.

MEL'S MIX: THE MAGICAL GROWING MEDIUM

At the root of the amazing results you will experience with the Square Foot Gardening method is the stuff that actually holds the plant roots: the specially formulated growing medium that over the years has become known as Mel's Mix. Years of experimentation led Mel Bartholomew to a simple mixture of equal parts peat moss, coarse vermiculite, and blended compost as the perfect growing medium for his revolutionary gardening method. Mel was forever experimenting and adapting his method, but although he recognized that there were circumstances under which gardeners might need to alter the ingredients in the growing medium, he never, ever found anything that could fully substitute for the original Mel's Mix formula. He felt genuinely sorry for any gardener who didn't grow with this unique mixture.

And longtime Square Foot Gardeners who have experimented report largely the same thing. Filling a Square Foot Garden box with ordinary garden soil is an assurance of disappointment. Using commercial potting-soil mixture may give better results than garden soil, but it is expensive and doesn't give nearly the same measure of success as Mel's Mix. Having a garden center blend topsoil and compost and deliver it to your home doesn't really work either.

The thing that makes a Square Foot Garden—and the thing that makes it work—is Mel's Mix.

The Mel's Mix mantra is simple:

1. Make a mixture of one-third garden compost, one-third peat moss, and one-third coarse vermiculite.
2. Add it to your Square Foot Garden box.
3. Enjoy amazing productivity!

There will be situations in which it's necessary and okay to substitute ingredients. We'll get to that in due course. But first, let's discuss why Mel's Mix is the best of all solutions for a growing medium in your Square Foot Garden.

ADVANTAGES OF MEL'S MIX

There are several principal advantages to filling your Square Foot Garden boxes with Mel's Mix, and they fulfill Mel's lifelong wish to make vegetable gardening more convenient and less time consuming.

- **No science classes.** Successful gardeners using old-fashioned methods often need to become amateur experts in soil science, developing working knowledge of subjects such as pH, macro- and micronutrients, and soil enzymes. Mel's Mix relieves you of that burden because the mixture is, by design, balanced in pH and offers a perfect balance of nutrients by virtue of the mixed compost that's included in the mix. When using Mel's Mix, you'll never have to buy a soil pH kit or take samples to the county extension office; you won't care that eastern US soils are slightly acidic while western soils are more alkaline. Mel's Mix works everywhere and every way, at any time and in any conditions.

- **No digging.** Success in traditional gardening methods requires a terribly labor-intensive process of digging (and double-digging, and double-digging again) the garden area to loosen the soil and adding hundreds of pounds of amendments to make the soil friendly to the roots of vegetables. None of that is necessary with the Square Foot Gardening method. Mel's Mix is always ready to plant in any weather and in any location. It's always loose and friable (meaning that it is loose and crumbly and easily worked), and it's ready whenever the time is right for planting.

- **Less watering.** Mel's Mix offers something unique for growing mediums: it holds moisture well, but also drains well. Peat and vermiculite both hold water very well, but they will hold only so much before they allow the excess to quickly drain away. This means that plant roots never drown is soggy soil but always have moisture to draw upon when they need it.

- **Less feeding.** Mel's Mix has all the nutrients, minerals, and trace elements that plants need, and you can largely forget about fertilizers and soil amendments because they simply aren't needed. And because the nutrients in Mel's Mix come from natural composts, you'll never need to worry about the question of organic versus synthetic—Mel's Mix is a completely organic method using nothing synthetic. When spring rolls around each year, there is no going to the store, no reading labels and lugging big bags or bales of soil additives, no laborious digging in of soil amendments in mucky wet soil.

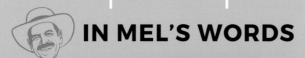

Three ingredients make up Mel's Mix: peat moss, vermiculite, and blended compost (clockwise from bottom right). Mel's Mix retains moisture, drains perfectly, and has all the nutrients and trace minerals a plant could ever want.

Through many experiments, I came up with the very best ingredients for that perfect growing soil. Of course, I made sure they were all inexpensive, readily available, and able to hold just the right amount of moisture for plants while not becoming too soggy for roots, which might drown your plants. I created a formula that holds moisture yet drains well.

At first this seemed like an impossible task, but then I thought about sponges. When you take a dry sponge and slowly add water to it, it just keeps soaking up water until it's finally saturated. At that point, any extra water just drains out the bottom. Well, it turns out that two of our ingredients—peat moss and vermiculite—do exactly the same thing. It takes a while to wet them and keep them moist, so you have to keep adding water, but finally, when they become saturated, any excess water just drains right out the bottom.

COMPOST

This key ingredient makes up one-third of the Mel Mix formula, and it is the only ingredient that you'll need to replenish after each grid square is harvested. It is also, arguably, the most important ingredient. So, what is it, and how do you make it?

Compost is, without question, the best material in which to grow plants. Good compost has all the nutrients needed for plant growth, and it is by nature loose, friable, and easily worked. Compost is easy to make, but good compost can be surprisingly hard to find. The best is the kind you make yourself in the backyard; the worst is single-ingredient material produced and bagged commercially.

Rather than tearing bags open, make neat cuts along the top. That way, when you finish making Mel's Mix, you can use the empty bags to store leftover mix.

WHAT IS COMPOST?

The subject of compost is a little confusing, partly because it's used both as a noun and a verb. As a noun, compost is a rich, crumbly, soil-like material frequently used in gardening as a soil amendment or a mulch. As a verb, to compost is to allow plant material to break down through the process of decomposition. In essence, when you compost, you are recycling organic, carbon-based material back into the soil, where plants can make access of the nutrients it contains.

Simple enough so far, but you also need to know that there are two forms of this breakdown process: aerobic decomposition (with air) and anaerobic decomposition (without air). Both processes are entirely natural and break down pesticide residue. The first form, aerobic, has no odor, causes the organic material to heat up, and does its job through the action of tiny microbes that essentially are digesting the plant material. On the other hand, the second form, anaerobic, is messy, smelly, and generally a little objectionable. More commonly, this process is called *rotting*.

The goal of good composting practice is to avoid the anaerobic form and maximize aerobic decomposition.

MAKING YOUR OWN: WHAT TO COMPOST

Although all organic materials will break down through decomposition, for garden compost the materials should be limited to materials that were at one time plants. This means that in addition to all the plant refuse from outdoors, you can add kitchen scraps of fruits and vegetables. But don't add any animal-based scraps, such as meats or bones. In general, animal byproducts are not good for your compost, though eggshells can be crushed up and sprinkled over the compost (they are a good source of calcium). Garden manure can also be added to compost provided it comes from plant-eating animals, such as cattle or sheep. Do not use manure from meat-eating animals, and under no condition should you use pet waste.

Make sure the plant ingredients you compost don't harbor any diseases or pests. Leaves and other plant parts with fungal spots or viral diseases, or materials laden with bugs, should be disposed of separately, not added to the compost heap.

IN MEL'S WORDS

Your home compost operation should include every different thing you can think of. Go to the grocery store and ask for the produce manager. Many stores throw out tons of spoiled vegetables and fruits they can't sell. These are from all over the world, so just think of the different soils and climates all that has grown in and what different vitamins, minerals, and trace elements they contain. If they're not diseased, chop them up and mix them in the compost pile. Any place people gather, there will be waste thrown out. Check out farmers' markets, local fairs or street carnivals, flea markets, and even places like Starbucks (guess what they would have for you there?). In addition to compost material, many of these food-serving places have big buckets used for pickles, mayonnaise, or oil that make great water buckets—all, often, free for the asking.

Garden compost that is ready to use will be dark and crumbly. Larger bits of sticks and other materials can be tossed back into the compost bin to continue decomposing.

Any plant material heaped together and left alone will break down into compost, given a year or two. But gardeners need the benefits of compost now, so the process of home composting is to hurry this process along by regular mixing, mashing, moistening, and moving (or "turning") the material.

HOME COMPOSTING REQUIRES BULK AND SPACE

Proper composting requires the right mixture of plant materials as well as the space to mix, mash, moisten, and move the materials around as the decomposition progresses. But efficient composting also requires a lot of mass, or bulk, in your compost pile. The more bulk you have in the pile (up to a certain point), the faster it will decompose into compost. Generally speaking, a volume of material 4 × 4 × 4 feet is about ideal. Larger than this and you may have trouble turning and moving the compost to mix in air—and without air, the process goes from aerobic to anaerobic, and your compost pile may begin to smell up and make the neighbors annoyed.

But if you don't have enough bulk—if the pile is less than about 3 × 3 × 3 feet—your pile may not do much of anything except break down in its own sweet time.

IN MEL'S WORDS

I had no idea people would be so confused about composting until I realized that only 10 percent of gardeners actually compost, another 10 percent say they don't ever want to compost, and the middle 80 percent say they would like to but are confused and scared by the process. Of course, much of that confusion comes from not knowing how to compost aerobically.

Let's summarize: keep everything moist, make a big pile, and keep turning it. How often? Every day if you want the compost in 2 weeks; every week if you want the compost in 3 months; or every month for it to be ready in a year. The ideal conditions for the fastest results are:

1. **Mix:** Add in as many different plant-based materials as you can find.

2. **Mash:** Chop everything into fine pieces.

3. **Moisten:** Not dry, not wet—just moist.

4. **Move:** Keep turning the pile toward the center, where all the action is.

The results will be the most amazing material you could hope for in your garden. It's often called black gold because of the color of the finished product.

PRACTICAL COMPOSTING TIPS

Mow those leaves. Save some of your leaves in the fall to add to the compost pile the following year rather than adding them all at once. After you rake them up, run the lawnmower over them to chop them up and then stuff into plastic bags (make sure they are dry) or, if you are a "beatnik" like me, store them in garbage bins along the wall of your compost operation.

Dry that grass. Others like to save their grass clippings the same way as leaves, but you have to be very careful. If piled up, fresh green grass will quickly turn into a black-hat, anaerobic operation that's a stinking, slimy, gooey mess. Grass clippings have to be dried before you add them to the pile or store them for later addition. It does seem counterproductive to dry the grass clippings only to moisten them in the compost pile, but now I'm sure you can see why we do it that way.

I compare it to my mother's meatloaf. She would dry bread and then crumble it to make breadcrumbs, then add milk to moisten everything. If she had just added moist, fresh bread, it would have gotten clumpy and gooey. The compost is similar. If material is put in wet, it packs down in clumps, preventing air from entering the pile, and then it rots and smells.

So, spread your grass clippings out on a tarp or the driveway and turn them a few times with a rake or flip your tarp before storing them or adding them to your compost pile. How long to wait? Until the grass is brownish and dry to the touch. It depends on the sun, humidity, and rain, as well as the climate of your location.

DETAILED LIST OF INGREDIENTS

YES *Each item should be under 20 percent of total compost by volume*	CAUTION—LIMITED AMOUNTS *Each item should be under 10 percent of total compost by volume*	NO *These items should not be added to a compost bin*
Straw	Corn cobs	Diseased or pest-laden materials
Hay (including salt hay)	Shredded twigs	Meat or bones
Leaves	Shredded bark	Grease
Grass clippings (dried)	Pine needles	Whole eggs
Old sod	Hedge trimmings	Cheese
Rejected or spoiled garden produce	Wood shavings	Seeds and fruit pits
Vegetable and fruit peels	Sawdust	Cat or dog manure
Newspaper (shredded)	Coffee grounds	Bakery products
Eggshells (crushed)	Peanut shells	Dairy products
Stable or poultry manure		Kitchen scraps
Tea bags		

MEL'S MIX IS MADE FROM:
One-third garden compost by volume

MEL'S MIX IS MADE FROM:
One-third peat moss by volume

TURNING AND MIXING

In any compost heap, the center of the pile is where the action is. This is the hottest spot (up to 150°F), the moistest spot, and the location where the most beneficial microbes are thriving, doing their job of breaking down the organic matter. The process of mixing (turning) the compost is all about making sure that all the plant material gets its turn at that sweet spot at the center of the pile, where all the magic happens.

An easy way to do this is by having two compost bins side by side. That way, as you move the material from one bin to the other, you can fairly easily make sure that newer material gets positioned near the center of the pile.

The most efficient composting occurs when the materials are mixed together in the most diverse way possible—brown material with green material, wet with dry, coarse with fine. Think about it this way: opposites attract, in a compost heap just like in life.

BUYING COMPOST

Ideally, the compost you use to make Mel's Mix should be homemade from ingredients you handpick.

MEL'S MIX IS MADE FROM:
One-third coarse vermiculite by volume

IN MEL'S WORDS

The parks and recreation departments of many municipalities have turned to composting as a way to keep landscape debris out of the waste stream. I really applaud these efforts, and I think they are environmentally responsible actions every town and city should take. The municipalities also usually offer the compost at low or no cost to local homeowners. Sounds like a great deal, right? Well, yes and no. As one of five types of compost in a Mel's Mix blend, this compost would be okay. Generally, though, municipal composts are based on wood products that don't produce very nutritious compost.

My other big concern is that municipal composts often contain a lot of weed seeds. If you notice a whole crop of weeds popping up in your brand-new SFG box, municipal compost is probably the culprit. It just didn't get hot enough to kill those weed seeds. If you can identify any of the pieces in a compost, such as wood chips, it isn't suitable for Mel's Mix. As a path or aisle cover, yes. As a Mel's Mix ingredient, no.

Finally, municipal operations also sometimes grind up treated timbers or painted scrap wood, which should not go into compost that will be used to grow edibles. Ask first.

But that can be a lot of compost, and not every gardener is up to the task—or has a large enough garden—to generate that much perfect black gold.

A perfectly good Mel's Mix can be created from purchased compost, but it is critical to buy a variety of commercial composts and blend them together. It is always a mistake to buy whatever is touted as the most popular compost, especially if it is sold loose rather than bagged. Commercial composts are always a byproduct from one industry only, such as lumbering, cattle farming, mushroom farming, vegetable canning, liquor production, cotton milling, or soybean production, each of which is trying to wring a little profit from whatever leftover materials they have. This is a noble enough idea—an environmentally friendly way to make full use of materials. But for a gardener, it means that the compost produced in this way will have one ingredient only, unlike the fabulous blend that occurs when you compost your own garden refuse.

The solution is pretty simple: buy a variety of compost types and mix them together thoroughly before measuring out your one-third quantity to put into Mel's Mix.

PEAT MOSS

The second key ingredient in Mel's Mix growing medium is peat moss. Peat moss is another completely natural material, the result of mass quantities of vegetative matter decomposing for millions of years. The greatest supplies of peat moss come from vast prehistoric bogs where huge amounts of living mosses were buried and very gradually dried out in preserved form. The age of peat moss can usually be determined simply by measuring the depth at which it is buried—the deeper it is, the older it is. Peat moss is one of the most common soil amendments used in gardening and agriculture because it makes soil lighter and more friable and improves its ability to retain water.

But the use of peat moss has become somewhat controversial in recent years because it is a nonrenewable resource whose global supplies are gradually diminishing. In the United States, most peat moss used in agriculture comes from the northern states and Canada, where active harvesting is still underway. In other parts of the world, though, supplies are virtually extinguished, and use of peat moss is carefully controlled.

It is critical to use it responsibly, and the Square Foot Gardening method is arguably one of the most efficient uses of peat moss there is. Square Foot Gardening uses only about 20 percent of the space used by traditional row gardens for a comparable yield, and this means you are using only 20 percent as much peat moss than you would be if you were amending a traditional garden. In addition, Mel's Mix uses this quantity of peat moss only once—after making the initial mixture, all you'll need to add is compost, which is entirely renewable.

SUBSTITUTES FOR PEAT MOSS

While Square Foot Gardening is a very efficient and defensible use of peat moss, you may live an area where supplies are limited or where the use of peat moss is legally controlled. There are a couple of alternatives you can use to take its place in your Mel's Mix.

Coconut coir. This material, also sometimes called coconut dust, is a byproduct of the coconut agricultural industry. Coir is the collected short fibers of coconut shells, leftover after the longer fibers are used for things such as upholstery stuffing, rope, and brushes. Once thrown away, these short fibers are finding renewed used as a kind of coconut "peat," with many of the same benefits as peat moss. When added to a planting medium, coir retains water well, absorbs moisture even more readily than peat moss, decomposes more slowly, and withstands compression better. A number of university studies have concluded that coir is a very good substitute for peat moss in garden use.

Coir is increasingly available at garden centers in compressed bricks at costs that are comparable to peat moss. It is an entirely renewable resource and can be used in exactly the same way, and in the same ratios, as peat moss.

Peat moss remains the tried-and-tested material for Mel's Mix, but coconut coir (shown here) and PittMoss are reasonable alternatives.

PittMoss. This commercial peat moss alternative is made from recycled newspapers and other cellulose materials. The creators of this product have touted it as offering merits that are superior to peat moss, but neither anecdotal evidence nor university research has yet proven this, although PittMoss does have some of the same merits in terms of water retention. Cellulose fibers will, however, break down rather quickly, so gardeners using this material should be prepared to replenish a soil medium that uses PittMoss.

Peat moss remains the gold standard for making Mel's Mix, but if you have reasons to look for an alternative, both coconut coir and PittMoss might be worth trying.

VERMICULITE

The third critical ingredient in Mel's Mix growing medium is vermiculite—another natural material that is available all over the world. Vermiculite is a nontoxic earth mineral created when mica is mined from the ground, then ground up and heated until it explodes and forms small pieces ranging from powder to the size of the end of your finger. The process causes each piece to contain nooks and crannies that can hold a tremendous amount of water while still breathing. When added to a growing medium, this makes the mixture extremely friable and loose, with plenty of available moisture for plant roots to find. The loose soil creates an environment in which plant roots can grow extremely fast.

VERMICULITE GRADES

Vermiculite is graded in several sizes—fine, medium, and coarse—and is also tested and approved for different uses. The coarse grade holds the most moisture while also lending friability to a soil mix, so always look for the coarse grade when shopping for vermiculite for Mel's Mix.

You may have heard stories about how vermiculite contains asbestos, and it's true that some vermiculite taken from one mine near Libby, Montana, in between 1919 to 1990 did include contamination from asbestos. We now know that this was not matter of the vermiculite itself containing asbestos but of naturally occurring asbestos in the same area contaminating the mined asbestos from that site. This contamination has posed a legitimate problem in homes where this vermiculite was used for pour-in insulation in walls and ceiling cavities, especially because almost 70 percent of all vermiculite sold in those years came from the Libby mine. And it continues to be a problem in older homes that haven't had the loose-fill vermiculite insulation removed.

But that mine was closed down in 1990, and ever since then, vermiculite has been meticulously inspected before it's mined for sale. Pure vermiculite is perfectly safe, and the granular vermiculite now sold is carefully inspected and tested for purity.

FINDING VERMICULITE

Obtaining the quantities of vermiculite you need can be a little challenging. Nurseries, garden centers, and home-improvement centers, if they stock it at all, may offer it in

Fine vermiculite is sold in small bags measured by the quart and is usually used for mixing soil for indoor potted plants. For a Square Foot Garden, you want large bags of coarse vermiculite measured in cubic feet.

small bags suitable for mixing a few indoor pots—and it is often finer-grade vermiculite, which would be prohibitively expensive to buy in quantities large enough for a Square Foot Garden bed. Your best bet is likely to do an online search for coarse vermiculite, which will produce a number of nursery-supply retailers that offer what you need.

Like peat moss, vermiculite is a dry, dusty product that you don't want to breathe. Make sure to wear gloves, long sleeves, and a particle mask when working with it, and do your mixing on a windless day or in a garage or other enclosed space.

ARE THERE SUBSTITUTES?

Gardeners who are nervous about the old asbestos worries, or those who find vermiculite too expensive, have experimented with various substitutes, such as pine needles, sawdust, and other materials. Some have doubled the amount of peat moss and omitted the vermiculite altogether. No one—including us at the Square Foot Gardening Foundation—has found much success with these other organic materials as a replacement for vermiculite. That is because a good growing medium in nature contains a fair amount of nonorganic mineral content, and without this, a growing medium just can't be as successful as Mel's Mix

One moderately successful substitute is perlite, another nonorganic mineral—specifically a volcanic glass. Perlite is cheaper than vermiculite, and it improves the friability of a growing medium in much the same way that vermiculite does, which is why many commercial potting soils use it instead of vermiculite. But perlite does not have the same moisture-holding capacity as vermiculite.

IN MEL'S WORDS

Perlite is another natural material mined out of the earth and used in agriculture for the same purpose as vermiculite—to break up and loosen poor soils and to retain moisture. I personally don't like or use perlite, and here's why. It is hard as a rock, rather coarse and gritty, and I don't like the feel of it in the soil mix. It doesn't hold moisture like vermiculite. It floats to the top of the soil mix as you water your garden, and because it's white, it looks rather unsightly and unnatural. And it makes me sneeze! Many people do use perlite instead of vermiculite, and, in fact, most commercial mixes are made with perlite because it's cheaper. It's a matter of preference and availability, but I know which one I'm using.

CALCULATING VOLUME AND BUYING INGREDIENTS FOR MEL'S MIX

Initially, you might find measuring the quantities of the three ingredients for Mel's Mix a little confusing, because the products are sold according to different standards of measurement—sometimes in pounds, sometimes in cubic feet, sometimes in quarts. And sometimes the products are compressed, which further complicates the process. You don't need to worry too much about this, though, because when you create Mel's Mix, all that matters is the volume—nothing else.

Calculating the volume of Mel's Mix you'll need for a Square Foot Garden box isn't as complicated as it first seems. For those of you interested in the precise math, we'll begin with a description of how to calculate the volume of a given Square Foot Garden box. But after that description, we'll also give you a chart that gives you volumes for various common box sizes. So, if you're not up to the math, just jump ahead to the table or try the soil calculator on www.squarefootgardening.com.

VOLUME OF A SQUARE FOOT GARDEN BOX

Determining the amount of Mel's Mix you need is a matter of calculating the volume of your Square Foot Garden box, and to do this, we need to go back to some basics of high-school algebra, where we learned (though have perhaps forgotten):

volume of a three-dimensional space = length × width × depth/height

Calculating the volume of a Square Foot Garden box, then, is a matter of multiplying the dimensions of the box, using a common unit of measurement. This could be done in any number of way, but the most convenient unit in our case is feet. In a standard, classic 4 × 4 box that is 6 inches (½ foot) deep, the math would look like this:

4 × 4 × ½ = 8 cubic feet

Pretty easy, isn't it? With this basic formula, you'll find it quite simple to calculate the volume of just about any Square Foot Garden box you might want to build. The most complicated part will be converting the height measurement to feet in instances where you alter the depth of the box. For example, if you make the box 10 inches deep using 2 × 10 lumber, the height factor of the calculation will be $^{10}/_{12}$ of a foot, or .83 feet. So, a 4 × 4 × 10-inch box will be calculated as 4 × 4 × .83, which gives 13.28 cubic feet.

For simplicity, here's a table that shows the total volume of some common square foot box sizes:

BOX DIMENSIONS	BOX VOLUME
4 × 4 feet × 6 inches (½ foot)	8 cubic feet
4 × 8 feet × 6 inches (½ foot)	16 cubic feet
4 × 12 feet × 6 inches (½ foot)	24 cubic feet
4 × 16 feet × 6 inches (½ foot)	32 cubic feet
2 × 4 feet × 6 inches (½ foot)	4 cubic feet
2 × 8 feet × 6 inches (½ foot)	8 cubic feet
2 × 12 feet × 6 inches (½ foot)	12 cubic feet
2 × 16 feet × 6 inches (½ foot)	16 cubic feet
1 × 4 feet × 6 inches (½ foot)	2 cubic feet
1 × 8 feet × 6 inches (½ foot)	4 cubic feet
1 × 12 feet × 6 inches (½ foot)	6 cubic feet
1 × 16 feet × 6 inches (½ foot)	8 cubic feet
4 × 4 feet × 12 inches (1 foot)	16 cubic feet
4 × 8 feet × 12 inches (1 foot)	32 cubic feet
4 × 12 feet × 12 inches (1 foot)	48 cubic feet
4 × 16 feet × 12 inches (1 foot)	64 cubic feet
2 × 4 feet × 12 inches (1 foot)	8 cubic feet
2 × 8 feet × 12 inches (1 foot)	16 cubic feet
2 × 12 feet × 12 inches (1 foot)	24 cubic feet
2 × 16 feet × 12 inches (1 foot)	32 cubic feet
1 × 4 feet × 12 inches (1 foot)	4 cubic feet
1 × 8 feet × 12 inches (1 foot)	8 cubic feet
1 × 12 feet × 12 inches (1 foot)	12 cubic feet
1 × 16 feet × 12 inches (1 foot)	16 cubic feet

One 5-gallon bucket = .668 cubic feet. One 4 × 4' × 6" garden box = 12 buckets of Mel's Mix.

MEASURING THE VOLUME OF MEL'S MIX INGREDIENTS

Okay, now that you have the volume of the Square Foot Garden box, it's simply a matter of dividing that volume by three to determine how much of each of the three ingredients you need. In a classic 4 × 4-foot, 6-inch-deep box, which has a volume of 8 cubic feet, you'll need 8 ÷ 3, or 2.66 cubic feet, of each of the three materials (compost, peat moss, and vermiculite) to create enough Mel's Mix to fill the box.

That's all well and good, but how in the world does one measure out each of these ingredients in cubic feet? If you wanted to be really precise, you could create a small box that's exactly 1 foot on each side and use this to measure out ingredients, 1 cubic foot at a time. A much easier way, though, is to use a standard 5-gallon pail, which is widely sold for utility use at just about every home-improvement center. A standard 5-gallon pail holds .668 cubic feet (about ⅔ of a cubic foot.) To be precise about the math, then, to use a 5-gallon pail as your measuring "cup," you would take the total volume of the ingredient you need, and divide this by .668 to determine how many bucketsful you need to measure out each ingredient.

In our classic Square Foot Garden box, 4 feet × 4 feet × 6 inches, we know that the total volume is 8 cubic feet and that we need 2.66 cubic feet of each ingredient. If a 5-gallon pail holds .668 cubic feet, the math looks like this:

2.66 ÷ .668 = 3.98 buckets (it's fine to round this off to 4)

In other words, to fill a classic Square Foot Garden box, you will need four 5-gallon buckets each of compost, peat moss, and vermiculite.

You likely don't want to have to do this math constantly though, so here's a convenient table to help you determine how many 5-gallon buckets you'll need to measure out common volumes. You don't have to be terribly precise about this, because a small amount of leftover Mel's Mix could be used to fill a small patio container or another small planter.

VOLUME NEEDED	5-GALLON BUCKETS
2 cubic feet	3
3 cubic feet	4.5
4 cubic feet	6
5 cubic feet	7.5
10 cubic feet	15
15 cubic feet	22.5

BUYING MATERIALS

The ingredients for Mel's Mix are measured out according to volume, but you may find that some materials, especially compost, are sold by the pound. And because the volume of different products of the same weight may vary, it's rather hard to make a blanket statement about how much volume there is in, for example, a 40-pound bag of compost. A 40-pound bag of mushroom compost may translate to a different volume than a 40-pound bag of composted cow manure. If you can't buy materials sold in cubic-foot measurements, there's really no alternative other than to buy bags and then determine how many bags it takes to fill your 5-gallon-bucket "measuring cup."

Peat moss is normally sold in cubic-foot bales, but here the issue is complicated by the fact that the bales are compressed for ease of shipping. Once they are unpacked, each of those bales expand to a volume that is considerably larger than a cubic foot. Here's how to understand how many cubic feet you are actually buying when you buy peat-moss bales:

Full bale = 3.9 cubic feet compressed = 8 cubic feet when unpacked and loosened.

Half bale = 2.2 cubic feet compressed = 4 cubic feet when unpacked and loosened

HOW TO CREATE MEL'S MIX

You're getting close now. Your Square Foot Garden box is (or boxes are) built. And with all the math out of the way, the fun now starts as you create the actual Mel's Mix and fill your garden box with the growing medium that will make the most productive garden you've ever seen. Before you get started, make sure that you know exactly where you want your Square Foot Garden boxes positioned in your yard, because once you fill them with Mel's Mix, it will be tricky to move them around.

The best place to mix is on a smooth, flat surface—a concrete driveway surface is ideal, or you can use a flat area of your yard where you can spread out a plastic tarp. The inside of your garage can work, provided you're not too concerned about dust getting all over your car or workshop items. The ingredients are quite dusty and dry, and you'll want to periodically mist down the Mel's Mix to keep the dust down as you blend ingredients. And make sure to wear a particle mask to avoid breathing the dust.

MATERIALS
The materials you'll need include:

- 16 × 16' plastic tarp
- Particle mask
- Shovel and rake
- 5-gallon bucket
- Compost (if using store-bought compost, buy at least five different kinds)
- Vermiculite
- Peat moss
- Wheelbarrow
- Water supply

CREATING THE MIX

1 Spread out a plastic tarp over a smooth area, such as a concrete driveway or flat area of the yard. If you can do your mixing close to where the Square Foot Garden box is positioned, it will simplify things. Begin by mixing the compost. Empty it onto the tarp and use a rake to do preliminary mixing of the compost.

2 With the assistance of a helper, drag the ends of the tarp back and forth to mix the compost thoroughly.

3 Once the compost is thoroughly mixed, add the vermiculite. Do preliminary raking, then complete the mixing by again rolling the tarp back and forth.

4 With the compost and vermiculite thoroughly mixed, add the peat moss and mix it in, using the rake then rolling the tarp.

5 Periodically mist down the dry mixture to keep dust from blowing around. If a garden hose is not available, a pressure sprayer can be used)

6 When the Mel's Mix is complete, use a wheelbarrow or the 5-gallon pail to transfer the growing medium to your Square Foot Garden box. This is best done before the grid is placed on the box.

7 Spread out the Mel's Mix into a uniform layer throughout the box before attaching the lattice grid over the top of the box. It's easy to see how perfect Mel's Mix will be for growing plants, because its structure and quality is vastly superior to garden soil.

8 Here's an easy way to fill your Square Foot Garden box if you have a helper or two. Just drag the tarp full of Mel's Mix over to your garden box and use it as a funnel to pour it in.

If you have leftover Mel's Mix, shovel it back into the empty plastic bags from your store-bought components and set it aside for reuse. It can be used for other planting containers and also makes a great medium for starting seedlings in four-packs. Or, you can use it to top off the Square Foot Garden boxes as the soil settles in a week or two.

IN MEL'S WORDS

You have now completed the most important and rewarding step in Square Foot Gardening. If you followed the formula correctly and didn't add any of your existing soil, it will stay loose and friable for 7 to 10 years, and you will be so excited and happy. You may have to keep one square open just for show; visitors to your garden will watch as you say "Just look at this soil!" as your run your hands through it. Many of you will then add, "Here—you try it. Just feel this soil." (But don't become a pest.)

Whether you are sowing seeds directly or planting transplants, the grid squares in your Square Foot Garden boxes make it easy to organize your garden.

CHAPTER

PLANTING YOUR SQUARE FOOT GARDEN

If you are following this book sequentially, you've now planned your gardens and given thought to how to lay them out in your yard. You've built your Square Foot Garden boxes, along with any trellises and accessories you want. You understand the magical growing medium known as Mel's Mix, and you've filled your Square Foot Garden boxes with this fabulous formula. Now comes the start of the actual gardening fun—planting your Square Foot Garden with the seeds and seedlings that will soon create the most productive and interesting vegetable garden you've ever seen.

THE ESSENCE OF SQUARE FOOT GARDENING

The SFG method requires a slightly different attitude toward planting than is usual for a traditional row garden. So, let's start with some background information you need to know as you get ready to plant your Square Foot Garden boxes.

VISUALIZING THE HARVEST

As we discussed in Chapter 3, the Square Foot Gardening method is considerably more productive than a traditional row garden, and this can easily lead to overplanting and a great deal of waste if you're not careful. It's important to visualize what your Square Foot Garden will look like in order to plant just enough and not so much that produce will go to waste. The Square Foot Garden method generally catalogs each vegetable into one of four categories to assist with visualizing:

- Extra-large vegetables: 1 plant per square (in some instances, 1 plant occupies two grid squares). Examples can include broccoli, cabbage, tomatoes, and peppers.

- Large vegetables: 4 plants per grid square. Examples include leaf lettuce and swiss chard.

- Medium vegetables: 9 plants per grid square. Examples include beans, beets, and peas.

- Small vegetables: 16 plants per grid square. Examples include carrots, radishes, and onions.

There are variations on this rule of thumb, of course, which you'll learn about in the Vegetable Guide in Chapter 12. The point, though, is that the SFG method calls for a denser planting arrangement than any other form of gardening, so proper visualization is necessary to prevent you from being wasteful.

The best way to really understand how much produce a given 1-foot square can grow is to look at the instructions on the seed packet. Look for "thin to" spacing directions; if the seed packet suggests that the seedlings be thinned to a spacing of 3 inches apart, you can easily figure out how many plants a single 12 × 12-inch grid square can hold.

It's really not necessary to get perfectly precise about this by using a measuring tool. If a vegetable requires 3-inch spacing and is being planted in a 12 × 12-inch grid square, that means that nine plants will fit (three rows of three plants each).

When it comes time to plant, just draw rough lines in the surface of the Mel's Mix with your finger, then use these lines to guide your planting.

FOSTER DIVERSITY

Unlike a traditional row garden, in which a single vegetable crop is planted all together, in the Square Foot Garden method we deliberately avoid that kind of monoculture and instead make sure that each vegetable has neighbors of a different type. There are several reasons why we recommend this:

- It prevents you from overplanting any single crop.

- It encourages you to stagger your harvest by planting one grid square this week and another of the same crop in two weeks or so later.

- It promotes conservation, companion planting, and crop rotation; allows for better plant hygiene; and reduces pest problems.

- It makes for a more attractive garden, with a blend of textures, heights, and colors.

One of the most common questions we receive at the Square Foot Gardening Foundation is from people who wonder why it's not okay to plant all 16 grid squares with, for example, leaf lettuce or spinach. But the most common problem new SFG gardeners experience is in overestimating how much they will consume and underestimating the fabulous productivity of a Square Foot Garden. Disciplining yourself to plant your garden so that each grid has a different crop will help prevent that problem, along with offering the other benefits mentioned. Many insect pests and diseases are plant specific, and a diverse garden is much less likely to get devastated by a single pest or disease.

The moral: to be a true Square Foot Gardener, practice diversity in your garden.

PLANTING TIME

Unlike traditional row gardens, which really need to be planted in late spring or early summer, a Square Foot Garden can really be planted in any season other than

DIVIDING YOUR SQUARES

As a rule of thumb, assume that each grid square in your Square Foot Garden can hold 1, 4, 9, or 16 plants. Here's an easy way to mark out the square for planting.

Extra-large plants are sown right in the middle of the square. This ensures a minimal amount of overlap into the neighboring squares.

For large vegetables, divide the square into four equal sections and poke a hole with your finger in the center of each divided section. These will be your planting spots.

For medium-sized vegetables calling for nine plants per square, divide the square into thirds in both directions and scribe lines in the soil with your finger. Mark the center of each section to mark nine planting spots.

For small vegetables calling for 16 plants per grid square, just divide the grid into quarters, then poke four holes in each section to mark planting spots.

PLANTING ASPARAGUS

1 Because asparagus is a perennial plant that will provide food over and over again over many years, this is an exception to the diversity rule. It's recommended to plant an entire box with asparagus, using bare roots.

2 Divide each grid square into quarters, then in the center of each section make a small mound about 3" high for each clump of bare roots.

3 Position the clump at the top of each mound and let the individual roots drape down over the mound. Press the plant down in place.

4 Cover the roots with more Mel's Mix to a depth of 2" or so. It can take 2 or even 3 years before you can harvest the asparagus. Avoid harvesting too soon, as the roots need to be well developed before they can survive harvesting.

winter. One thing newcomers quickly come to realize about a Square Foot Garden is that the growing season is much longer than it is with other methods—running from early spring to late fall. And if you happen to live in place like Texas or California, Square Foot Gardening is truly a year-round affair.

But for the sake of discussion, let's look at how the Square Foot Gardening season differs from traditional gardening in a midcontinental climate—a place that freezes in the winter.

In the early spring, because it is a raised bed and filled with nicely porous Mel's Mix, a Square Foot Garden will warm up enough to germinate seeds considerably earlier than garden soil that is still lying on top of winter frost 1 or 2 feet below the surface. Plus, the size of a Square Foot Garden makes it relatively easy to protect against cold snaps that might hit in early spring. And because one of the main principles of Square Foot Gardening is crop rotation, early cool-season crops can be planted in some of the grid squares while others remain open in preparation for the warm-season crops you'll plant in summer.

In all but the coldest climates, you can likely get two to three crops a year out of each grid square in your garden. There are two types of crops to consider as regards the impact of weather. The first, known as cool-weather plants, do best in the cooler temperatures of spring and fall and don't thrive very well in the hotter months of summer. The second group is the warm- or hot-weather crops, which need the heat of summer to thrive and don't do well in the cooler weeks of spring and fall. The magic of a Square Foot Garden is that any given grid square can grow a full crop of a cool-season vegetable, then be planted with a warm-season crop, and then rotated back to another cool-season vegetable once the warm-season vegetable has been harvested.

The compact size of a Square Foot Garden makes it very easy to protect plantings from a late-spring or early-fall frost. Chapter 6 will give you some ideas for protective accessories to extend your growing season.

Not all plants are the same. Just as is true with people, some vegetables handle heat, cold, dryness, or high humidity better than others. Those that handle cold temperatures readily are categorized as hardy, while those that are easily killed by cold temperatures are known as nonhardy. Each of the four seasons has three time periods—the early season, the midseason, and the late season. If you're thinking about a spring crop, for example, there may be some vegetables that grow well only in the middle portion of spring and will collapse from heat near the late part of the season. It takes some experience for any gardener to become accustomed to the particulars of each vegetable and figure out how it best fits into a planting schedule.

Understanding a plant's hardiness is not an exact science, because conditions vary considerably even within a particular geographic region. If you live in a deep valley, conditions might be quite different than they are on hilltop location just a few hundred yards away. Be patient—simple experience will soon teach you the best time and the best rotation rhythm for the vegetables you want to grow.

IN MEL'S WORDS

Looking through a seed catalog is not the best way to decide what to grow. Suppliers make everything look so good and sound so exciting that you can easily get carried away. I recommend you review your shopping list from the past week and the past month. That eliminates the impulsive thoughts of "Oh, I'd like to grow that!" or "Wouldn't it be fun to grow peanuts?" Start simple and easy with the foods you already eat regularly. Expand and experiment later on.

So often I hear, "But I'm so anxious to start my Square Foot Garden. I've always wanted a garden, and I want to grow everything." Well, if you've been wishing and wanting to grow for 20 years, spending the first year getting experience and confidence with the Square Foot Gardening method won't make any difference. Then spend the next 40 years enjoying your garden. Don't ruin a lifetime hobby by starting off too big.

Frost dates. If you're in the habit of thinking of March 20 or 21 as the first day of spring, well, lose that habit right now. Your plants really don't care what the calendar date is—it's the weather, and particularly the soil temperature, that they respond to. The date you should really be paying attention to is the date of the last frost in your area. This is the key date that tells us when to plant. Each different crop—both cool-season and warm-season—has an ideal planting time that is measured in weeks before, or weeks after, the last frost date.

The end of the growing season in the fall is keyed to two dates. The first frost will kill off some tender plants, but it's the freeze date—the day when a hard freeze kills everything to the ground level—that truly marks the end of the growing season for the year. This is the time when root vegetables need to be harvested. Once the top growth is dead, the root vegetables should come out of the ground immediately.

How do you find your local frost dates? The easiest source of information is probably the Internet, where you can find pretty detailed information on average frost dates for your region. You can also call your local county extension agent or a local nursery. Be aware, though, that these frost dates represent averages compiled over recent years. There is no guarantee that because your average last frost date is April 15, for example, you won't have frost until May 1 in a particular year. This why some nurseries will routinely recommend planting dates that are at least two weeks past the average last-frost dates. They may even void any warranties if you plant before the dates they recommend.

Air temperatures and germination rates Proper spring planting time is not just about the simple last frost date. Different vegetable seeds germinate and sprout at different rates depending on air temperatures. Some regions get quite warm very quickly after the last frost date, and here many vegetables will sprout and shoot up considerably faster than in a region where the spring warmup is quite slow, even if the last frost date is earlier.

Soil temperatures, which are of course influenced by air temperatures, can vastly influence sprouting times. For example, if you plant carrot seeds in the summertime when the soil temperature is between 60°F and 80°F, the seeds will likely sprout in less than a week. But the same seeds planted in early spring while soil temperatures are 40°F may take 6 full weeks to sprout. Each 10°F of soil temperature can amount to a difference of 2 weeks in sprouting time.

Seeds planted in soil that is too cold may not sprout at all but instead become subject to rot or fungal disease or become food for insects and birds. This is why it makes sense to delay your planting until the Mel's Mix in your Square Foot Garden boxes reaches a temperature suitable for fast sprouting, as suggested in the chart on page 260. If you are really eager to see greenery shooting up, then start some seedlings indoors—but don't plant them outdoors until the soil temperatures are suitable. Fortunately, the Mel's Mix in a Square Foot Garden typically warms up faster than ground soil, so you won't wait too long.

PLAN ON FALL CROPS

In Square Foot Gardening, as soon as the summer crop is finished, you're ready to plant cool-weather crops for the approaching fall. These will be crops that are frost hardy—meaning that both young and mature plants can tolerate air frosts that don't penetrate the ground. This makes the Square Foot Garden method quite a lot different from traditional row gardening, in which once a crop has produced, that spot of the garden sits idle until planting time next spring.

Seeds or transplants you put in at the end of the summer will sprout quickly because the soil is warmer. Transplants may no longer be available at garden centers by that time, so many Square Foot Gardeners sow seeds and grow fall seedlings indoors in late summer as they wait for the summer crops to finish up.

Fall crops also benefit from the gradual cooling that occurs in late summer and early fall. What ends the production of cool-season vegetables planted in spring is actually the intense heat of midsummer, which causes many crops to flower and set seeds—this ends the production of crops like lettuce and spinach. The same cool-season crop planted in late summer will last much longer, because the air temperatures will be cooler just at the time the crop is fully ripening. In cool weather, these crops feel no urgency to complete the growing cycle by flowering and setting seeds, so the crops slow down their maturation processes, which allows them to maintain their flavor and remain harvestable for much longer. If the plant happens to be a frost-hardy crop, such a kale, you may be able to harvest it right up through the first snows.

In other words, with a Square Foot Garden, fall is a great time to garden, provided you plant the proper crops.

PLANTING FROM SEEDS

Like any form of gardening, you have the option of planting your crops from seeds you sow yourself or from transplants purchased at a garden center. Or, you can combine the skills, sowing your own seeds indoors until they sprout into seedlings, then transplanting them into your Square Foot Garden box when the conditions are right.

Buying transplants has its appeal, of course, in terms of time and effort saved, but Square Foot Gardening places a premium on efficiency, and for this reason we generally favor sowing our own seeds. There are plenty of advantages to growing your own transplants from seeds you sow yourself and storing the remaining seeds in their packets until they are needed next year. First, seeds cost just pennies, while a single transplant may cost you several dollars. And you'll have many more options available, because seed catalogs may offer dozens of varieties of a single crop while your garden center sells only few different types of transplants.

The only real setback is that it takes some time and effort to grow your own transplants. If you are a new gardener, you may want to wait until you have a year of Square Foot Gardening under your belt before tackling seed-starting. Or, you can practice on some easy seeds to begin with and plant the rest of your garden with store-purchased transplants until you get your feet wet. Seed starting is fun, but don't tackle it if it seems like too much work. Square Foot Gardening is meant to be fun, and if fun means buying transplants rather than growing them yourself, there's nothing wrong with that. Later in this chapter, you'll learn how to plant those transplants, whether you've grown them yourself or are buying them.

STORING SEEDS

In the Square Foot Gardening method, we waste no seeds at all. Rather than sowing seeds thickly, then thinning them out to the desired spacing once they sprout, our method is to plant exactly the number to produce the plants we want. For this reason, a single packet of seeds can last for several years. If seeds are stored properly, they will last for many years. Contrary to the views of the gardening industry—which has an interest in seeing you buy a fresh packet

Store surplus seeds in their packets in jars with screw lids. Group similar seeds together so that they are easy to find when the next planting season rolls around. Keep the jars in the back of your refrigerator with the lid tightly sealed to keep moisture out.

of seeds every year—it's just not necessary to buy fresh seeds every year or to sow the entire packet and then thin them out once they sprout. With the Square Foot Garden method, you can plant just a pinch of the seeds, then store the rest for next year. Seed companies guarantee that a certain percentage of the seeds will sprout, and this number is quite high—usually around 90 percent. Careful Square Foot Gardeners can easily make a single packet of seeds last for 5 years, if they properly store them.

How best to store those seeds for future years? The ideal storage conditions for seeds is exactly the opposite of the moisture and warmth that makes them sprout. Store them in a cool, dark, dry place—look for a storage area that maximizes these conditions. Some people freeze their seeds, but Mel Bartholomew discovered that the best method was to refrigerate them in a wide-mouth jar with a screw lid. Label the containers and store them on the back wall of your refrigerator. To prevent them from absorbing any air moisture in the jars, put a small packet of desiccant in each jar—desiccant packets are found in each of those little over-the-counter medicine or vitamin bottles you buy, or you can add a little powdered milk wrapped in tissue paper to each jar.

PRACTICE PLANTING

Some seeds are large enough that pinching one or two to plant in Mel's Mix is easy. But others are so tiny they are nearly microscopic. It's a good idea to practice your planting skills before you kneel down next to your Square Foot Garden box. You can do this indoors before you start your garden.

Practice with different types of seeds, from the tiniest to the largest, and practice picking up and dropping a pinch of seeds onto a sheet of white paper to count the results.

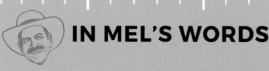

IN MEL'S WORDS

Some seeds require special preparation or planting methods. These seeds are so few, though, that it's not worth going into detail. It's not something you have to remember or study because seed companies, bless them, print any special instructions or requirements right on the seed packet.

Kids can very much enjoy this game. Some people have no trouble with this at all, but other gardeners, such as those with arthritis or other dexterity problems, may find it easier to use a small tool, like a spoon.

PRESOAKING SEEDS

Before planting your seeds, it's a good idea to give them a head start by presoaking them. Soaking can soften the hard seed shell and make sprouting easier. With some seeds, this will be recommended by the seed company, but it's a good idea for most seeds. While some can be soaked overnight, others will fall apart after only an hour, so some experimentation is necessary. Big seeds should be soaked for only about 30 minutes to 1 hour. Bean and pea seeds, which look shriveled up, will swell and break in half if you soak them too long. Be careful when handling, because some seeds may get slippery when wet. A plastic spoon may be helpful in handling them.

HOW TO SOW SEEDS IN GRIDS

WATCH YOUR DEPTH

Planting depth can be pretty critical to proper sprouting of a seed. The proper depth really depends mostly on the size of the seed and the quality of the soil in which it's being planted. Generally speaking, a seed's planting depth should be 2 to 4 times the thickness of the seed itself. With tiny lettuce seeds, this means barely covering the seeds at all, while thick, large pumpkin seeds may need to be a full inch or more under the soil.

It's important to place your seeds below a moist surface to prevent them from drying out. If they are too close to the surface, hot sun may dry them out. Once the seed has "broken dormancy" and begins sending up green shoots, it is critical to continue to keep the soil moist, because it will die if it dries out. For this reason, if your garden experiences very sunny, hot conditions, you may want to consider blocking the sun with a canopy of shade cloth during these critical first few weeks.

1 Use your finger to divide each grid square into smaller sections to guide your planting, as described on page 145. (In our example, we're dividing into quarters for large plants.) Poke a hole in the center of each section.

2 Tip out the seeds onto the palm of your hand and pinch two or three seeds between your thumb and forefinger.

3 Drop the seeds into the hole, paying attention to the planting depth recommended by the seed packet. Lightly cover the seeds with a small amount of Mel's Mix.

4 Lightly water the grid square, using a watering can or a cupful of water from a sun-warmed bucket of water. If you water from a cup, filter the water through your fingers to create a sprinkling effect. Heavy watering can uncover the seeds, so water lightly. Keep the surface of the Mel's Mix moist until the seeds sprout.

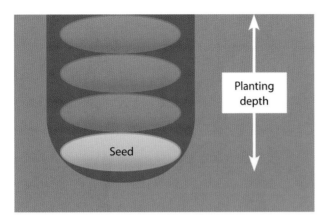

Plant the seeds at a depth 2 to 4 times their diameter. If you are starting them early, you can transplant the individual sprouts into four-packs once all the seeds have sprouted. When they're large enough—roughly the same size as purchased transplants—you can move them into their own SFG grid square.

Because Mel's Mix is so loose and friable, it's not too much of a problem if you place your seeds a bit too deep. If the seed is deeper than recommended, nature will soon direct it to reach upward once it receives a little water, and because Mel's Mix is so loose, this won't be much of an issue.

BE PATIENT

It's all too common for a new gardener to plant seeds, water them, and walk away expecting seedlings to sprout up very quickly. Some vegetables do just that, but others will take a little time. Before you jump to the conclusion that you're a bad gardener, or that the seeds were bad, you should consider that some seeds may have successfully sprouted but are beginning their journey by sending roots down into the soil to begin seeking the nutrients and water that will give them the energy to send green growth poking up into the light. If you give up on the seeds and stop watering at this crucial time, the seeds will indeed die—if the soil dries in the root zone 1 to 2 inches below the surface, the tender roots will wither away. But if you keep the soil lightly but constantly moist for the critical 1 or 2 weeks after planting, chances are good that you'll be rewarded with a healthy seedling at each and every spot you planted.

How long does it take seeds to sprout? It varies from crop to crop, and you can learn the details in the appendix chart found on page 260. Remember that temperature plays a factor here—in warmer temperatures, seeds will sprout faster, and it can also affect the percentage of seeds that sprout. This information can be crucial to timing your planting. If you know ahead of time that it's going to take 10 days for the seeds to sprout at an average outdoor temperature, then you won't be anxiously looking for sprouts until that time, and you'll know it's important to keep the soil moist during that period. And because temperature affects sprouting percentage, you'll know, for example, that cool conditions may require a couple of extra seeds in each planting location to accommodate a higher failure rate.

KEEP RECORDS

It's a great idea to keep detailed notes on your seed planting each year, including details such as:

- Seed company
- The date you sowed, and the conditions at the time
- Your watering habits
- How long it took the seeds to sprout
- Rate of germination—how many seeds, if any, failed to sprout
- How healthy the resulting plants were

This might sound a lot like bookkeeping, but many gardeners enjoy recording these details, and some even set up computerized spreadsheets to tally up this information. If you enjoy it, it can be a great way to help you learn and measure your progress as a Square Foot Gardener.

MOVING SEEDLINGS

Because a Square Foot Garden is small, and because Mel's Mix is so loose and friable, it's completely possible to move seedlings—or even mature plants—around in your garden. In particular, as you're getting started in Square Foot Gardening, it's common to recognize mistakes in how you've planned the grids or to rethink what and where you want to plant. For more experienced gardeners, this is more like an art form—moving plants around to achieve a visual effect or to make harvesting easier. The key here is to simply be careful. With caution, most every seedling or young plant in a Square Foot Garden can be successfully shifted to another grid square.

It's a great idea to start your own transplants from seed in indoor garden flats, but not in the manner used by this gardener. Even in garden flats, it's best to sow sparingly so as to not waste seeds.

SPROUTING SEEDS AND GROWING TRANSPLANTS INDOORS

Most crops can be pretty easily started from seeds sown directly into your Square Foot Garden grids, but there are situations in which you might want to sprout the seeds indoors and grow them into good, strong young plants that can then be planted outdoors. Your goal here is create the same kind of strong transplants you would otherwise have to buy at the garden center. If you live in a cold climate with a short growing season, for example, it can be helpful to get your crops started indoors so that you can take full advantage of a short growing window. Or, you might simply be so eager to get gardening that starting some crops from seeds indoors is the perfect way to spend spare time in the late winter or early spring.

The process takes some time but is simple enough:

1. Sprout the seeds.

2. Move the sprouted seedlings into four-packs.

3. Grow the seedlings up into healthy young plants.

4. Prepare the transplants for the garden by hardening off.

5. Move the transplants into the Square Foot Garden.

HOW TO START SEEDS INDOORS

1 Poke some drainage holes in the bottom of a disposable plastic cup or shallow container. Fill the container with fine vermiculite and pour water around the edge of the container.

2 Add enough water so that the vermiculite is fully damp. It will take on a darker appearance as it soaks up water. Pour a few seeds from a seed packet into the palm of your hand.

3 Pinch a few seeds between the thumb and forefinger of your hand.

4 Sprinkle the seeds across the surface of the vermiculite.

5 Cover the seeds with a thin layer of vermiculite. (Don't cover the seeds if the seed packet indicates the seeds need light in order to germinate.) Keep the vermiculite moist until the seeds have sprouted and produced their first sets of true leaves.

The materials you'll need are quite simple: a few cups and saucers, some fine vermiculite, some peat or plastic four-pack seedling containers, a plastic tray, and a few cups of Mel's Mix.

INDOOR SEED SPROUTING

The first step to growing indoor transplants is to sprout the seeds. Rather than using a commercial seed-starter mix, we have found that the best method of sprouting seeds is to use a cup or shallow dish filled with ordinary vermiculite. Once it's used to start the seeds, the vermiculite can be used to make future batches of Mel's Mix. Once the seeds have sprouted, they'll be moved to four-packs filled with Mel's Mix to grow on into full-fledged transplants.

SPROUTING INDOORS, PLANTING OUTDOORS

Although sprouting seeds indoors is most often done when you are growing transplants indoors, it's also possible to sprout seeds indoors, then plant those tiny sprouts into the outdoor garden right away. The easiest way to do this is to place seeds on a moist paper towel, then put the paper towel in a shallow tray or dish. Keep the seeds and towel moist and warm (a plastic bag can help with this). Check daily, and when you see the seeds sprouting, carefully cut the paper towel into small sections and lift each one out with a knife. Now you can take each tiny seedling outside and plant it into Mel's Mix in your Square Foot Garden. This method gives your plants a bit of a head start—instead of 14 days, you might see the first leaves in 6 days or so.

MOVE THE SEEDLINGS INTO FOUR-PACKS

When you're sprouting seeds in vermiculite, it's best to transplant them into the four-pack as soon as the tops have sprouted and you see the first two leaves, called the seed leaves or cotyledons. These will have a different appearance from the subsequent sets of "true" leaves.

Most garden experts advise waiting until you have two "true" leaves, but experienced Square Foot Gardeners have found that if you wait until the set of true leaves develops, the roots may already be so long and tangled that it's hard to transplant upward into the four-packs. The cotyledon comes first, and it's usually a fairly flat, large leaf that doesn't look like the plant's regular leaves. When these appear, it's time to transfer the tiny seedlings into four-packs to grow on into full plants. Here's how it's done:

1. Fill peat or plastic four-pack transplant containers with Mel's Mix and place into a plastic tray alongside the containers where your seedlings have sprouted in vermiculite.

2. Use a pencil to bore a hole in the center of the soil in each cell of the four-pack.

3. Now turn to the seedlings growing in vermiculite. Carefully hold on to one the seedlings by gripping one of the leaves between thumb and forefinger.

4. Use a pencil to carefully dig into the vermiculite under the tiny plant and lift it out—root and all. Make sure to touch only the leaf, not the stem.

5. If the roots are very long, trim off the bottom one-third with a pair of scissors.

6. Transfer the seeding to the four-pack, carefully tucking its roots down into the hole in the Mel's mix.

7. Use the point of the pencil to lightly pack the Mel's Mix around the seedling. Take care not to damage the stem or the leaves.

8. Give the seedling some water, either by misting from above or by adding water to the tray so that the Mel's Mix soaks it up.

9. Put the tray in a spot that is light but not in direct sunlight.

GROW THE SEEDLINGS INTO TRANSPLANTS

Mel's Mix is a very good growing medium for seedlings, and you should have few of the problems that sometimes occur with indoor seed starting. The peat moss in Mel's Mix is slightly acidic, and this can lessen the chances of a common fungal problem known as damping off. Keep your four-pack trays moist, but not saturated, and place them in a location that gets good air circulation but without strong drafts. In the early days of growing, keep the plant in a location that gets plenty of light but isn't in direct sunlight. As the plants develop more sets of true leaves, they can be gradually exposed to increasing amounts of direct light, either from sunlight through the window or from some form of commercial grow light.

Do not fertilize your young plants. They are getting all the nutrients they need from Mel's Mix, and adding more will do more harm than good.

PREPARE THE YOUNG PLANTS FOR THE OUTDOORS

You should have a good idea of when the proper planting time is for outdoor plants, based on your region's last frost dates and recommendations from your garden center or county extension agent. But even though your carefully grown indoor transplants may look completely sturdy and healthy, it can be devastating for them to go instantly from carefully controlled indoor conditions right into the Square Foot Garden grids. No matter how pleasant the weather is, it is a tremendous shock for a plant that's been luxuriating in indoor conditions to go directly into the garden.

We recommend that in the 3 or 4 weeks prior to the proper outdoor planting time, you gradually acclimate your plants to outdoor conditions. This is pretty easy to do. Begin by picking a nice afternoon with mild winds, and move your four-packs in their trays into a shady but warm location outdoors to get 1 or 2 hours of exposure. Then bring them indoors as temperatures begin to fall in late afternoon.

Gradually increase the amount of time each day your plants enjoy the outdoors. At some point, allow them some time in direct sunlight outdoors. And near the time when outdoor planting is coming, allow your plants to sit outdoors all night, provided the weather report predicts mild overnight temperatures.

This process of gradually acclimating transplants is known as "hardening off," and it is essential if you want

Modular trays with cells allow roots to develop individually without encroaching on their neighbors. This allows for easy transplanting.

your plants to successfully make the transition into the garden and quickly grow into vibrant, productive adults. It is much like the way that we introduce our children to a big-time swimming pool by first letting them get their feet wet in a warm wading pool, then gradually getting them familiar with deeper waters.

PLANT THE TRANSPLANTS INTO YOUR SQUARE FOOT GARDEN GRIDS

Whether you have grown transplants yourself indoors from seeds or purchased them from a garden center, it's very likely that some or all of your garden crops will be started by planting young transplants into the grids. This is a very simple process that looks the same whether you are planting very small transplants from four-packs, or much larger transplants from quart-sized containers purchased at the garden center.

HOW TO PLANT TRANSPLANTS

1 Mark the grid for planting in the same way you would for planting seed. Make a hole large enough to hold the transplant that will fit there. For small transplants, you can use a pencil to simply move soil around to create an opening. For larger transplants, you may need to scoop out hole with a small trowel.

2 Remove the transplant from its container, being careful not to damage the roots or the stem. If the root clump is tightly bound together, untwine it with your fingers or cut into it to free the clump.

3 Settle the transplant into the planting hole. Gently firm the soil around the base of the plant, creating a slight depression around the base to hold water. Gently water the plant and keep it moist for several days until it gets established. If sunlight is very warm, you may want to protect the plant with shade cloth for the first 1 or 2 weeks.

4 This newly planted bed of salad crops has been planted with careful spacing so that all plants can grow without competing with one another.

A 3 × 3 Square Foot Garden box planted with quick-growing and easy-to-harvest crops, such as salad greens, is a great way to introduce kids with the fun of Square Foot Gardening.

IN MEL'S WORDS: SQUARE FOOT GARDENING WITH KIDS

I've always considered Square Foot Gardening a family-friendly activity. It's a great way to get children out of the house, away from video games and the computer, and get them some fresh air and exercise. It's also a wonderful way for children to learn everyday lessons from nature as well as become more self-sufficient. It's really fulfilling to see your child's eyes get big as he says, "Look what I grew!" Of course, getting kids involved in Square Foot Gardening means keeping in mind that you're dealing with little people who have short attention spans, unlimited creativity, and tons of energy.

I always try to encourage parents to see all the learning possibilities in a garden, and that carries over to inside the house. There are lessons about math, science, biology, nature—all kinds of things your child can learn from his or her Square Foot Garden. Always keep an eye out for teachable moments because they pop up all the time in the SFG process!

OFF TO A GOOD START

Start as you would for any Square Foot Garden: with the location. Let your child pick a location, but guide them toward one that gets all the sun the plants will need and is as close as possible to a door that your son or daughter regularly uses. (Don't forget, it can be the front door as well as the back!) You want your child to pass it often and be able to see it out of the house—that way they are more likely to interact with their Square Foot Garden. I think it would be great if you could position their box so that your child can see it from her room. Wouldn't it be wonderful for her to look out her window and see it every day? That would work especially well for a child's bedroom on the second floor. It's just a real treat if you can send your child out to pick strawberries for her cereal in the morning. That's a special way for kids to learn the value of a garden.

Older kids can easily garden in a classic 4 × 4 Square Foot Garden box. You can even dedicate an entire box to each child.

BOXED FUN

With the location selected, you'll want to build the box. I try to let kids do as much as possible in creating their SFG. That's why I say include them in the whole process of building the 3 × 3-foot Square Foot Garden box. Help them in shopping for the lumber, cutting it, drilling holes, and screwing the box together. Even with you helping them out, it gives your child a real feeling of accomplishment, the pride in knowing that they did it.

Of course, if you don't have tools or if your child is too young, you may want to use a prefab box rather than building from scratch. You can still keep them involved with the construction process, even if it's just joining the sides together with a corner block. (Remember to buy a 3 × 3-foot box for kids younger than eight.)

Children often like to personalize their boxes, which is fine, as long as they don't get any toxic materials on the inside of the box or underside of the grid. Let them paint the box with soy-based or other nontoxic paints. Or here's an idea: let them stamp the sides of the boxes with their own rubber stamps that you can find in a crafts store. You can even help your child stencil their name on the outside of the box! Just let their imagination go (preferably before assembly), and you're sure to see some interesting designs.

GROWING A CHILD'S SQUARE FOOT GARDEN

Children really become engaged in a Square Foot Garden when they start thinking about what they'll plant. Start with a seed catalog. It's fun to sit down with a child on a rainy day or at night inside and look through those beautiful pictures and wonderful descriptions. Make a list of the things that your child wants to plant, and then sort through the different varieties available. Or go to a nursery with the list and look through the seed packets on the rack.

If you want to get a jump on the season and start building excitement in your son or daughter for their new garden, start some seedlings on a well-lit windowsill. Fill small cups with vermiculite, plant the seeds, and keep the vermiculite moist. You can imagine the delight on children's faces when they see those seeds start sprouting. They'll be checking them every morning when they get up.

Here's a list of some of the best plants for kids—the ones that will yield the most and grow the fastest.

Radishes. An all-time kid pleaser, radishes grow in as few as 3 weeks. There are cool- and hot-weather varieties,

When gardening with kids, a prefab Square Foot Garden box purchased on the Internet or in a garden center will allow your child to share the fun of assembly.

and one SFG square can support 16 radishes. Plus, they are pretty much fail-safe.

Lettuces. You might not think this would be such an interesting crop for kids, but they love it. That's because it's quick-growing and gives little ones a way to interact with their garden using their scissors (cutting that dinner salad every night). Choose leaf varieties, which mature more quickly than head types. You can also select from different colors, which are sure to grab a child's interest!

Cherry tomatoes. Every gardener loves tomatoes, but younger gardeners will really appreciate these smaller varieties. When the fruit ripens, your children can just pop them in their mouths for a healthy, tasty treat as they run around playing in the yard. Cherry tomatoes are started by transplants, so take your little gardener with you when you head to the nursery and discuss the different labels on the transplants to pick out the variety that will provide the most interest. Regardless of which type you choose, cherry tomatoes are abundant when they mature, with all those little fruits on a long stem. It's very impressive and worth bragging about. Your child can bring his or her friends over and say, "Look—I grew that!"

Bush beans. Easy and fast growing and high yields make this a kid's garden favorite that grows in many colors

and sizes. Kids also get a kick out of growing pole beans up a vertical support. You can teach them about different seasons and the natural crop rotation of Square Foot Gardening by replacing the bush beans with snow peas in the fall.

Carrots. Just like radishes, kids seem to love carrots. You'll have to temper their anticipation and desire to pull the carrots before they are mature. But even if they do, you'll just enjoy baby carrots for dinner! I think this is a great opportunity to bring some math into the garden. Carrots take two or three times as long as radishes to grow, so if a radish takes 20 days, ask your little Jane or Johnny how long the carrots will take. How many months is that?

Corn. Choose short varieties, and don't be afraid to try unusual types with multicolored kernels for added fun. This is also a great way to teach children how to protect their garden bounty from birds and other thieves! But for success, you'll need at least several squares of corn so that they can pollinate. You may even want to plant a whole separate box of corn (and maybe a square of sunflowers for an attractive pairing). One thing's for sure: corn on the cob never seems to go to waste! It's as fun to eat as it is to grow.

Sunflowers. Kids flip over these tall garden flowers, which are beautiful and fun to grow, and they will enjoy eating the seeds after the flowers are dried. Choose short-stalk varieties so you and your child don't need to stake the sunflowers and so the flowers will be closer to the child's eye level.

Nasturtiums. These are considered prime flowers for a children's Square Foot Garden. They are easy to grow, durable, and pretty—and, as a bonus, the blossoms can be tossed onto a salad to really amaze your kids!

The Square Foot Gardening grid system is educational for kids, teaching them basics of geometry and calculating fractions.

Young Square Foot Gardeners need not enjoy their fun only when the harvest is done. A square foot box can be decorated and staged for Halloween fun.

IN MEL'S WORDS

As you've learned, you can use your fingers to divide up individual squares for planting. So can your children. When I'm working with little ones in the garden, I like to teach them my "Zip, Zap, Bing, Bing, Bing" method.

For instance, for nine plants per square foot, take two fingers, and spread them apart. Draw two lines horizontally (zip), which divides the square into thirds, and then two vertically (zap), so that you've got nine sections. Folks from Texas like to use the "Hook 'em Horns" sign using the index finger and pinky finger.

For those with smaller hands (kids love doing this), have them use their thumb and index finger, or take one finger and draw two lines separately going each way. Poke nine holes (bing, bing, bing) in the middle of the drawn squares and you're ready to plant your seeds.

It's even more fun marking the 16 plantings per square foot. Remember: there is no measuring. Divide the square in half each way (eyeball it) by drawing lines in the soil with your finger, the same zip-zap (one vertical line and one horizontal line, each dividing the square in half) as described for four per square foot. Then, take two fingers, your index and middle fingers, and punch holes in the soil.

The holes should be spaced about 3 inches apart. Give your kids a ruler and show them how to read it so they can practice their finger spacing. In each of the four squares, go *bing, bing* with your fingers, marking two holes each time so there are four holes in each small square.

You'll probably need to help out with smaller seeds, because unreliable motor skills and excitement can lead to way too many seeds being planted. We don't want that, because we want to show our children that gardening is fun—not the unpleasant backbreaking toil that my mother's row garden was for me!

You can make a fun game out of practicing picking up a pinch of smaller seeds indoors, on a table over a piece of white paper. The kids can count how many they picked up and dropped.

WATERING

Keeping plants from getting thirsty is a great way to teach kids proper watering methods. You can actually show them how wasteful it is to stand around with a hose, spraying everything—or to use a sprinkler system, because they were meant to spread water over wide areas, not Square Foot Gardens. The way we water in Square Foot Gardening is also a chance to teach children about treating plants gently, as they pull aside the lower leaves and slowly pour a cup of sun-warmed water right over the roots. And it's a great time to discuss why we use sun-warmed water—wait until you hear some of the answers they'll come up with!

KID QUIZ

Here's a good question for children to think over. Which part of a seed sprouts first? Is it the top stem with its leaves? A fun children's book would have the tops popping out of the ground—looking around and if it likes what it sees and wants to stay, calling down to the root and saying, "Anchor me in." But that's a fairy tale. For all seeds, the root sprouts first and goes down. How does it know to go down? Gravity! After the root gets started and secured with little feeder roots so it can start taking up moisture and nutrients, it calls up to the top and yells "all clear below," then the top sprouts and goes straight up against gravity. It is not because of darkness or light or any other reason—strictly gravity, and the all-clear signal, of course.

ENJOYING THE CROPS

Harvesting a Square Foot Garden is the really fun part, and it's the most rewarding stage for children. You can amaze them by pulling up a bright red radish, swishing it around in the sun-warmed water bucket, and popping it into your mouth. Just imagine the look of delight on their faces when they learn that everything in the garden is ready to eat . . . right now. You'll have to show them how to determine whether a fruit or vegetable is mature (without dampening their enthusiasm), but after that, they'll get in the fun habit of harvesting salad makings every night.

They'll be able to say with pride, "I grew that!"

CHAPTER 9

MAINTAINING YOUR SQUARE FOOT GARDEN

Maintaining a traditional row garden is a laborious task from early spring to the end of harvest—months filled with churning up the soil with power tillers and digging in amendments, hours spent fertilizing and weeding throughout the growing season. Watering a traditional garden requires either lugging heavy buckets of water up and down rows to individual plants or using long hoses to broadcast water over the entire garden, most of which will just soak into the ground rather than quench the thirst of your vegetables. Serious traditional gardeners fill garages or large sheds with dozens of tools and dozens of pest-control solutions and specialty plant foods to address any and every problem that comes up.

Say goodbye to all that, because almost none of it is necessary if you are a Square Foot Gardener. The nature of the Square Foot Garden box means that weeding tasks are nearly nonexistent and nearly all plant nutrients are provided by the compost in Mel's Mix. Most gardeners go the entire growing season with no need for additional feedings at all. Watering a Square Foot Garden is incredibly easy and efficient because the garden is compact with access on all sides, and you will water less often because the peat moss and vermiculite in the mix retains water so well.

Gone are all the power tillers, hoes, rakes, spades, and other equipment necessary for a traditional row garden. In fact, Mel Bartholomew was fond of saying that the only tools you need for a Square Foot Garden are a hand trowel, a pencil, and a pair of scissors or small pruner. You might also find a small foam kneeling pad and a pair of garden gloves useful, but that's about it. Your entire tool collection for a Square Foot Garden could be stored in the same 5-gallon bucket you used to measure out the Mel's Mix when you created your garden.

Let's look at just how easy it is to maintain a square foot garden.

TILLING

Quite simply, tilling and churning the soil is just not necessary with a Square Foot Garden because the Mel's Mix you've created to fill it is perfectly loose, friable, and perfect for plant roots right from the start. Part of the reason a traditional row garden needs annual tilling is that people are constantly walking between the rows, stomping the soil down and packing it into rock-hard density. The only way to loosen compacted garden soil is to rent a tiller and churn it all back up each spring so that water and air can get back down into it. But a Square Foot Garden is built so you have easy access on all sides and never need to walk on the soil. Water and air can easily circulate down in the mix.

The only real mixing that is necessary occurs after you've harvested a grid square in your garden. At that point, you'll want to replenish the square with fresh compost, using your handy trowel to mix the fresh compost in with the remaining Mel's Mix in that grid square. And at the beginning of each spring as you prepare to plant again, you'll be topping off the garden with fresh compost, again using a simple hand trowel to blend in the compost.

All you really need to maintain a Square Foot Garden are a trowel, a pencil, and a pair of scissors.

IN MEL'S WORDS

The first of the three tools you need is a trowel. I've found that the one-dollar variety is really the best buy. They're attractive, strong, and neat looking. They have all the features of a six-dollar trowel. So, instead of just one, now you can afford six—one for every SFG box! Why not buy an assortment of colors? You can have one in every box just sitting there waiting so that you don't have to go looking for a tool when you walk by and see a square that is ready for replanting. Of course, if you see an occasional weed, your big, strong weeding tools are your own thumb and forefinger!

The trowel is for transplanting, for mixing in an added trowelful of compost when you replant each square foot, and for loosening up and turning over the Mel's Mix in an individual square or even an entire 4 × 4 grid. In the spring you won't believe how perfect the soil will be if you follow the Mel's Mix formula and start with a perfect soil.

The other two tools you'll need are a pencil (yes, that's a tool) for poking holes and lifting out young seedlings to transplant and a pair of scissors for harvesting beet, lettuce, or swiss chard leaves for supper; cutting off dead blossoms; and snipping off extra seedlings if more than one seed sprouts in a hole. Here again, because SFG tools are so simple and inexpensive, I love to splurge and keep one of each at every 4 × 4. That way, I never have to look for a tool.

I like to buy children's pointed scissors in August when you can find back-to-school sales. Usually I can purchase them for about 50 cents—an affordable price that allows for several pairs around the garden.

It would be fun to list all the tools that you no longer need if you have a Square Foot Garden. In fact, you could probably just go into your garage or toolshed and see them all right there—poor, lonely tools. Maybe you have some old-fashioned single-row friends who just can't give up all that hard work and could use some extra heavy-duty tools. You could rent them out and maybe make a few bucks.

The same 5-gallon bucket you used to measure out Mel's Mix ingredients can be used to store your kit of garden tools near your Square Foot Garden.

SUPPORTING PLANTS

Here's the one task you do need to pay attention to with a Square Foot Garden. Because Mel's Mix is so loose and friable, tall plants may have a little trouble staying upright in the garden box. Large vegetables such as tomatoes or peppers will benefit from support cages, just as in a traditional garden. With tall plants, drive plant stakes firmly down through the Mel's Mix and into the underlying soil and use them to tie the plant stems in place so they don't topple over. You can use commercial plant stakes for this or repurpose any stake-like materials you have around your property, such as lengths of copper plumbing pipe, metal rebar, or wooden stakes. The plant-support grid shown on page 118 is also a good way to support your plants.

WEEDING

A Square Foot Garden has few or no weeds, which you will quickly learn if you are new to the process. "How is this possible?" you may wonder. The answer is the ingredients used in Mel's Mix. Vermiculite and peat moss contain no seeds, and if the compost is correctly made, temperatures of 150°F or higher kill all the weed seeds that might be in the materials that go into it. So, with no viable weed seeds in the Mel's Mix to begin with, there aren't any that will sprout in your Square Foot Garden box. Add to this the layer of landscape fabric you laid down at the bottom of your garden box, and it means that weeds can't even sprout up through the bottom of the box.

If you've removed weeds and grass from the area below your Square Foot Garden box, then covered the ground with landscape fabric, it will be virtually impossible for weeds to grow up into your Square Foot Garden.

Eventually, of course, a few weed seeds will arrive in your Square Foot Garden on the wind or delivered by birds, but these will be very, very easy to remove. Mel's Mix is so loose as a growing medium that even the most tenacious weeds can simply be plucked out with your fingers. How can you tell if a new sprout is a weed? If it's not in a precise location where you planted seeds or looks out of place among transplants, it's almost certainly a weed. With a little practice, you'll quickly learn to distinguish vegetable seedlings from weeds.

Taller plants may need some support from traditional plant stakes.

FEEDING

If you come from a background of traditional row gardening, you may automatically want to continue the practice of monthly feedings using liquid or granular fertilizers in your Square Foot Garden.

This is completely and totally wrong. It could not be more wrong. Mel's Mix has all the nutrients, minerals, and trace elements that plants need, so forget about fertilizers.

There are gardeners who insist there are *some* plants that benefit from additional feeding even in a Square Foot Garden. If you insist on being one of these rebels, be very, very conservative about it, using greatly diluted organic fertilizers. It is very unlikely, though, that your vegetable garden will need additional feeding. It is more likely to be an issue if you are using your Square Foot Garden bed to grow showy, ornamental flowers, which are notoriously heavy feeders.

Mel's Mix is by nature laden with nutrients, but it is also somewhat on the acidic side due the presence of peat moss in the growing medium. There are some plants that thrive more in soils that are on the alkaline side of the pH scale, so in rare instances, you may want to add a small amount of granular lime in the form of ground limestone to the grid squares where some of these vegetables are growing. Veggies that might prefer a slightly more alkaline soil include:

- Cabbage
- Cauliflower
- Celery
- Cucumber
- Okra
- Peppers
- Yams

There is no reason to go overboard with this. A small handful of ground limestone mixed into the grid squares where these vegetables are growing is all it takes.

REPLENISHING THE MEL'S MIX

In the very beginning, the Mel's Mix in your Square Foot Garden box may settle a little, and before planting it's wise to add a bit to bring the level up to just below the grid lines. After this there's never a need to add more Mel's Mix, though it will be necessary to mix in a little more compost periodically, because this is the material that gets "consumed" as the plant roots break down the compost and take up its nutrients. A single trowelful of fresh compost will rejuvenate a Square Foot Garden grid and prepare it for replanting.

This is a pretty simple matter. As you harvest each square of your grid, mix in a single large trowelful of fresh mixed compost to rejuvenate the Mel's Mix in that square before planting the next crop there. Mix it in well, then replant late-season seeds or transplants as you wish.

At the beginning of the next planting season, do the same thing to each square in the grid, bringing the level of the Mel's Mix in the box to just under the lattice grid. Over a growing season, the lowering of the Mel's Mix volume occurs because the compost is breaking down

Weeds are rare in a Square Foot Garden but usually can be identified because they will be out of place within the plant spacing. And weeds will be easy to pluck out because Mel's Mix is so loose.

and being consumed—so it is the compost that needs to be replenished.

Does Mel's Mix last forever? The answer is no. Eventually the peat moss too will break down, and as that happens you will need to mix a new batch to refill the boxes. But experienced Square Foot Gardeners have shown that you can get up to 10 years of good life from a batch of Mel's Mix if you rejuvenate it with additional compost regularly. Making a batch of Mel's Mix is the most expensive part of creating a Square Foot Garden, but when you consider the money saved on fertilizers and the extreme productivity enjoyed in a small space, it becomes a bargain.

MULCHING

In much of the country, mulching a Square Foot Garden is not necessary. Normally, mulching is done to minimize weeds and keep the soil moist, and the nature of Mel's Mix means neither issue is much of a problem in most regions. But instructors and gardeners working in the hot southwest regions of the United States have found that keeping the soil cool and moist under the harsh sun there can be a challenge. The answer is to lay down a layer of mulch over the Mel's Mix in the grids. Some mulches, such as cocoa beans, shredded wood, and bark chips, are also quite attractive—you may want to consider a mulch for aesthetic reasons even in moderate climates.

IN MEL'S WORDS

You can grow a healthy Square Foot Garden even in a desert climate with just a few simple steps. Once your plants are growing and established, the first order of business is to lay down a thick layer of water-conserving mulch. This can be wet newspapers or cardboard, chopped-up straw, or even dried grass clippings. Some people use black plastic, but you might want to cover it with another mulch material—there's no reason your Square Foot Garden should be anything but beautiful. Conventional mulch, such as wood chips or bark, will work as well. However, whenever I use wood chips in a Square Foot Garden, I always put down a barrier first because wood chips can pull nitrogen from the soil as they decompose, and your plants aren't going to be happy about that.

In a desert environment, the wind can be as much a concern as the sun. We've had a lot of success making windscreens from the floating-cover type of cloth sold at nurseries and large garden centers. Stick a steel fence post outside each corner of the 4 × 4 square and then wrap the cloth around the stakes and the box sides, just like you might see around a tennis court.

WATERING

One of the biggest advantages of Square Foot Gardening is that the combination of the condensed size and the nature of Mel's Mix mean your garden requires much less water and much less watering effort than a traditional garden.

MEL'S PREFERRED WATERING METHOD

Mel Bartholomew taught that the best method for watering your garden is to leave a bucket of water to warm in the sun next to your Square Foot Garden box, then to water each plant whenever it needs a drink by dipping a single cupful of water from the bucket and applying it directly to the root zone below the plant. Some people have argued that this method takes too long, to which we point out the following:

- Your Square Foot Garden is only a fraction of the size of a traditional garden, and you are watering only when a plant needs its drink.

- You're no longer broadcasting water over the entire plant, instead only applying it to the place it is needed—the base of the plant, where the roots are located. Mel's method is a supreme water saver.

- Mel's Mix is specially formulated to absorb and retain moisture, so you'll need to ladle water on the roots far less often than you might think.

A single cupful of water dipped into the bucket and poured over the roots at the base of a plant is sufficient for seedlings. Larger plants may need several cupfuls.

A bucket of sun-warmed water is the ideal source of irrigation water for your Square Foot Garden. Keep a full bucket near your garden box and use it any time a plant is drying out.

We have found that sun-warmed water is best partly for the same reasons that people prefer to shower in warm instead of cold water. A more scientific explanation is that plants will absorb nutrients in the soil more effectively if the soil and water temperatures are warmer. Irrigating with sun-warmed water helps warm the soil, which means that seeds will sprout quicker and transplants will shoot up faster.

LESS WATER, MORE OFTEN

Gardening newcomers very often overwater their plants—maybe out of kindness or maybe out of fear of failure. This can be a big problem in traditional row gardens or container gardens, as overwatering can literally drown the roots of plants. To grow well, plant roots need air as well as moisture, and keeping the soil saturated with water shuts off air to the plant roots. This is much less problematic with Mel's Mix, because you really can't overwater. Mel's Mix is so loose and friable that excess water quickly drains away, opening up the essential air spaces between particles.

This quick draining does, however, mean that Mel's Mix does dry out a little more quickly than other growing mediums after watering. Rather than saturating a garden once a week or so as you would do with a traditional row garden, the best strategy for irrigating a Square Foot Garden give each plant a little drink whenever they "ask" for it.

IN MEL'S WORDS

Think of your plants in your garden the same as you do your children. If they've been out in the hot sun and playing hard and one of them looks a little droopy and wilted, you know right away to inspect that child a little closer to make sure he or she is properly hydrated.

The secret is to watch the plants. A daily walk around your 4 × 4 Square Foot Garden will quickly teach you how to spot the plants asking for water. They may signal this with a slightly wilted look, or maybe the branches will droop just slightly, or maybe the color will be just slightly off. At that point, just give that plant a little drink from the sun-warmed bucket of water. They key here is to wait for each plant to ask for its drink. Practicing a little tough love here will teach your plants to seek water in the soil by building extensive root systems. Your vegetables will actually be more vigorous if you water when they ask for it rather than giving them more water than they need.

WATERING BY HOSE

For those of you who like traditional methods, yes, you can always use a garden hose to water plants. It can be a nuisance to roll out and roll back up each time you need it, so if possible the best strategy is to leave the hose extended out into the garden, perhaps with the excess coiled up right next to the Square Foot Garden box, where the water in the hose can be warmed by the sun. You should be careful, though, not to spray water that has been heated too much, as scalding-hot water is just as bad for plants as ice-cold water. As you begin spraying, feel the water with your hand and let it get lukewarm before beginning to water the base of your plants.

With a garden hose just lying there, it will be tempting to saturate the entire garden, but here too the best strategy is to water only those plants who are asking for a drink. Make sure your hose is equipped with one of those shut-off valves right at the end so you have complete control over the force and amount of water. There are many types of extension wands, long and short, equipped with spray nozzles on the ends. This allows you to water directly under the plants at the root zone, turning the wand on and off for each plant to avoid wasting water.

HOW TO INSTALL A DRIP IRRIGATION SYSTEM

While the absolute most efficient watering is to apply water to individual plants only when they ask for it, another very efficient watering method is to install a drip irrigation system that uses a series of small plastic tubes running along the soil beneath the leaves of the plants to deliver small amounts of water precisely where it's needed at the precise time you want it to. There are many different manufacturers of drip irrigation kits (sometimes they are called microwatering kits), but all kits are similar in that they include plastic or vinyl tubing about ¼-inch in diameter, small drip-emitter heads, and stakes to hold the tubing and drip heads in place. Installing one is really just a matter of cutting and fitting the parts to the configuration of your garden. It is possible connect a drip irrigation system to an automatic timer to automate the watering process, but we advise Square Foot Gardeners to inspect the garden regularly and turn the drip system on and off when it is clear the garden is asking for water. There is no substitute for regular, close contact with your garden.

MATERIALS
The materials you'll need include:

- Drip irrigation kit include tubing, T-fittings, drip emitters, and stakes
- Pipe clamps
- Faucet backflow preventer (if spigot is not already equipped with one)
- 25-psi pressure regulator (included with most kits)
- Hand pruner or utility shears

A) Hand pruners
B) ½" tubing
C) ¼" tubing
D) Instant (puncture) tool
E) Pipe clamps
F) Emitters
G) Regulator assembly
H) Tubing stakes
I) T-fittings

ASSEMBLY

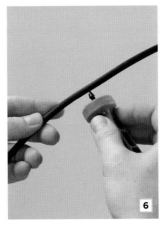

1 Install the backflow preventer on the faucet spigot, if it is not already equipped with one. Run a garden hose from the spigot to the Square Foot Garden box location. Attach the pressure regulator to the end of the hose. This regulator lessens the water pressure to a level that will not damage the drip tubing or compromise the fittings.

2 Connect the hose adapter to the pressure regulator, then install the length of ½"-diameter feeder tubing to the hose adapter. These are barbed fittings that secure simply by forcing the tubing into the fitting.

3 Run a ½" tube along one side of the box and attach it with pipe clamps. This tube will then feed the ¼"-diameter feeder tubes running down the length of the garden box.

4 Punch holes in the ½" tubing where you want to run the flexible ¼" drip tubing. Most drip irrigation kits come with a puncture tool for this purposes, but if yours doesn't, you can use an awl or nail to punch holes.

5 Cut sections of ¼" tubing to run the length of the garden box, and attach one end to a barbed elbow fitting and insert into the holes in the ½" tubing. Install a barbed cap on the other end.

6 Use the punch tool to poke holes in the flexible ¼" tubing where you want emitters to be inserted. Kit designs vary, so follow the manufacturer's instructions regarding this. On some kits, simple holes in the small tubing provide the drip irrigation, while other kits use a small plastic emitter inserted into the holes. Use the stakes included with the kit to secure the tubing in place. Turn on the hose and make sure the emitters are all operating properly.

HOW TO BUILD A WATERING GRID

Square Foot Gardeners are a clever, inventive group, and over the years many different designs have been created for a watering system that doubles as a planting grid. Online gardening forums are full of designs for this kind of watering accessory, with gardeners challenging one another to create the most full-featured system for the lowest cost.

The system described here is a very simple one that just about anyone can build using ordinary ¾-inch PVC plumbing pipe and fittings, and a few other parts, all available at hardware stores or big-box home-improvement centers. The essence of the system is a grid-work of hollow PVC pipes with holes drilled in them to emit water. At one corner, a fitting is installed to allow you to hook up a garden hose. The short pipes are joined together with cross-fittings, and the ends of the grid pipes are covered with endcaps attached with plumbing solvent cement—except at one corner, where threaded caps are used so you can unscrew the caps at the end of the season and drain the system before storing it away.

The trickiest part of this project is making the corner fitting to attach a garden hose to the watering grid. The stub-out is made with a simple PVC elbow, a short length of pipe, and another threaded elbow fitting known as a street elbow. But in order to attach the male threaded end of a garden hose onto the male threaded end of the PVC street elbow, a short length of hose with two female-threaded fittings is needed. We have used a short hose fitting called a hose protector, but there are also other solutions you could use, such as an ordinary water-supply hose meant for washing machines that that has female-threaded fittings on both ends.

This design is intended for a classic 4 × 4 Square Foot Garden box, with part measurements appropriate to a box of that size. If you have a box with different dimensions, make sure to sketch out the project and adjust measurements and part quantities appropriately.

MATERIALS
The materials you'll need include:

- ¾" schedule 40 PVC pipe, 10' long (2)
- Drill and ³⁄₁₆" bit
- ¾" cross-fittings (3)
- ¾" elbow (1)
- ¾" male-threaded street elbow (1)
- ¾" PVC stand pipe, 6" long (1)
- ¾" threaded transition fittings (2)
- ¾" female-threaded caps (3)
- ¾" pipe caps (9)
- Saw or PVC pipe cutter
- PVC solvent cement
- 6" hose protector
- Teflon plumber's tape
- Eye and ear protection
- Work gloves

ASSEMBLY

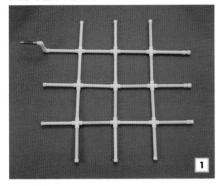

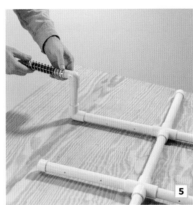

1 Cut the straight lengths of PVC pipes for the grid. The lengths may vary depending on the size of your box and the size of the cross fittings, but in our 48" SFG, the pipes are 10" long. Lay out the basic grid using pipe lengths and cross fittings. Dry-fit the grid, and test-fit to make sure it fits inside the boundaries of your SFG box. Make sure there is room for the caps on the ends of the pipes.

2 Disassemble the pieces, then drill two ³⁄₁₆" holes through each pipe, spaced evenly. These will be the emitter holes that distribute water out of the sides of the pipes.

3 Use solvent glue to assemble the watering grid pipes and cross fittings. Apply a thin layer of solvent cement on both the outside of the pipes and the inside hub of the cross-fitting. Make sure the watering holes are aligned horizontally.

4 With the completed grid lying on a flat surface, attach an elbow fitting to one corner end pipe using solvent cement. Make sure the open socket is pointing up. Attach a short vertical standpipe in the open socket on the elbow.

5 Attach the street elbow to the top of the standpipe. Keep in mind the direction from which the garden hose will reach the watering grid when "aiming" the street elbow. Attach a short hose protector to the stub-out, first wrapping the threads with Teflon plumber's tape. This hose protector will be the point where you attach the garden hose when watering. When the grid is not in use, you can cap off the stub-out by removing the hose protector and threading a cap onto the stub-out threads.

COMPLETION

6 At one corner of the watering grid, attach a threaded transition to two adjacent pipes using solvent cement. Cover the ends with threaded caps. These caps can be removed for draining or flushing the pipes. On all remaining open pipes, install caps with solvent cement.

7 Your watering grid can now be positioned in your Square Foot Garden box. It will serve both as planting grid and an ingenious watering system.

PESTS AND PLANT PROBLEMS

It's difficult for one book to anticipate and address all of the kinds of insects and diseases you are likely to encounter in your region, but you will be happy to know that Square Foot Gardens suffer fewer of these problems than do traditional row gardens, and when they do occur, the problems are easier to cure thanks to the fact that Square Foot Gardens are smaller and more accessible than traditional gardens.

COUNTY EXTENSION AGENTS AND MASTER GARDENERS

Your community very likely has some great resources on which you can call. In every county in every state in the country, some tax dollars go toward the training and maintenance of a staff of horticultural experts trained by the nearest land-grant university—the county extension agents. Commercial farmers lean heavily on these experts, so why not you? Look under the directory of county officials to find your extension agent. We at the Square Foot Gardening Foundation often direct gardeners to this great local resource.

In addition, most land-grant universities, in conjunction with the county extension agencies, offer training for group of local volunteers as part of a Master Gardener program. As part of their commitment, these master gardeners volunteer time to helping local gardeners find solutions to problems and answering their questions. An online search for master gardeners in your county will produce a telephone number or website where you can quickly get all sorts of questions answered. Be prepared to e-mail a photo of your pest or disease problem, as this will greatly help the experts diagnose your problem.

At one time, both country extension agents and master gardeners leaned toward traditional row gardening and were not very knowledgeable about Square Foot Gardening. That is really not the case any longer, because the merits of Square Foot Gardening are now proven and well known.

A GUIDE TO COMMON PEST SOLUTIONS

Many pests are common across all gardening regions. The treatments below are listed in ascending order of severity and the order in which they should be used. Notice that we don't recommend any synthetic chemical sprays. These chemicals are available, and they work, but we don't recommend their use on your edible garden. If you do go the synthetic chemical route, please read product labels carefully, especially any cautions about toxicity to humans.

Remember that not all insects are damaging to your garden. A healthy vegetable garden will have a variety of beneficial insects, such as this lady beetle, who will feast on damaging aphids. Consider that some pest solutions will also kill the beneficial insects.

INSECT	AFFECTED PLANTS	TREATMENT
Aphids (tiny, pear-shaped bugs, usually found in groups; can be many different colors; slow moving; found on underside of leaves and tender stalks of plants)	Wide variety; aphids attack leaves and new growth	• Spray off with hose • Homemade garlic spray • Insecticidal soap
Cabbage worms (adults are white or cream-colored moths with dark spots on wings; damage-causing caterpillars are fuzzy, green and slow moving)	Cabbage, broccoli, cauliflower, kale, and similar crops	• Floating covers early in the season • Handpick worms and drop in soapy water • Spray with Neem oil • For serious infestations, spray with *Bacillus thuringiensis*
Corn borers/earworms (striped green, brown, or pink caterpillars [ear worms], pink or reddish caterpillars with darker spots)	Corn, peppers, and beans	• Plant resistant hybrids if corn borers or earworms are an ongoing problem in your area
Flea beetles (dark, shiny, sometimes metallic greens and blacks on small bodies; these beetles can hop when disturbed)	Beans, squash, lettuce, turnips, broccoli, sunflowers, corn, and other plants such as mustard and eggplant	• Sticky traps • Apply beneficial nematodes at the start of the season
Japanese beetles (large-bodied iridescent insects; winged but slow moving and slow flying)	Roses and a wide variety of vegetables and flowering plants	• Handpick and use insecticidal soap • Neem oil at first sign of beetles • Pheromone traps (use carefully to avoid drawing more beetles into your yard)
Slugs and snails (soft-bodied slugs are green to yellow, slimy, and 1 to 2 inches long; snails are similar but brown, with brown shells and prominent antennae)	Tender young seedlings and transplants	• Handpick and drop in salty or soapy solution • Set out flat beer in shallow saucer near susceptible plants
Cutworms (ugly gray-brown worms, about 2 inches long, with a noticeably greasy appearance)	Most vegetables and other garden plants, as seedlings or transplants	• Protect seedlings and transplants with cardboard collars, such as toilet paper tubes, or wrap stalks in aluminum foil • Apply beneficial nematodes to the soil
Tomato hornworms (green worms with white bands and red horns)	Tomatoes, eggplants, peppers, and potatoes	• Cut off affected leaves and dispose of the hornworm and leaf in the garbage (don't touch hornworms because they can leave an awful smell on your hands)
Spider mites (green or amber insects about the size of a pencil lead; amber or white eggs; wispy white webs)	Most leafy plants	• Garlic spray • Spray of equal parts water and alcohol

It's hard to know what kind of spray to use if you're not sure what type of pest you have, so whenever possible, take a sample to an expert. You can clip off damaged leaves, but a live critter is the best way to determine exactly what you're dealing with. Your local nursery professional will usually be able to tell you what you've got, but the county extension service agent will definitely be able to identify the pest and give you guidance on the best spray (or other treatment) to use on it. Actual samples are the best, but it's also fine to take a close-up photo and e-mail it to the local extension service office.

PREVENTING PEST PROBLEMS

PHYSICAL BARRIERS

From the perspective of an environmentally conscious gardener, the best way to deal with pests is to deny them access by using one or more physical barriers. You can stop most garden invaders by simply not letting them get to your plants in the first place.

Larger invaders, such as deer, raccoons, squirrels, and other wildlife, are easy to foil with the simple wire cage on page 116. (It's also a great way to keep family pets and even the occasional soccer ball away from your plants!)

Floating covers are fine mesh nets that you place over early-season plants to prevent insects such as the cabbage moth from laying eggs on their leaves. You can cover individual squares by just wrapping the floating cover around the plant. Air, light, and water can still get in, but the insects can't.

A simple perimeter of crushed eggshells can keep most slugs and snails away from your plants. Epsom salts (above) can serve the same function.

PREVENTIVE SPRAYS

Make a pest spray by boiling ingredients—in this case garlic and cayenne pepper, which make one of the most effective sprays—for several minutes. Allow the liquid to cool to room temperature, then strain it into a spray bottle using a strainer or cheesecloth over a funnel.

When spraying plants, make sure to spray the undersides of leaves, where many pests like to hide. Spray every day or every 2 days and immediately after any rainfall.

REMOVAL

Sometimes, the best solution to insect problems is simply to remove the pests by hand. Insects tend to be pretty slow-moving creatures, and many, such as that common villain the aphid, can be washed or picked off plants. There are also traps available to remove many flying insects.

Physical removal is one of the most effective and easiest ways to catch problems when they start and prevent them from taking hold. This is true for both insects and diseases.

The same holds true of diseases when they show up on your plants. Square Foot Gardens are much less susceptible to fungal, bacterial, and viral diseases than traditional row gardens due to the garden being planted in a diverse manner, with the species interspersed. When spots do appear on leaves and fruit, it's best just to cut them and dispose of them with household waste (do not compost plant material that appears diseased). Keeping the Square Foot Garden box free of leaf litter will further reduce the likelihood of diseases.

and bacteria that can be a problem in traditional garden soils. The compost that forms one-third of your garden is pathogen-free by virtue of the heat generated during the composting process. And the other two ingredients—vermiculite and peat moss—are sterile at the time you buy them.

Second, the strategy for planting a Square Foot Garden means there is inherent diversity because the species are interspersed in a way that makes it difficult for any pathogen to overcome a large portion of your garden. Garden pathogens tend to be specific to species, and while a single tomato plant, for example, might succumb to a virus, unless your Square Foot Garden is planted only with tomatoes, the problem will likely be confined to one plant. In fact, if you are intent on planting the same species in many grid square, it's best to have several Square Foot Garden boxes and spread the plant among them.

REMOVING DISEASED PLANT PARTS

A plant disease will be pretty evident by the look of the plant's leaves, roots, and stems. Diligence will help here. Your routine should involve a daily stroll around your garden anyway, and when you see a plant with shriveled

Disinfect garden shears after removing diseased leaves from each plant. Viruses, bacteria, and fungi can be spread between plants. It's also a good idea to wash your hands if you are simply picking off diseased leaves by hand.

SOLVING DISEASE PROBLEMS

Accomplished Square Foot Gardeners have contacted us from time to time on other issues and problems they have with the method, but there are relatively few questions regarding viruses, bacterial diseases, and fungal diseases. One reason for this is that Mel's Mix is relatively sterile to begin with, free of the various spores, viruses, leaves, rotten fruit, or other signs of problems, pick away the diseased portions immediately and discard them. Do not add this plant material to your compost pile, because some pathogens are very long lived—if the compost pile fails to generate the proper heat, they may infect your entire compost supply and spread it to living plants when you use the compost.

To solarize a Square Foot Garden box, cover it with clear plastic and allow it to set in the sun for 4 weeks. The heat generated inside should kill all pathogens. If the soil inside the box is slightly moist, it will help the process. Note: If solarizing to kill weeds, use a black plastic sheet.

If the plant's problems are severe, remove the entire plant, root and all, and discard it. You'll know when this is necessary. Don't mourn too much about it; losing an occasional plant is part of gardening.

In rare instances, a pathogen might remain in the soil after you remove a diseased plant. This is especially true of some fungal diseases, like *Verticillium* wilt. If a problem reappears the next season, there are several options. First, you can choose to plant species other than the affected one in this box; because so many pathogens are species specific, there's a good chance that other plants will be entirely unaffected by it. Second, you can choose to discard the existing Mel's Mix and replace it with fresh mix that is entirely pathogen-free once more. The expected life expectancy of Mel's Mix is about 7 to 10 years anyway, so if

IN MEL'S WORDS

Choose solutions, just as you will choose pest-fighting strategies: by starting with the mildest. Only when simpler tactics fail should you move on to the more serious treatments, such as pesticides. However, I avoid synthetic chemicals of any kind in my SFG. Chemical treatments are unpredictable and can stay in the soil for a long time. I'd rather lose a few tomatoes or even a whole harvest than risk growing produce with potentially harmful toxins.

Neem oil is a widely available, nontoxic spray that works well on insects, provided it is applied at the right time. Follow label directions precisely.

a soil pathogen seems stubborn, it may be time to replace the growing medium. Finally, you may be able to sterilize the soil by solarization. To do this, simply cover the garden bed with clear plastic, weight down the edges with bricks, and allow it to sit in the sun for 4 weeks. The heat that builds up within the box will very likely kill any pathogens lurking there.

The Square Foot Garden method results in a harvest that is far more productive than that of a comparable traditional garden.

CHAPTER

HARVESTING YOUR SQUARE FOOT GARDEN

Gardening the Square-Foot way is fun and rewarding from start to finish, but the very best time you'll spend is in harvesting delicious crops from your garden. The problem with a traditional garden is that there is often too much produce, which is not only backbreaking work to harvest but also a source of waste, as most people have trouble eating all the produce the garden produces. All that changes with a Square Foot Garden. Because you have planned so carefully (Chapters 2 and 3), you are growing pretty much exactly what you need.

A Square Foot Garden also has the advantage of having a good, long harvest season, meaning that there is not one time when the work becomes overwhelming. In a Square Foot Garden, crops will begin bearing earlier, allowing you replace those that bear once for a second harvest. For those crops with a long, continuous bearing period, you'll find that the harvest lasts even longer, often running right up until frost time—or even later if you protect the Square Foot Garden with a frost cover.

This chapter will cover three topics: timing the harvest so you are picking your crops at their peak ripeness; storing your harvested crops the right way for best longevity; replanting a grid square after the first crop is harvested; extending your harvest so that you are picking produce earlier in the spring and later in the fall; and putting your Square Foot Garden "to bed" once everything is harvested and you're ready to relax and dream about next spring.

TIMING THE HARVEST

Especially for first-time gardeners, it's not always easy to know exactly when to pick your crops. After spending so much time planning, planting, and tending your garden, you deserve to know how to pick the produce at the moment of perfect ripeness. With some crops, ripeness will occur suddenly, and you'll need to harvest the entire crop fairly quickly if you want maximum flavor. Other crops bear fruit gradually, allowing you a window of several weeks or even months to harvest. A few vegetables, including some herbs and leaf vegetables such as kale, can be harvested pretty much from the moment they produce leaves right up through a fall frost.

JUDGING RIPENESS

One important clue as to when a crop will be ready for picking is found right on the seed label. Most seed packets will list a time period after planting or sprouting when the vegetable is usually ready to harvest. But this can vary considerably depending on conditions, so the following chart offers some tips for how to know when a crop is ripe:

CROP	RIPENESS INDICATORS
Asparagus	• Harvest spears when 7 to 9" long • Harvest in the morning, when temps are cool
Basil	• Harvest continually with scissors to keep growth coming • Remove flower buds before they open
Beans	• Harvest when pods are firm and evenly green • Beans are past prime when pods get lumpy • Remove by pinching stems with fingers
Beets	• Harvest when shoulders push up aboveground
Broccoli	• Harvest when heads are full but before buds open • Cut stalks 4" down from top of head
Brussels sprouts	• Harvest heads that are 1 to 2" in diameter • Ripe sprouts will twist off easily with fingers
Cabbage	• Harvest when leaves are tight against head, not loose • Harvest by cutting stem off at base
Cantaloupe	• Harvest when skin turns from smooth to rough • Underlying skin color should be golden or buff colored
Carrots	• Ripeness is indicated when shoulders begin to push aboveground • Harvest when diameter is ¾ to 1"
Cauliflower	• Usually ripe when heads are 6 to 8" in diameter • Head should be tight, with segments not yet separating • Cut head from stem at ground level
Celery	• Any stalk longer than 6" is ripe • Cut off 2" up from soil line
Chives	• Start harvesting when plants reach 3" tall • Cut down to 1" above soil line

Cilantro
- Harvest when plants are 6 to 8" tall
- Harvest outside leaves, leaving stems intact

Collard greens
- Harvest when plant is about 1' tall
- Cut individual leaves from stem
- Leaves more than 8" long are overripe and will be tough

Corn
- Ripe ears are rounded at the top and will feel firm and plump
- Harvest in the morning, holding stalk with one hand and tearing away the ear with the other hand

Cucumbers
- Most varieties ready to harvest at 5 to 8" in length
- Ripe cucumbers will be firm and uniformly dark green

Eggplant
- Harvest as soon as skin becomes glossy
- Fruit may be overripe if skin has turned black

Garlic
- Harvest when leaves on bottom half of stem are brown
- Move into shade immediately after harvesting

Kale
- With most varieties, harvest leaves at 6 to 8" long
- Harvest leaves from bottom of stem, leaving top leaves to grow

Leaf lettuce
- Harvest leaves on outside of stem using scissors after they are 3" long
- When plant bolts (sets flowers), leaves will be overripe and bitter

Leeks
- Harvest when roots are at least 1" in diameter
- Root stalks more than 2" in diameter may be woody and inedible

Mint
- Harvest younger, smaller leaves regularly to keep plant productive
- Mature plants can be cut down to 2" above ground level to rejuvenate them

Okra
- Harvest pods when 2 to 3" long using a sharp knife
- Pods that are hard to cut off will be inedible

Onions
- Ripeness is usually indicated when leaves turn yellow and fall over
- Harvest when shoulders push up aboveground
- Let dry in sun after harvesting

Oregano
- Harvest anytime after plant is 4" tall
- Harvest individual leaf clumps down to just above a leaf pair
- Harvest in midmorning for best flavor

Parsley
- Start harvesting when plants reach 6"
- Harvest individual stems, from the inside of the plant outward

Peas, snap
- Pods are ripe when full and rounded but not overly large
- Peas inside pod should be obvious to touch
- Pods should snap rather than bend

Peas, snow
- Harvest when pods are thin and light green, with peas inside just visible

Peppers, bell
- Fruit walls will be thick

Peppers, jalapeño
- Harvest when fruit is 2 to 3" long

Peppers, cayenne
- Harvest when small for milder flavor or when large for more heat

Peppers, habanero
- Harvest when fruit is round and 1 to 2" in diameter

Potatoes
- Harvest "new" potatoes when plants start to flower
- Harvest mature potatoes when vines begin to die
- Harvest on a dry day using a garden fork

Pumpkins
- Fruit is ripe when rind is hard enough to resist a fingernail scratch
- Pumpkins are usually ripe when they reach the predicted color
- Maturity is indicated when stems begin to shrivel and dry out

Radishes
- Most varieties are ripe at about 1½" in diameter
- Harvest by pulling up on the greens
- Radishes that have split open are overripe and will be too spicy

Sage	• Can be harvested anytime by pinching off individual leaves
	• Pick on a dry morning after dew has dried.
Scallions	• Harvest as soon as there is 6" of top growth
	• Leave in ground to allow scallions to ripen into onions
Spinach	• Harvest as soon as leaves are large enough to use
	• Harvest frequently to prevent flowering
	• Plants are past prime and inedible once plants bolt (set flowers)
Squash, butternut	• Harvest when rind is hard and deep tan in color
Squash, acorn	• Fruit is ripe when rind is dark green and stem withers and dies
Squash, hubbard	• Harvest when vines begin dying
Strawberries	• Harvest as soon as fruits have become completely red by twisting to break stems
Sweet potatoes	• For best taste, harvest just before first predicted fall frost
	• Cut vines away at ground level, then dig tubers up with garden fork

Swiss chard	• Harvest leaves for salads when plants are between 8" and 2' tall.
	• Cut leaves stems to 2" above ground level
	• Never cut away more than one-third of leaves at one time
Thyme	• Harvest at any time, cutting leaf stems down to just above a leaf pair using sharp scissors
Tomatoes, hybrid	• Pick when fruit is nearly all red and skin is firm but with a slight "give"
Tomatoes, cherry	• Harvest when fruit is dark red, but before skins split
Tomatoes, heirloom	• Harvest when "shoulders" of fruit are still green; these varieties ripen quicker than hybrid tomatoes
Turnips	• Harvest when roots are between 2 and 3" in diameter
Watermelons	• When thumped with knuckles, ripe fruit will make a hollow sound rather than pinging noise.
	• Ripeness is indicated when tendrils coming off vine turn brown
Zucchini	• Best ripeness occurs when zucchinis are 6 to 8" long
	• Harvest by cutting stems about 1" from end of fruit

TECHNIQUES FOR HARVESTING

Pick, pluck, twist, or cut . . . what's the right way to harvest a crop? That depends on the plant, of course, but there are a handful of simple but important tools you should have for effective harvesting.

- **Scissors** for snipping leaves from leaf vegetables and herbs. With clean cuts that don't damage plant stems, leaf vegetables will continue producing for a long time.

- **A sharp knife** for severing fruits with thick stems. In most cases, it is better to cut off crops like melons, peppers, and tomatoes rather than pulling them off by force in order to prevent damage to plant stems.

- **A garden fork** for digging large root vegetables, such as potatoes and sweet potatoes.

- **A hand trowel** for harvesting smaller root vegetables, such as carrots and beets.

- **Pruners** for harvesting crops such as peppers, eggplant, and tomatoes.

It's important to keep any tools you use clean, especially as you move between your crops while harvesting. Viruses, bacteria, and fungi can be transmitted from one plant to another as you snip the stems to harvest crops such as tomatoes and peppers. An easy way to sterilize tools is by wiping them with a cloth moistened with isopropyl alcohol. Do this before you start harvesting and again each time you move between plants.

Children can help harvest many plants, provided they are taught how to use tools safely.

A sharp knife is essential for harvesting some crops, such as cauliflower, cabbage, and broccoli.

Fruit such as eggplant or peppers can be harvested with either a sharp knife or pruners.

 ## IN MEL'S WORDS

A little bit of this, a little bit of that . . . you don't have to wait for the plant to mature to its maximum size. Go out at harvest time (which might be half an hour before lunch or dinner) with your pair of scissors and a small basket or salad bowl, and cut off a few outer leaves, perhaps one from each plant. To harvest a varied salad, just take four lettuce leaves from one plant, parsley leaves from another, and perhaps beet greens from another. Each square may contain a different variety and color of lettuce. You might pull one radish and one carrot, even though they've only grown to half size, wash them off in your bucket of sun-warmed water, put the tops in the compost bin, and then continue around your Square Foot Garden, taking just a little bit here and a little bit there of this and that. Soon your harvest basket is full, and yet you can look at your garden and cannot even see that anything is missing.

Lettuce can be harvested just as soon as the leaves are large enough for salads or cooking. For best continued growth, harvest one or two outer leaves from each plant each time you harvest.

You'll get the most out of leafy vegetables, such as leaf lettuce, swiss chard, and herbs, by harvesting continuously. This will delay the time when the crops will set flower heads (called bolting) and keep the produce tasting great as long as possible. You can't delay the inevitable forever, though. Sooner or later all plants will go to seed; this will happen fairly soon for cool-weather crops. When the crop sends up seed stalks, it has effectively finished growing for the season and is no longer of much use for harvesting. Take one last harvest, then remove the plant and prepare that grid square for replanting.

REPLANTING

As soon as you finish harvesting one grid square, it's time to pull out what's left of the crop stalk and roots, prepare the growing medium, and plant the next crop in that square.

The process of preparation for replanting couldn't be simpler:

1. Remove any debris, such as dead leaves, stems, or roots.

2. Add one trowel of fresh compost, then thoroughly mix it in and smooth it over.

Just that easily, you are ready to plant the seeds or transplant seedlings for your next crop. The whole process can be finished in about 60 seconds.

If you are replanting as summer ends and fall approaches, make sure the next crop to get planted in a grid square is a cool-season vegetable. In many regions, this will be the third planting for a given grid square. Spinach can be a good choice for this last cool-season crop of the year. Many people find that a workable three-crop rotation will begin in the spring with a root crop, such as carrots; proceed to a warm-season fruit crop, such as cherry tomatoes or eggplant; then finish off with a leaf crop, such as lettuce, spinach, or swiss chard.

In traditional row gardening, experts often advice you to rotate your crops—to make sure the same ground is not planted with the same crop repeatedly. The theory is that soils can have their essential nutrients depleted if you plant and replant the same crop in the same locations year after year. But in a Square Foot Garden that uses Mel's Mix as a growing medium, this traditional reason for crop rotation is really not an issue. Because Mel's Mix consists of 33 percent compost, which is steadily replenished each time you plant

IN MEL'S WORDS

If your garden is close to your door, you'll probably use it much more than if it were across the yard. You'll enjoy fresh greens and salad more often, eat healthier, and feel better. Square Foot Gardening can be part of a weight-loss program, if you ask me! On top of all that, you'll have fun doing it. Don't forget to share the fun with your spouse, children, or grandchildren—the wonder of growth and harvest is priceless. Harvest a few small plants with a child, and that child will remember the experience forever.

a new crop in a grid square, plants will get a steady supply of all the key nutrients and trace elements automatically.

There is a second reason to rotate crops, though, and this one does apply to a Square Foot Garden: pests and soil pathogens particular to a given crop may persist in the soil after the harvest. If you plant the same crop in the same grid square twice in a row, the new planting may become prey to the same problems that were found in the earlier crop. If you make a point of planting a different crop when it comes time to replant a grid square, there's little chance of the same diseases or pest problems continuing on to the next rotation. Fortunately, the Square Foot Gardening style makes this kind of rotation almost automatic.

HANDLING AND STORING CROPS

Experts at the University of California, Davis, have determined that 25 percent of all fruits and vegetables are not eaten because they are damaged or begin to spoil before they can be eaten. Those statistics include the enormous quantities of grocery-store vegetables that go to waste, but home gardeners too can see a lot of produce go to waste because they harvest too late or don't know the best way to handle and store crops after they harvest them.

Minimizing waste is really just a matter of knowing the fine points of how to handle the produce you grow. Some fruits and vegetables are more or less prone to heat and cold, for example. Some store very well long-term, while others will begin to spoil in just a few days. Even such simple practices as when you wash a bunch of garden greens can dramatically affect how long a vegetable remains at peak edibility.

HANDLING DURING THE HARVEST

The best safeguard is to handle produce with the utmost care from the moment you pick to the moment you consume it. When digging potatoes, don't toss them into a bucket but set them into a basket gently. When picking strawberries, don't pile them into a deep container where the weight might crush them but lay them out on a shallow tray as you harvest them.

Safe handling also means that you should isolate good, healthy fruits and vegetables away from diseased specimens. This means not only that you should reject any vegetables that are damaged as you harvest but also that you should pay attention to problems during the course of the growing season. If you have steadfastly inspected your plants over the growing season and eliminated all the "bad apples" as you spotted them, the barrels of produce you later harvest are likely to be healthy and unspoiled.

STORING PRODUCE

What you do with your produce after you've carefully harvested it also has a great impact on its shelf life. Most vegetables and fruits begin to change immediately after you harvest them. Some will begin a slow change, gradually ripening to a greater degree. Tomatoes are one such crop—they can be harvested when they are just short of ripe, then will fully ripen as they sit on the countertop. Other vegetables, though, begin to deteriorate the moment they are picked and should be eaten immediately. Strawberries have a notoriously short shelf life; it's best to eat them the same day you pick them unless you are freezing or canning them. Still others remain pretty much at a steady state in exactly the same condition as you pick them. Onions, for example, will keep for many months, and potatoes also have a long shelf life if stored correctly.

If you are a Square Foot Gardener, the art of canning might be a great secondary hobby. If you have the space, "putting up" the fruits and vegetables you grow will make it possible to enjoy them throughout the year.

SHORT-TERM STORAGE

CROP	PANTRY NOTES
Artichokes	Moisten, then refrigerate for up to 5 days in plastic bag
Asparagus	Place ends in jar of water, cover with plastic bag, refrigerate for up to 7 days
Beans	Refrigerate, unwashed, in plastic bag for up to 7 days
Beets	Leave 1" stems; will stay fresh on countertop for 3 days or in refrigerator for 10 days
Brussels sprouts	Refrigerate, unwashed and untrimmed, in plastic bag for up to 7 days
Cabbage	Refrigerate in plastic bag for up to 2 weeks
Carrots	Refrigerate, unwashed, in tightly wrapped plastic bag for up to 3 months
Cauliflower	Refrigerate unwashed heads in loose plastic bag for up to 3 weeks
Celery	Cut stalks into segments and store in lidded jar, in refrigerator, for up to 7 days
Corn	Refrigerate with husks on; use within 2 days
Cucumber	Dry, then place in tightly wrapped plastic bag and refrigerate for up to 10 days
Eggplant	Keep on countertop for 2 days or refrigerate in perforated bag for up to 7 days
Garlic	Store whole cloves in cool, dark place for up to 4 months; do not refrigerate
Herbs	Place in a plastic bag with moistened paper towel; refrigerate for up to 3 weeks
Kohlrabi	Refrigerate in loose plastic bag for up to 3 weeks
Lettuce	Wash and pat dry, wrap in paper towel, and place in plastic bag; refrigerate for up to 1 week

CROP	PANTRY NOTES
Melons	Refrigerate for up to 5 days
Okra	Refrigerate, unwashed, in perforated plastic bag for up to 4 days
Onions	Store in cool, dark, dry place for up to 6 months; do not refrigerate
Peas	Place unwashed, unshelled peas in perforated plastic bag and refrigerate for up to 4 days
Peppers	Store unwashed and fully dry in perforated plastic bag for up to 3 weeks
Potatoes	Store in dark, dry, moderately cool place for up to several months
Radishes	Refrigerate in sealed plastic bag for up to 2 weeks
Spinach	Wash and pat dry, wrap in paper towel, and place in plastic bag; refrigerate for up to 1 week
Strawberries	Leave stems on; refrigerate, unwashed, in partially opened container for up to 7 days
Summer squash	Dry carefully, then refrigerate in tightly wrapped plastic bag for up to 2 weeks, or until they begin to shrivel
Swiss chard	Store, unwashed, in tightly wrapped plastic bag for up to 5 days
Winter squash	Store in a cool, dark, dry place for up to 4 weeks; do not refrigerate
Tomatoes	For best flavor, store for no more than 2 days on countertop; may be refrigerated for up to a week, though flavor will be compromised
Zucchini	Dry carefully, then refrigerate in tightly wrapped plastic bag for up to 2 weeks, or until they begin to shrivel

Here are some ways to prolong your enjoyment of the produce you have grown.

- **Juicing.** Many fruits and some vegetables can be turned into healthful juice drinks as they begin to move past full ripeness but before they begin to spoil. A good blender or juicer and a recipe book will help you make full use of the berries and vegetables you grow.

- **Canning.** It takes some work, but canning and other forms of preserving are great ways to keep ripe fruit and vegetables to eat whenever you want them. A vast number of fruits and vegetables can be canned, pickled, fermented, or otherwise preserved so that you can enjoy them from the first frost in the fall to the last frost the following spring. There is little cost to this and enormous rewards. Two or three tomato bushes can provide enough tomatoes to fill a long pantry shelf with canned tomatoes. Carrots and asparagus can be pickled to serve as elegant appetizers at dinner parties. Cucumbers make for wonderful pickles when canned in a brine solution.

- **Drying.** Other fruits and vegetables can be dried to preserve them. The drying process generally increases and concentrates the flavor while maintaining all the nutritional value. Many fruits and vegetables can be air-dried, but you can also buy a dehydrator to speed up the process.

- **Freezing.** Many vegetables can be quickly frozen when they are at their peak ripeness, then thawed out whenever you need them for cooking through the winter months. Here are just a few:

Tomatoes can be cut into cubes and frozen, then used in recipes or salsas. Kale leaves can be frozen for up to 6 weeks but may turn bitter after that. Corn can be frozen either on the cob or shelled and packaged in plastic. Strawberries and other berries will keep up to a full year when frozen whole. Zucchini keeps well frozen when it is chopped, sliced, or grated. Herbs can be frozen and will keep almost indefinitely. Cucumbers are best frozen by first peeling, then slicing them.

SETTING UP A ROOT CELLAR

A traditional way to store fall harvests over the winter is in a root cellar. If you happen to live in a climate where homes are built with basements, you can have a reasonable facsimile of classic root cellar in a corner of your basement. But even if you don't have a basement, you can create the conditions of a root cellar, because this is really more about climate and conditions than it is about location. You simply need to create a space that has the following conditions:

- **Humidity.** Find the wettest, most humid corner of a basement or utility space—root crops prefer a humidity level of 80 to 90 percent. If you live in a dry climate, you might be able to turn a spare closet into a root cellar by adding a small humidifier. Basements may already have this kind of humidity level.

Sun-drying concentrates flavors, which is why it is a favorite preservation method for crops such as tomatoes and hot peppers.

- **Ventilation.** Root cellars need to have a good airflow. In a genuine root cellar, there will be both an intake and an exhaust fan, but you may be able to get by with simple house fans to keep air circulating.

- **Shelving.** Your storage space should be fitted with shelves that can tolerate the weight of the produce and also the humid conditions required. It's best if your shelving units are adjustable, because humidity levels will vary with height—in a basement, humidity levels are highest near the floor.

Some gardeners go all-in and construct a formal root-cellar closet complete with equipment to ventilate and control humidity. If you are seriously into a self-sufficient lifestyle and Square Foot Gardening, you might want to consider it.

EXTENDING THE HARVEST

One of the huge advantages of Square Foot Gardening is that the effective gardening season can be stretched both in the early spring and into the late fall in order to produce 30 to 50 percent more produce. Doing so requires some more advanced techniques and add-on accessories, though, so if you are a beginning Square Foot Gardener, you might want to wait 1 or 2 years before tackling it. And extending the seasons only makes sense if you really want more produce or want it much earlier or later than what is otherwise possible.

In most parts of the continental United States, the average growing season extends from May until September—6 months in length. But it is entirely possible to extend that growing season by a month in each direction, adding 33 percent to the growing time and as much as 50 percent to the total harvest. For the average gardener, working this magic is a matter of pride and a sense of accomplishment; for the self-sufficiency crowd and food-canning buffs, this becomes a more practical need.

START EARLY, HARVEST EARLY

The most obvious way to extend the garden year is by starting earlier in the season. It is possible to add a full cool-season crop in the early spring or late winter and harvest it in late spring, with plenty of time to rotate a grid square to a warm-season crop once the early cool-season crop has finished.

Growing out of season—both in the early spring and in the late fall—is really just a matter of keeping the cold temperatures away from your plants and away from the soil. Doing this involves providing your Square Foot Garden box with some extra protection against the severe conditions of early spring.

Covering and protecting your crops serves the same function as a greenhouse: it creates an artificial environment that keeps the cold air out but lets sunlight in. This is really all it takes to get in that early cool-season planting. The same protective structure will make it possible to plant warm-season crops at least 2 weeks earlier. You can get in a full extra planting of vegetables such as lettuce, spinach, and radishes during the summer months, paving the way for an extra cool-season crop in the late fall.

By now, you're probably getting the idea. In a climate zone with an average 6-month-long growing season, careful planning allows a Square Foot Gardener to get as many as four crops out of a grid square. There are a variety of structures you can use to protect your Square Foot Garden in the cool spring months, but one of the easiest is the protective dome structure described in full detail in Chapter 6.

Here's a basic process for preparing a Square Foot Garden box planting in the early spring:

1. Begin by warming up the Mel's Mix in your Square Foot Garden box. Spread a sheet of clear or black plastic over the top of the box and weight it down with a brick at each corner.

2. After 2 or 3 sunny days, remove the plastic and take off the grid, then mix up the soil with a trowel so that the warmer surface soil is blended into the cooler lower layers of soil.

3. Cover the box again with plastic. After another 2 or 3 sunny days, the soil will be at the right temperature for planting seeds and seedlings. Keep the box covered with plastic until planting time, mixing up the soil every few days until you plant.

4. On a warm afternoon, plant your cool-season crops in their grid squares. The techniques are no different here than for any other type of planting, but it can help if you've already started your seeds

indoors and grow them into transplant seedlings (page 153). If you start seedlings early, be sure to harden them off before planting them into the early spring garden.

5. Immediately after planting seeds, cover the Square Foot Garden box again, either with sheet plastic or with a protective dome. If you have planted seedling plants, then use the protective dome.

6. Control the climate in your early-spring garden. Even in early spring, direct hot sun on the protective dome can cause heat to build up inside it. This hot air needs to be vented or your sprouting seeds and seedlings will be killed. As the weather warms up, lift the dome away from the box slightly, then lift it a bit further each week until the time comes when you can remove it entirely. A light frost will not hurt cool-weather plants that are well established, but too much heat will definitely kill them. It takes some experience to learn how to control the climate under a protective dome, so don't worry too much if your first experience doesn't go exactly as you want.

EXTENDING COOL-SEASON CROPS INTO SUMMER

Normally, cool-season vegetables such as lettuce, radishes, spinach, and cabbage are over and done with by the time midsummer rolls around, but if these are favorites of yours, you may be able to add a second planting of one or more cool-season crops and grow them into summer. This requires that you pick varieties known to tolerate heat. Look for words such as "long-standing," "slow to bolt," and "heat resistant" on the seed packet or seedling label.

If you provide some shade to cool-season crops such as lettuce and radishes, you'll find it possible to keep them growing well into summer. Protecting them from noontime sun is especially important. Carefully placing a Square Foot Garden box so that shade shelters the garden during the heat of the day, or using a commercial shade cloth to block some of the sun, makes it possible to prolong many crops quite a few weeks into the summer.

A thick layer of mulch on the soil will also keep the soil temperature down and make cool-season vegetables last longer, as will providing extra water to them as the soil gets warmer in midsummer.

STARTING WARM-SEASON SUMMER CROPS EARLY

As the spring season begins to draw to a close, you can give some of your warm-season summer vegetables a head start. Planting these seeds in their designated grid squares and covering them with a protective cage about 2 weeks before the typical planting time will produce seedlings much sturdier than those grown indoors.

In addition to the do-it-yourself protective dome described in Chapter 6, there are many types of protective covers you can buy from garden retailers and online vendors for this purpose. They range from water-filled walls that absorb and radiate sun warmth to special covers designed to heat up the soil very quickly. Experiment with these products to learn which ones suit your needs.

EXTENDING WARM-SEASON SUMMER CROPS INTO FALL

Many warm-season crops can be extended well into the fall, provided you are willing to put forth the effort. Some gardeners, though, find it easier to rotate the grid squares to cool-season crops that will tolerate cool temperatures and light frost. But it is not uncommon in many regions to see the first frost followed by several weeks of very nice warm weather, so if you want to keep your tomatoes, peppers, and other warm-season crops churning along, you'll need to figure out some way to protect the garden boxes from the cold spells that fall between warm days. To protect your crops from frost, consider using the PVC arch or covered-wagon frame described in Chapter 6. Low-growing crops can be covered with a loose layer of straw that you remove when the weather warms after a cool morning.

To protect vine crops from frost, throw a blanket or tarp over the vertical frame so it drapes over the sides of the box.

PLANTING IN FALL

Some gardeners choose to begin closing down the garden as the season enters fall, but it's also possible to use this as an opportunity to get in one more round of cool-season crops before extremely hard frosts hit. Depending on when the average first frost date is for your region, you may well be able to plant and harvest a number of vegetables within the fall season.

IN MEL'S WORDS:
COLD STORAGE OF YOUR HARVEST

The only secret of successful storage is actually very simple—learn each vegetable's best storage conditions and provide them. There are really only two: cool and dry or cold and moist. The list of vegetables that need cool and dry conditions is easy to remember because there are only a few—pumpkins, winter squash, and onions. The temperature should be around 50°F to 60°F, and the humidity needs to be fairly low, at about 50 percent.

Try to find a cool corner of your garage or basement where the temperature stays above 35°F but below 60°F. If you think your storage area might freeze or get too warm at times, you can build two walls to enclose a corner to provide an even-temperature fruit closet. Add some insulation, and remember to allow plenty of air circulation. Don't stack produce up in a big pile—spread your vegetables out evenly on a shelf (not on the floor).

Handle produce as gently and infrequently as possible. When you're out harvesting, treat each vegetable as if it were an egg. Any bruise or cut will be the first spot to spoil. Lay each harvested vegetable separately in a box of sawdust or crumpled newspaper; don't pile them all together. Do not wash or scrub the produce. Leave the bottom of the root on root crops, and at least an inch of the top growth. For vine crops, leave as much of the stem on as possible. Only store produce that is in really good condition.

Vegetables in the group that need cold and moist conditions are all root crops—beets, carrots, turnips, white potatoes, winter radishes, and all of the cabbage family. This group also includes fruit, especially apples. The ideal storage temperature for them is as cold as you can get without actually freezing—35°F to 45°F.

Actually, the simplest way to store root crops is not to dig them up at all. Roll a bale of hay over the planted area; this will break their tops and stop the plant's growing cycle while keeping the ground from freezing. When you're ready to harvest, simply roll the bale over, dig up a few vegetables, and then replace the bale. Regular radishes won't hold up too long in freezing weather while the winter radish will last almost indefinitely. Carrots and leeks also do quite well through the entire winter. If you're feeling adventurous, you can experiment with leaving different root crops in the ground to see which last through the fall and winter so you'll know what to expect the following year.

Cabbage and other leaf and head crops can also be stored in the garden, but they won't do well under a solid bale of hay. Instead, it is better to use a loose, fluffy covering of straw or leaves. To keep the wind from blowing this loose covering around, try placing a 2-foot-high fence of chicken wire around your garden areas and anchoring the wiring at each corner with stakes.

Another storage method for root crops is to bury a container in the ground and pack your vegetables in layers of moist sawdust, peat moss, or sand. You can sink a plastic or metal garbage can straight into the ground while keeping the top a few inches above the surface so no water gets in. Make sure the cover fits tightly, then pile at least 12 inches of hay or leaves over the top. Keep everything dry by covering it with a weighted-down plastic sheet or tarp. Watch out for leaks in the container that can allow groundwater to seep in. If you can, select an area on high ground to locate the storage container. The ground will not freeze under or around this container, and your vegetables will be maintained in very even and moist conditions.

These carrots were lifted from the garden in fall and stored in trays of moist peat moss in a garden shed. Stored this way, carrots and similar vegetables can keep until spring.

As fall progresses and winter approaches, it is critical that you keep an eye on temperatures and provide temporary shelter when you think they might dip low enough to kill your crops. You may be surprised to realize that different parts of your yard have their own microclimates. A walk around your property on a cold night might make this evident. Low-lying areas will collect cold air that rolls in from higher areas—a phenomenon knowns as cold air drainage. Once you understand this pattern, you'll see the benefits of locating a garden on the top of the south side of a slope rather than in a low area. On nights when borderline-freezing temperatures are predicted, it will be the garden boxes in low-lying areas that you should cover with a protective structure for the night. Frost can and often does occur in low-lying areas while just a few feet away, a garden box that is just slightly higher can escape unscathed. If a body of water is nearby—even a small landscape pond—it can reduce the chances of frost in a nearby Square Foot Garden.

In general, the very early morning hours are the coldest, especially when the air is still and calm at night. Misty or rainy nights are less likely to see frost in these borderline times between fall and winter.

Watch the daily weather forecasts, and be ready when frost is predicted. Most cool-season crops will tolerate a light frost with temperatures at or just below the freezing point of water. A light frost may blacken the edges of warm-season vegetables and flowers but usually does not kill them; cool-season vegetables usually tolerate this light frost just fine. A hard frost, though, when temperatures dip down into the 20s and below for extended periods will kill all warm-season crops and flowers, and some cool-season crops will also succumb to this kind of frost. You'll know you've had a hard frost if you hear a crunchy sound when you walk on the ground and see a thin film of ice on the surface of your birdbath. Many cool-season flowers (such as mums and asters) and many fall vegetables (such as turnips, kale, and cauliflower) will survive these first hard frosts even without a protective cover.

The longer you're willing to play watchdog and protect your crops against cold snaps, the longer you can grow those crops. For most gardeners, though, there comes a point when cold temperatures are so prevalent that surrender is inevitable.

GROWING IN WINTER

If you are really ambitious and want to continue growing into the winter, you need some special materials and techniques in order to provide special protection to a limited range of plants. The challenge is to keep a small portion of the ground from freezing and to provide sunlight to that area. In many parts of the country, it's possible to continue growing special varieties of lettuce and spinach, as well as hardy leaf crops such as kale. There are also some East Asian vegetables you may be able to grow all winter long. Some members of the onion family (onions are technically perennials) can be planted in fall to overwinter in the ground and produce crops the following spring and summer.

Winter gardening is most practical in USDA climate Zones 5 and above. While winter Square Foot Gardens have been known to work in Zone 4 and even Zone 3, it becomes much more difficult in a climate that regularly sees winter temperatures of 0°F or lower. In this kind of climate, winter Square Foot Gardening is suited only for gardeners who get a lot of fun out of a serious challenge.

Winter gardening is really a matter of experience. If you're dedicated to extending the seasons as long as possible, a few growing seasons of experimentation will teach you what you need to know. Once you have the knack, it's actually possible to harvest salad right from your garden during the coldest months of winter in some regions. First, it requires that you select fast-growing vegetables for your fall planting, such as hardy salad greens and root crops that are bred especially for cold tolerance. This will be identified with names such as "Arctic" or "Frost King."

If you are seriously interested in winter Square Foot Gardening, here's the basic process:

1. Pick the sunniest, most sheltered spot you can find for the winter garden. A spot next to the house or garage is ideal because the structure may reflect some heat back onto the garden, especially if it is painted white or made from brick. Remember that winter sun is very low in the sky, so the sunniest spots in your yard may well have changed from where they were in summer. Make sure to keep your garden away from building overhangs where snow can avalanche onto it. If the spot you've chosen is relatively sheltered from wind and gets maximum winter sunlight, there's a good chance you can succeed.

2. When you plant your winter box, be aware that the crops will grow very slowly, and because you will be harvesting them almost as soon as each leaf is ready, you can plant the seeds considerably closer than you would for a spring or summer garden.

3. Insulate around the walls of the Square Foot Garden box using soil or bales of hay. A good deal of the soil warmth will be radiated out the sides of the box, so whatever you can do to minimize this heat loss will improve the performance of your winter Square Foot Garden.

4. Provide a tight-fitting cover for your garden box. Unlike the dome covers used for early spring and fall, which could be rather loose, this one should fit as tightly as possible to trap as much solar heat as is possible. Cover it with thick, clear plastic, doubling up the layer if possible. On snowy days, brush off any accumulating snow so that when the sun appears, your garden can absorb as much warmth as possible.

5. On especially cold nights, cover your garden with an extra tarp or blanket, and leave it there until the sun again beats down on the garden.

PUTTING YOUR SQUARE FOOT GARDEN TO BED

While winter gardening is possible, most Square Foot Gardeners in all but the mildest climates will find that there comes a time when the gardening season is over and it's time to put the garden boxes "to bed" in anticipation of the next planting season approaching in a few months. We know of no better description of this process than the words of Mel Bartholomew himself.

CROPS YOU CAN PLANT IN FALL

5 TO 10 WEEKS BEFORE FROST
Broccoli
Cabbage
Cauliflower
Beets
Carrots
Lettuce
Spinach

0 TO 5 WEEKS BEFORE FROST
Lettuce
Radishes

IN MEL'S WORDS: AFTER THE HARVEST

When it is time to put the SFG to bed, we do this the same way we put our children to bed. You wouldn't think of sending them to their room and paying no attention to them, would you? Instead, we encourage them to prepare for bedtime—to brush their teeth, get one last drink, fix the bed just the way they want it—and then spend some time reading a bedtime story. Then it's finally lights out.

Well, treat your garden the same way. Don't leave it a mess, with dead plants and debris lying about. Tidy it up and make it look good. Now is an excellent time to mix a little extra compost into each box and smooth and level it out so it will be all ready for the spring planting. That's never happened before with single-row gardening. Now it's not only possible, but also very practical.

The little extra work you do in the fall will keep your garden attractive and neat-looking all winter and make your springtime garden easier to begin. You'll simply go out, rake off the mulch cover (remember your rototilling neighbor?), and start planting either at the regular time or early.

Grids in winter. You can remove, clean, fold, and hang up the grids or leave them on the boxes all winter, which will remind you of how much fun you have now with gardening. What I'm suggesting for the end of the season is really no different than what I recommend you do all season long. Keep your garden neat, tidy, and attractive. If you keep it in tiptop condition (and that's not too difficult with a no-work garden), you will enjoy it so much more.

Take notes. The only thing you might want to do is record in a notebook or journal some of the highlights of this past year—notes for improvements, special varieties of plants, and tips for next year.

Decorate for the holidays. You'll enjoy Square Foot Gardening much more if you keep your garden neat and attractive at all times.

Because you no longer have to hoe the weeds or dig and cultivate the soil, you'll have time and energy for the pleasant things like trimming off yellow or dead lower leaves and blossoms or, in the case of pest damage, possibly removing entire plants.

But what about winter? There's not much work to do after putting the garden to bed, but you might think about decorating the garden so it still looks nice all winter long—or at least for the holidays.

At Thanksgiving, make a nice arrangement in one or more boxes of a fall scene, like a stack of corn with pumpkins. Some of the boxes could just have a bale or two of hay or straw. Maybe even a scarecrow in a box. Those boxes could be covered with cloth (like white floating garden covers) or old colored sheets tacked or stapled down.

For the Christmas season, here are some ideas that will make your SFG festive during the bleak winter months.

1. Make holiday boxes out of your garden boxes by using old colored or striped sheets, a tarp or tablecloth, or floating garden covers.
2. Think ahead when you go to yard sales or the thrift shop. Many fabrics could serve double duty as frost covers in the fall, then decorative covers in the winter.
3. Use wide, colorful ribbon or rope or contrasting colored strips of sheets, to tie bows on the boxes. Tuck in greens and pine cones, even lights if you can get an extension cord to the garden. (Remember now, your garden no longer needs to be way out back; it can be right near your back door where you'll see it more often.)
4. Decorate your vertical frames with lights, pine branches, pinecones, and bird feeders.
5. After Christmas, stick a discarded Christmas tree in the center of each box and make them into bird feeders, with or without lights. Tie a string from each box corner to the treetop for support.

OUTSIDE THE BOX: COMMUNITY OPPORTUNITIES

Until the day he passed away, Mel Bartholomew championed the potential for Square Foot Gardening to be more than just the best, most efficient way to grow a home garden. He also believed that the Square Foot Gardening method could transform kids' lives, transform neighborhoods, and help the world's poor and underprivileged citizens become more independent and lead better lives. Mel always dreamed big, and he fully believed that the incredible efficiency of the Square Foot Gardening method had the potential to solve the world hunger issue. And perhaps he was right—if you're going to dream, you might as well dream big.

Square Foot Gardening is a perfect activity for a variety of community outreach projects.

Square Foot Gardening is now a global activity. The Square Foot Gardening Foundation's outreach program has traveled to dozens of countries to spread the benefits of this method, which can be used in even the most demanding climates of the world.

Over the years, we at the Square Foot Garden Foundation have seen many of Mel's aspirations fully realized. Square Foot Gardening is indeed more than just a technique for home gardeners. This innovative gardening system is infectious, spreading out into communities in ways that might surprise even Mel himself. In schools all across the country—and around the world, for that matter—kids are learning how to garden the SFG way, having fun as they learn the most productive, most efficient gardening method there is. In urban areas where there is little backyard room for individual gardens, empty land and parking lots are sprouting up Square Foot Garden farms to both beautify neighborhoods and provide inner-city dwellers with inexpensive, fresh, healthful produce. Care homes for the elderly are building elevated Square Foot Gardens as a form of recreational and occupational therapy for their residents.

Do you want to be part of this revolution? Here are some ways you can do it.

IN MEL'S WORDS

If you want your community garden to produce the most bang for the buck, I'd suggest looking for sites where it will help those most in need. These days, there are so many families who could really use inexpensive (or free) healthy food. The people who need it most are usually those who are least equipped to grow it. Here are some sites you might want to approach in your community to get the biggest "return on investment" possible from your Square Foot Garden community garden.

Houses of worship. Many run soup kitchens, preschools, and other programs that are just darn near perfect for matching new gardeners and needy families and individuals to a community Square Foot Garden. You can usually find a little bit of land around a church or even set up the boxes in a corner of a parking lot.

Homeless shelters. Not only are people in homeless shelters just about as much in need of fresh, healthy food as you can get, they are also a willing group of potential gardeners. Many hands make quick work of a community Square Foot Garden placed out back of a homeless shelter.

Food banks. What better places to put a community Square Foot Garden than next to an organization set up to distribute food to those who need it? The staff in the food bank usually knows exactly what types of fresh produce are best for distribution, and they also have community contacts to help recruit new gardeners and others to help out in the garden.

COMMUNITY GARDENS

With the right leadership behind it, a community garden offers a neighborhood a means of fostering relationships, boosting pride by creating a sense of accomplishment, and feeding many, many people. The Square Foot Gardening method is particularly well suited to community gardens because it is easy to maintain and grows a lot of produce in a very small space. Make no mistake about it, though—organizing and running a community garden of any kind takes a leader (or leaders) with energy and vision. It is a big challenge for the organizer to deal with the many different people necessary to keeping a community garden humming along. Then there is the day-to-day maintenance of the garden, which creates its own set of challenges. For the right organizer or group of organizers, though, few activities offer more chance for reward.

When looking for a place to start a community garden, begin by contacting your local parks and recreation department's website for existing community gardens that might be adapted to include Square Foot Gardening. Then contact the officials in charge. To begin, just ask if they are open to the idea of converting a corner of the larger community garden to square-foot boxes. Be ready to do some educating if the powers that be aren't familiar with the Square Foot Garden method. Once they understand the efficiency and productivity of the method, however, city officials will likely be friendly to your proposal.

If you're having trouble finding a place for a community garden, you can reach out to individual city council members or to a local county extension agency or Master Gardener program. One of these resources almost certainly will have ideas on how to get your program launched.

If an established community garden program doesn't exist, you still might be able to talk your municipality into devoting one corner of a park, a playground, or even a vacant lot as a temporary spot for Square Foot Gardening. Strips of right-of-way or street boulevards on lands owned by the city might be made available to you for a community garden.

A local school principal or clergy member may be willing to offer up part of the schoolyard or churchyard for a general community garden. Finally, local businesses with land available might be willing to lend you space for your community Square Foot Garden. One advantage of the SFG method is that the garden boxes can be placed on concrete or asphalt, so even abandoned parking lots can become a vibrant and productive community garden.

LAYING OUT A COMMUNITY SQUARE FOOT GARDEN

The basic layout of a community Square Foot Garden is really not much different from that of a large private garden with

Most cities and some smaller towns have active community-garden resources, managed by a parks and recreation department or city planning office. These programs will already have a list of accessible land for community gardens. Establishing a square-foot community garden can involve blending Square Foot Gardening into an existing traditional community garden or establishing it from scratch on lands designated for community gardening.

multiple boxes. You need to give each gardener the proper amount of space for the garden box, plus enough space for aisles between them. In a community environment, you might be well served by increasing the width of the aisles between boxes to allow more space between gardeners.

A community garden also benefits from a fence around the entire project, which will serve to keep both feeding animals and unwanted human visitors out of your garden. Another nice feature is a shaded sitting area where gardeners can sit and visit or rest during work sessions. Other nice add-ons are things such as a large compost bin, a trash barrel, water barrels, or a hose spigot.

Here are some dos and don'ts of community gardening:

Don't

1. Give too much space to any individual gardener. This is a common mistake in community Square Foot Gardens. Not only is it not necessary, given the fabulous productivity of the SFG method, but it can lead to hard feelings between gardeners who feel they are not getting their fair share. All any gardener really needs in a Square Foot Garden is a space about 15 × 15 feet. This can easily provide all the produce a single family can use. And limiting the size will keep everyone happy. In most community gardens, there are waiting lists for people wanting plots, and limiting the size will provide an opportunity for more people to participate.

2. Allow row crops. If you are creating a Square Foot Garden from the beginning, some neighbors might instinctively try to bring row-gardening methods to it, which will serve only to gobble up space that could be put to better use with square-foot boxes. Rather than demeaning those who still row garden, discuss with them why Square Foot Gardening is a more successful method and encourage them to give it a try. If you have talked local leaders into giving you a portion of a larger community garden for your SFG project, be sure to clearly define the section that is a Square Foot Garden and strictly enforce the "SFG only" rule for that portion.

Do

1. Post the rules All good community gardens have rules, and a Square Foot Garden is no exception. Come up with set of common-sense rules to cover obvious issues, such as hours when the garden is accessible, plants that are forbidden due to their invasive nature, how disputes will be settled, and other aspects of neighborly behavior.

2. Space aisles correctly. When you are working in a shared space with defined borders you sometimes need to be a little adaptable as far as box sizes and spacing. While planting as many 4 x 4 boxes as you can fit in without cramming them too close together might work, you also might need to adjust the size and shape a little bit to maintain the minimum 3-foot aisles (if you have to cheat the 3 feet just a little it is not the worst thing in the world, but do try to make sure the aisle spacing is at least 3 feet and preferably a bit more where one gardener's box adjoins another's. This will go a long way toward preventing unhappiness from gardeners

brushing up against their neighbor's crops or stepping on plants that have spilled outside the boundaries of a garden box. Don't allow individual gardeners to fence off their sections, as this can quickly make navigating through the community garden very difficult.

3. Hold classes. When starting a community Square Foot Garden from scratch, there will be gardeners who don't understand the method and will make mistakes. They may, for example, fill their garden boxes with plain dirt rather than Mel's Mix. Or they may not understand the principles of crop layout or rotation. So, it is a great idea to hold periodic afternoon classes during which you can teach the

PREVENTING VANDALISM IN A COMMUNITY GARDEN?

Unfortunately, community gardens sometimes get damaged, especially in economically depressed neighborhoods, where a community garden can feel like an intrusion from outsiders. The best way to avoid this is to make sure the project is well publicized and that its goals are understood by everyone in the neighborhood. Put up a large sign that announces a community garden is coming to serve the neighborhood. Once the garden is expected and its goals understood, it is less likely to suffer damage at the hands of vandals. Alert the local neighborhood watch or residents who have homes overlooking the garden to keep their eyes peeled for any problems. Let local law-enforcement agencies know the garden is there and ask them to patrol the area occasionally. Most importantly, get as many people as possible involved. The more people who are involved, the more people who will be watching out for the community garden. Vandals are unlikely to touch a community garden if they know someone who grows food there.

basics of how to construct boxes, how to create Mel's Mix, and the basics of tending a Square Foot Garden.

4. Charge modest fees, if appropriate. It's standard practice in some community gardens to charge modest annual rental fees for space in the garden. A small fee can have the effect of making gardeners more serious about the activity, and in some community gardens it is used a screening method if garden space is in high demand. Square Foot Gardening philosophy believes it is quite appropriate to charge modest fees to offset the costs of running the garden, such as building fences or having lumber or Mel's Mix ingredients delivered for the use of the plot holders. A minimal rental fee can also cover the costs of liability insurance for your community garden (see #6).

5. Give everyone a chance. After a season or two, you may have a waiting list of people wanting to garden, and you should do everything you can to allow as many people as possible to participate. This might involve seeking out new locations for additional community-garden plots, reducing the size of plots in order to squeeze more people in, or establishing a lottery system that allows more people an opportunity to have a garden.

6. Take out liability insurance, if necessary. It's possible the owner of the property—whether it is a private homeowner, church, or business—may already have liability insurance on the space where your community garden is located. If not, it's a good idea to take out a liability policy. All that's needed is a general policy to cover any injuries sustained in the garden. Any broad-service insurance company can provide such a policy; shop around for the best prices.

GRANTS FOR YOUR COMMUNITY GARDEN

If you are looking for help with your community garden, there may be grants available. Some grant programs award funds to be used in the manner specified in the grant application. Others sources provide materials to be used for the garden. Some programs will offer both types of assistance. Here is a short list of grants you can apply for:

- The Lorrie Otto Seeds for Education Grant Program (www.wildones.org/seeds-for-education) provides small monetary grants to nonprofit programs that have an educational component. If your Square Foot Garden community project is one set up to teach children about gardening, it may qualify for a grant.

- The National Gardening Association provides many grants through their Kids Gardening program (www.kidsgardening.org/garden-grants). Grants are awarded based on whether the project keeps with the NGA's "vision of a greener future and belief in the powerful impact gardening programs can have on the mental, physical, and psychological health of individuals."

- Stonyfield Farms (www.stonyfield.com) provides both monetary and product-materials grants to projects directly aimed at organic gardening or climate-change issues.

- Seeds of Change (www.seedsofchange.com/grant) offers seeds to programs that have an educational purpose through a program called Sowing Millions, Growing Minds. They are especially supportive of school-based programs.

- The Captain Planet Foundation (www.captainplanetfoundation.org) provides thousands of grants each year, ranging from a few hundred to several thousand dollars. They specifically aim at funding hands-on environmental projects that empower young people by teaching about the environment.

- Ashoka's Youth Venture (www.youthventure.org) funds projects founded and operated by teenagers. This organization focuses on awards for sustainable projects, offering a great way for teenagers to get involved while learning entrepreneurial stills and the satisfaction of nonprofit work.

BECOMING A SQUARE FOOT GARDENING INSTRUCTOR

Organizing and running a community garden can be simpler if you take the next important step in developing your credentials. The Square Foot Gardening Foundation offers education for gardeners who want to become certified instructors of the Square Foot Gardening Foundation. There are a couple of ways to qualify, including home study and online study. The instruction focuses not only on the basics of the Square Foot Gardening method but also on the many gardener questions we've fielded over the years. By the time you complete one of the courses, you will be a full-fledged expert on Square Foot Gardening.

The advantages of being a Certified Square Foot Gardening Instructor? For those seeking to organize and run a community SFG program, these credentials will bring a certain authority to your applications for grants to help fund and run your community garden. Certified Instructor credentials can also help you if you seek to get involved in a school program aimed at teaching children the principles of self-sufficiency and healthy eating through gardening.

As a Certified Instructor (we'll soon know you as a CI) you'll develop the expertise needed to make a positive impact on the environment and on the lives of others in your community. Some CIs go into service around the world, teaching the benefits of efficient, self-sufficient gardening. CIs teach in schools, community gardens, transitional homes, prisons, places of worship, and urban neighborhoods. Wherever they find themselves, their mission is to help others to help themselves.

As a Certified Square Foot Gardening Instructor, you may even be able to help some in your community achieve a level of financial independence by learning how to sell produce in their communities through community garden sales and at farmers' markets. Some CIs hold seminars in libraries, schools, and other places where groups can gather to share knowledge.

The Certified Instructor Program sponsored by the Square Foot Gardening Foundation is ever evolving, so refer

Certified instructors are available in just about every geographic area to coach new gardeners on the SFG program. They especially love working with kids either individually or through schools.

to our website, www.squarefootgardening.org, for the latest information. The website also offers a standard home-study course to prepare you for being an instructor. Once you fulfill the requirements and become a Certified Instructor, you will gain access to the online portal where specially designed support and marketing materials are available. You will also have access to other Certified Instructors around the country who can share with you their practical tips on how best to teach this most practical, foolproof way to grow a home garden.

SQUARE FOOT GARDENING IN SCHOOLS

Square Foot Gardening offers many educational opportunities for subjects ranging from plant science to geometry, so a school is a natural place for a Square Foot Garden. If you have school-age children, reach out the principal of the school to ask about starting one or more boxes in a spare corner of the schoolyard or playground. Or, with the permission of the school administration, you can reach out to individual teachers within the school. If you are willing to spend 1 or 2 hours once a week teaching the Square Foot Garden process to kids, many teachers will be thrilled to partner with you. There are many instances of a single Square Foot Garden box tended by the kids in one classroom gradually becoming a project involving dozens of Square Foot Garden boxes tended enthusiastically by everyone in the school. When summer break comes around, many of the families of these kids happily continue tending those gardens until the fall session starts and kids learn the magic of harvesting the fall crops.

- A school program can start with a single Square Foot Garden box tended by one class, then expand so that each student has his or her own garden box. If you are a Certified Instructor (or find one to participate), consider holding a Saturday seminar and inviting school parents to come and learn how they can garden the SFG way in their own backyards.

- When school science fair time rolls around, a Square Foot Gardening project is a perfect way for kids to learn the basics of plant science and plant propagation, as well as principles of self-sufficiency.

- Square Foot Gardening can fit nicely into school science, technology, engineering, art, and math (STEAM) programs. Reach out to science teachers in your area schools to discuss possibilities. Many schools run after-school programs that seek interesting activities that are both fun and instructional, and Square Foot Gardening is a perfect fit.

OTHER OUTREACH OPPORTUNITIES

Just about any civic organization, especially those devoted to the needs of children, can offer an opportunity to extend Square Foot Gardening into the community. If you or a someone you can partner with is a Certified Instructor, the list of opportunities for community service is nearly endless. A few of the organizations you can reach out to:

A COMMUNITY GARDEN SUCCESS STORY

St. John Baptist Church in Columbia, South Carolina, already maintained a food pantry that handed out hundreds of pounds of food every week in partnership with the Columbia Harvest Hope Food Bank. St. John's also had a community garden—a traditional row garden that was badly neglected and full of weeds. At the same time, Columbia College had been working on a community program to fight Type II diabetes involving a model for health awareness that included a walking program, a cooking program, and a gardening element. The hope was that these three components would help teach people about their disease and how to proactively manage it—as well as any other health problem—rather than turning first to prescription drugs. St. John's, Columbia College, and the Square Foot Gardening Foundation then joined forces to realize the gardening leg of the program, building a 10-box Square Foot Garden in one weekend in an empty lot on church property. The garden quickly flourished with organic fruits, vegetables, herbs, and flowers. As is often the case with successful community gardens, the project in Columbia demonstrated how different elements within a community can come together to create a valuable community asset.

- Local chapters of the Boy Scouts of America and Girl Scouts of America
- YMCA and YWCA family centers
- Boys and Girls Club of America centers
- 4-H clubs
- Senior citizen organizations and centers
- The Red Cross and other aid centers
- Local hospitals
- Civic volunteer offices

MAKING MONEY FROM SQUARE FOOT GARDENING

For most private home gardeners, the advantage of Square Foot Gardening lies in having lots of healthful produce to eat that costs you very little to grow. A family with four to six Square Foot Garden boxes can save hundreds of dollars each year versus the costs of buying the same fresh produce at a grocery store. But if you are innovative and willing to work hard, Square Foot Gardening can also offer the opportunity to generate a modest ongoing cash flow. Here are some of the ways people have made money as Square Foot Gardeners:

- **Selling produce.** Selling the produce from your Square Foot Garden can be as sophisticated as supplying produce to a commercial farmers' market or roadside vendor or as simple as letting your kids set up a folding table along the sidewalk to sell tomatoes, cucumbers, and zucchini. Some gardeners sell their produce in the workplace to fellow colleagues. In terms of payback on investment, selling tomatoes will give you a good profit margin. If you make a point of growing organically and market your produce as such, your vegetables will be worth 20 to 40 percent more than nonorganic produce.

- **Building and selling materials.** If you are handy with tools, consider building Square Foot Garden boxes and selling them to friends and neighbors. You may even be able to whip up a large batch of Mel's Mix and sell that to the people who buy your boxes.

- **Tending gardens for a fee.** Consider printing up a flyer and offering your services as a gardener. If you are building and selling Square Foot Garden boxes, you might think about offering this service to your customers. In particular, people with mobility challenges might very much like to have someone tend their gardens for them.

- **Teaching for a fee.** Many organizations may be willing to pay modest speaking fees if you are a skilled gardener and you have credentials as a Certified Square Foot Gardening Instructor.

A SCHOOL SCIENCE PROJECT

Kids get a big kick out of rooting tomato-plant suckers (the side branches) cut off a mother plant. This project is also a great way to learn about and demonstrate one of the key methods of plant propagation. If you are working with a classroom, this can be an interesting project to conduct during weekly teaching visits. The project takes about 4 weeks from start to finish. For each team conducting the experiment, it requires:

- One large cup of vermiculite
- One large cup of water
- Scissors

In the first teaching session, have your teams of kids cut off two suckers from an established tomato plant and set the cut end of one into a cup of water and the other into the cup of vermiculite. Instruct them to keep the water level in the one cup topped off and to keep the cup of vermiculite constantly moist.

Place the cuttings in a sunny, warm location, such as a south-facing window. Once a week, have the kids carefully remove the suckers from their cups to inspect and measure the amount of root growth. Then have them chart the root growth in each medium to determine which is more successful at rooting new tomato plants. By the time you have concluded this exercise, you may well have created a room full of new tomato plants—and new Square Foot Gardeners.

A TEACHER'S STORY

Hi—my name is Sandy, and I am a fourth-grade teacher. I've found Square Foot Gardening to be the perfect vehicle for learning. Though I teach in the California public school system, I find my students learn best when I'm learning about something that interests me, right alongside of them. That is how Square Foot Gardening came to be the center of my classroom. Growing my own vegetables appeals to me on many levels. I love to eat fresh food, am interested in being healthy, and like to share what I cook with the people I love.

Gardening has always been on the list of things I wanted to add to my life. But I had never attempted to grow anything more than a houseplant, and truthfully, not very successfully.

I strongly believe that I can learn and be successful at whatever I choose and decided it was time to give gardening a serious try. I searched the Internet for the most efficient and successful gardening method I could find. I wanted to start with a small garden that would be easy and manageable. As I researched, Mel Bartholomew's Square Foot Gardening method stood out. It met all my requirements and stirred enough optimism in my ability to succeed that I ordered his book. As I began to read, I was inspired to give it a try and was as sure as he was that I'd succeed.

I find the things that inspire me will inspire my students. So, I brought my interest and enthusiasm for Mel's book into the classroom and shared what I was doing with my students. I asked them whether they would be interested in doing the same. They matched my curiosity and optimism step for step. I sat them down in front of me, opened the book, and began to read. As I read, we chatted about what we might be able to do at our school. Mel's voice came through clearly, enough so that my students wanted to write him a letter. So, we wrote him a letter.

The students each contributed a question or comment that we composed together into one e-mail, and we sent him our thoughts. We were very excited when Mel responded. And he not only responded to us as a group—he wrote back speaking to each student about the comment or question he or she had written.

That was very powerful.

I work hard to teach the students that no matter who an expert or hero is, that expert was once a child sitting in a classroom just as they are now, people who followed their own interests and curiosities. In this case, Mel was the author of a book on a subject he felt passionate about, and we were studying it to build a successful garden. This opens up endless possibilities in these little learners about becoming the author who learns about and shares, in some way, the information on whatever topic sparks their interest.

The math, reading, writing, science, art, and social studies lessons evolved naturally as we made our way through researching, building, and growing our SFG. There is something delightful that happens when a skill is learned in the midst of discovery, rather than from a workbook. In our pursuit of a successful school garden, the students and I found an abundance of opportunities that stirred curiosity, a need to find answers, or a desire to experiment with just how a certain aspect of the SFG would work for us. I had specific standards to teach according to district and state guidelines. I used what the students did with their SFG to teach and apply those skills, which facilitated their learning. I remember feeling excited as the teacher and watching my students get excited about what we'd be doing next with our garden as the school days progressed. That feeling is something neither my students nor I feel when we work on skills out of a workbook. If you're a teacher, in any capacity, I invite you to take Square Foot Gardening into the classroom. You and your students will be truly amazed at the results.

Each vegetable has slightly different preferred conditions and maintenance needs. Understanding them will let you maximize your harvest.

12

THE SQUARE FOOT GARDENING GUIDE TO VEGETABLES

E ach vegetable you grow has different needs and requires its own form of care. Each of the profiles on the following pages has all the basic information you need to obtain, plant, grow, and harvest the vegetable and herbs listed. These profiles are just a starting point, though, as you will also find information specific to individual varieties on the seed packet or plant tag for the variety you buy. You can also use online resources and other books to learn more about individual crops.

ALL ABOUT ASPARAGUS

ASPARAGUS

BOTANICAL INFORMATION
Latin Name: *Asparagus officinalis*
Height: up to 5'
Spacing: 1 per square
EDIBLE SEASON
Spring and early summer

Seed to Harvest/Flower: 2 years
Seed Storage: NA
Weeks to Maturity: NA
Indoor Seed Starting: NA
Earliest Outdoor Planting: Early spring for production in subsequent years
Additional Plantings: NA
Last Planting: NA

Asparagus takes two to three years to mature, then will reliably reappear each year. The spears should be harvested in the spring when they are 7 to 9 inches tall; later spears will be woody and should be left in place to fuel development of new roots. Many gardeners devote an entire Square Foot Garden box to this delicious crop.

STARTING
- **Location:** Full sun.
- **Seeds Indoors:** NA
- **Transplanting:** Plant root crowns in early spring as soon as soil can be worked. Dig trenches 6 inches wide and about 10 inches deep. Create a mound in the trench then spread root crowns over mound, about 15 inches apart. Barely cover the roots, then keep adding soil as stems grow, until trench is full.
- **Seeds Outdoors:** NA

GROWING
- **Watering:** Keep well-watered.
- **Maintenance:** Keep beds covered with a 6-inch layer of mulch. Cut down dead foliage in fall. After harvest, allow the ferns to grow, which will replenish the roots for next year's production.

HARVESTING
- **How:** Do not harvest until second or third year. Cut spears off with a sharp knife when they are 7 to 9 inches long.
- **When:** Asparagus is at its tender best in spring and early summer; harvest lasts for 2 to 3 weeks.

PREPARING AND USING
Asparagus can be used in recipes or the spears can be steamed and served alone. Asparagus freezes well.

COMMON PROBLEMS
Asparagus beetles, cutworms, slugs; crown rot, rust

ALL ABOUT BASIL

Basil is part of the mint family. It is commonly used in Italian cooking as well as in many Asian dishes. Basil also comes in different flavors, such as cinnamon, licorice, and lemon. If you are fond of Italian cooking, you may want to grow several different varieties.

STARTING
- **Location:** Full sun.
- **Seeds Indoors:** Start seeds indoors 4 to 6 weeks before the last frost. Seeds germinate quickly.
- **Transplanting:** Set out after all danger of frost has passed and the soil has warmed. Basil will stop growing if the weather is cool and then take a while to catch up, so wait to transplant it until the weather is starting to feel like summer.
- **Seeds Outdoors:** Sow basil seeds where the plants are to be grown in warm soil. Seeds germinate in 7 to 10 days, and the plants grow quickly.

GROWING
- **Watering:** Keep well watered.
- **Maintenance:** Pinch the basil tops often to keep the plant bushy. Harvesting basil for cooking will also keep the plant strong and bushy. For energetic, tasty plants, remove flower buds as they appear.

BASIL

BOTANICAL INFORMATION
Latin Name: *Ocimum basilicum*
Height: 1 to 2'
Spacing: Small varieties, 4 per square foot; large varieties, 1 per square foot
EDIBLE SEASON
Summer

Seed to Harvest/Flower: 12 weeks
Seed Storage: 5 years
Weeks to Maturity: 4 to 6 weeks
Indoor Seed Starting: 4 to 6 weeks before last frost
Earliest Outdoor Planting: After soil has warmed
Additional Plantings: 3 weeks and 6 weeks
Last Planting: NA

HARVESTING
- **How:** Pinch stems just above leaf nodes where new stems will sprout. Use only the leaves in cooking.
- **When:** Harvest basil anytime. In fact, the more you pinch off leaves and stems, the more it will grow.

PREPARING AND USING
Use fresh leaves in cooking, discarding stems. Dried basil does not retain its flavor. Excess basil can be processed with olive oil, wrapped tightly in plastic wrap, and stored in the freezer for up to three months.

COMMON PROBLEMS
Aphids, Japanese beetles; *Fusarium* wilt

ALL ABOUT BEANS

Beans are one of the easiest vegetables to grow. They come in two types: bush beans and pole beans. Pole beans are climbers, great for vertical gardening along the back row in your Square Foot Garden. Bush beans grow lower to the ground; each plant yields one large crop all at once, with a smaller crop a few weeks later. Pole beans take longer to grow but provide a steady continuous yield all season long. A single planting of pole types is adequate, while additional plantings of the bush types are needed to have a constant harvest.

STARTING
- **Location:** Full sun.
- **Seeds Indoors:** NA
- **Transplanting:** Does not transplant well.
- **Seeds Outdoors:** Presoak seeds for 30 minutes for faster sprouting. Plant seeds about 1 inch deep and water right away. Seeds sprout in 5 to 10 days. For a continuous harvest of bush beans, plant a new square of a different color or variety every 2 weeks all summer long.

GROWING
- **Watering:** Beans must be regularly watered. Do not allow the soil to dry out, but keep the leaves dry.
- **Maintenance:** Weed weekly if you see any weeds sprouting.

BEANS

BOTANICAL INFORMATION
Latin Name: *Phaseolus vulgaris*
Height: 12 to 18" (bush); 4 to 7' (pole)
Spacing: 9 per square (bush); 8 per square (pole)
EDIBLE SEASON
Summer

Seed to Harvest/Flower: 8 weeks (bush); 10 weeks (pole)
Seed Storage: 3 to 4 years
Weeks to Maturity: 8 weeks (bush); 9 weeks (pole)
Indoor Seed Starting: NA
Earliest Outdoor Planting: Immediately after the last spring frost
Additional Plantings: Every 2 weeks
Last Planting:

HARVESTING
- **How:** Break or cut each stem holding the bean pod. Do not pull on the plant when harvesting.
- **When:** For the best flavor, pick beans when they are still small and tender. Once they get large or pods bulge with seeds, they are past their peak and the plant will stop producing.

PREPARING AND USING
- Wash and refrigerate if not using immediately. Beans do not store well, so try to use them the same day they are picked. Beans contain a lot of vitamins A, B, and C as well as calcium and iron.
- Beans are good eaten raw when they are small. Remember—the smaller the bean, the more tender it will be.
- Cook any size bean. They can be steamed or stir-fried, then served individually with a little seasoning, grated cheese, or parsley. Beans are excellent additions to soups, stews, or mixed vegetable dishes. Leftovers can be added to a salad; Marinated beans can be added to a sandwich, along with lettuce, tomato, and cheese.

PROBLEMS
Aphids, Japanese and Mexican bean beetles; birds, rabbits, woodchucks, deer; blight, rust, mildew

ALL ABOUT BEETS

Beets are a wonderful vegetable to grow because they're easy and both the roots and the greens (tops) are suitable for eating. They are mostly pest and disease free and resistant to both fall and spring frosts. The root gets very hard when grown in the hot summer season.

STARTING
- **Location:** Partial shade or full sun.
- **Seeds Indoors:** NA
- **Transplanting:** Does not transplant well.
- **Seeds Outdoors:** Each seed in the packet is actually a cluster of two to five individual seeds, so several sprouts will come up from each seed planted. Plant one presoaked seed in each space ½ inch deep 3 weeks before the last spring frost. To have a continuous harvest, plant a new square every 3 weeks except in the hottest part of the summer. After the sprouts are about 1 inch tall, cut off all except the strongest plant from each seed cluster.

GROWING
- **Watering:** Plants need constant and even moisture.
- **Maintenance:** Keep damaged leaves picked off, mulch in hot weather, and weed weekly.

BEETS

BOTANICAL INFORMATION	
Latin Name: *Beta vulgaris*	**Seed to Harvest/Flower:** 8 weeks
Height: 12"	**Seed Storage:** 4 to 5 years
Spacing: 9 or 16 per square depending on variety	**Weeks to Maturity:** 8 weeks
	Indoor Seed Starting: NA
EDIBLE SEASON	**Earliest Outdoor Planting:** 3 weeks before last spring frost
Spring and summer	**Additional Plantings:** Every 3 weeks
	Last Planting: 8 weeks before frost

HARVESTING
- **How:** Pull up the entire plant with the largest top. If you're not sure of bulb size, dig around the root with your fingers to uncover the top and check the size. To harvest greens, individual leaves can be cut at any time, but don't take more than one or two from each plant.
- **When:** Roots are the most tender when at half size, so start pulling when the roots are approximately the size of a table tennis ball and continue until they are full size. Leaves are usable at any size.

PREPARING AND USING
Use greens whole or chopped in fresh salads or cook them like spinach. Roots are rich in iron and vitamin B. Serve hot—steam or bake with the skin on, then squeeze them to take the skin off (your hands will turn red when you do this). Try quickly sautéing shredded raw beets and serve hot, or try them cooked and chilled (shredded, sliced, or diced) in salads or mixed with cottage cheese. Small whole beets can also be cooked and served with an orange sauce, salad dressing, or a spoonful of sour cream. Try them in borsht, a type of Russian soup that can be served hot or cold.

PROBLEMS
Cutworms, slugs and snails, leaf miners; rabbits, woodchucks, deer; relatively disease free

ALL ABOUT BOK CHOY

Also called Chinese cabbage, bok choy is a cool-season vegetable that grows best in spring and in fall. It is fairly easy to get two crops of year, because bok choy, which is usually grown from seed, takes 45 to 50 days to mature.

STARTING
- **Location:** Full sun to partial shade.
- **Seeds Indoors:** Start seeds indoors 4 to 5 weeks before the last frost.
- **Transplanting:** When nighttime temps reach 50°F.
- **Seeds Outdoors:** Plant 2 to 3 weeks before the last frost date.

GROWING
- **Watering:** Keep moist; drought will cause plants to bolt.
- **Maintenance:** Provide shade in hot weather to prevent plants from going to seed; cover plants to prolong season in the fall.

BOK CHOY

BOTANICAL INFORMATION	
Latin Name: *Brassica rapa* subsp. *chinensis*	**Seed to Harvest/Flower:** 45 to 50 days
Height: 1 to 2'	**Seed Storage:** Up to 4 years
Spacing: 4 per square	**Weeks to Maturity:** 50 days
EDIBLE SEASON	**Indoor Seed Starting:** NA
Spring, for fall harvest	**Earliest Outdoor Planting:** 2 weeks before predicted last spring frost
	Additional Plantings: Every 2 weeks
	Last Planting: NA

HARVESTING
- **How:** Cut off baby greens; snap off mature ribbed leaves.
- **When:** For baby greens, when plants are 4 or 5 inches tall; mature leaves can be harvested when they are 12 to 18 inches long, anytime before the plants bolt.

PREPARING AND USING
Bok choy is a crisp leaf cabbage that is great in soups, salads, and stir-fry dishes. It is one of the most nutritious of all vegetables, containing ample supplies of vitamins C, A, B6, and K as well as calcium, manganese, potassium, and iron. Wash leaves thoroughly before cooking, as they can be gritty otherwise.

COMMON PROBLEMS
Cabbage loopers, cabbage worms, flea beetles, slugs

ALL ABOUT BROCCOLI

Broccoli requires cool weather but is great in a Square Foot Garden. It is very frost hardy and grows well in the spring and fall; it doesn't do well in the summer heat. Broccoli is a great source of fiber and is filled with vitamins A, K, and D. It has excellent allergy-fighting properties.

STARTING
- **Location:** Needs full sun.
- **Seeds Indoors:** Plant 5 to 10 seeds in a cup of vermiculite– or place one seed ¼ inch deep in potting soil in each individual compartment of a seedling tray–approximately 12 weeks before your last spring frost. Seeds will sprout indoors in 5 to 10 days at 70°F. Keep seeds warm until sprouted; move to full sunlight as soon as the first shoots appear.
- **Transplanting:** Plant outside approximately 5 weeks before the last spring frost.
- **Seeds Outdoors:** Not satisfactory, as the season is too short before hot weather arrives.

GROWING
- **Watering:** Like all members of the cabbage family (also called the cole family), you're growing leaves and flowers, which need consistent moisture. Never let broccoli dry out or wilt.
- **Maintenance:** Weed weekly; mulch in warmer weather.

BROCCOLI

BOTANICAL INFORMATION
Latin Name: *Brassica oleracea* var. *italica*
Height: 18 to 24"
Spacing: 1 per square
EDIBLE SEASON
Spring and fall

Seed to Harvest/Flower: 16 weeks
Seed Storage: 5 to 6 years
Weeks to Maturity: 9 weeks
Indoor Seed Starting: 12 weeks before last spring frost
Earliest Outdoor Planting: 5 weeks before last spring frost
Additional Plantings: NA
Last Planting: NA

HARVESTING
- **How:** Cut off the main central head at its base with a sharp, serrated knife or clippers, leaving as many leaves on the plant as possible. Within a few weeks, new side shoots (miniature heads) will form and grow from the original plant to provide you with a second harvest.
- **When:** Harvest as soon as a head appears full and tight. The head is actually a flower head, which you want to harvest before the flower buds open. If you have several plants, don't wait too long to cut the first one after the heads start forming, even if it looks a little small. It's still edible when it's small.

PREPARING AND USING
Broccoli contains vitamins A, B, and C as well as calcium, phosphorus, and iron. Wash under running water and soak in cold salted water for two hours if there's any chance that a green cabbage worm is present in the head. Refrigerate if not using immediately. Broccoli can be served fresh and raw with hummus or any dip, or it can be chopped fresh into a salad. To cook, you can steam or stir-fry it. Try it plain with just a little dressing or sour cream, or topped with a cheese sauce or just plain lemon juice. It's an excellent addition to any stir-fry dish; mix it with interesting combinations of meats and vegetables.

COMMON PROBLEMS
Cutworms, root maggots, green worms, cabbage worms; club root

ALL ABOUT BRUSSELS SPROUTS

This member of the cabbage family is a cool-weather crop that is long growing but also long bearing. It is best in spring for fall harvest. It tolerates very cool weather, even light frost. Seed-starting recommendations vary widely from variety to variety, so refer to seed packet instructions.

STARTING
- **Location:** At least 6 hours of sun per day.
- **Seeds Indoors:** Sow indoors about 6 months before first fall frost.
- **Transplanting:** Plant seedlings outdoors about 5 months before first fall frost.
- **Seeds Outdoor:** Plant seeds outdoors 4 weeks before last spring frost.

GROWING
- **Watering:** Water regularly, 1 to 1½ inches per week.
- **Maintenance:** Mulch to keep the ground cool and moist; brussels sprouts may require shade protection in hot conditions. Plants need the mineral boron, so additional feeding is sometimes necessary.

BRUSSELS SPROUTS

BOTANICAL INFORMATION
Latin Name: *Brassica oleracea* var. *gemmifera*
Height: 2½'
Spacing: 1 per square
EDIBLE SEASON
Spring to Fall

Seed to Harvest/Flower: 5 months
Seed Storage: 4 years
Weeks to Maturity: 4 months
Indoor Seed Starting: 6 months before first fall frost
Earliest Outdoor Planting: 5 months before first fall frost
Additional Plantings: NA
Last Planting: NA

HARVESTING
- **How:** Twist heads until they break away from the plant.
- **When:** Harvest when small heads are 1 to 2 inches in diameter; in fall, heads may be harvested through the first frosts.

PREPARING AND USING
Refrigerate fresh sprouts in plastic bags for no more than 3 days. Brussels sprouts are delicious when coated with olive oil, garlic powder, salt, pepper, and lemon juice, then baked for about 15 minutes until browned. For a nuttier flavor, try roasting or searing them quickly in a pan. Greens can be used in salads.

COMMON PROBLEMS
Harlequin bugs, cabbage loopers, cutworms, aphids; powdery mildew, rust

ALL ABOUT CABBAGE

Cabbage is a very easy vegetable to grow. It's frost hardy and takes very little work. Cabbage comes in a variety of shapes, sizes, colors, and leaf textures and can be grown as an early- to late-season crop; the early-season variety is smaller and faster growing, while the late- or long-season variety is usually bigger. All varieties grow best in cool spring or fall weather.

STARTING

- **Location:** Full sun.
- **Seeds Indoors:** Plant seeds ¼ inch deep in potting soil in individual compartments of a seedling tray 12 weeks before your last spring frost. Seeds sprout in 5 to 8 days at 70°F. For a second crop in the fall, repeat the process anytime in the middle of June (or 16 weeks before your first fall frost date). In most places you can usually start seeds for a new crop as soon as you've harvested the previous one. Keep warm (70°F) until sprouted; move to full sunlight as soon as first shoots appear.
- **Transplanting:** Don't let transplants get too large before planting them outside. Late transplants do not form good heads and sometimes flower the first year if allowed to get too large.
- **Seeds Outdoors:** The season is too short to plant seeds directly in the garden for the spring crop, and starting the fall crop from seed outdoors would tie up too much valuable garden space that could be used more productively. Start all seeds in individual containers for transplanting into the garden.

CABBAGE

BOTANICAL INFORMATION
Latin Name: *Brassica oleracea* var. *capitata*
Height: 12 to 18"
Spacing: 1 per square
EDIBLE SEASON
Spring and fall

Seed to Harvest/Flower: 16 weeks
Seed Storage: 5 to 6 years
Weeks to Maturity: 9 weeks
Indoor Seed Starting: 12 weeks before last spring frost
Earliest Outdoor Planting: 5 weeks before last spring frost
Additional Plantings: NA
Last Planting: NA

GROWING

- **Watering:** Cabbage needs lots of water to head up properly, but after the head is formed and while it is growing to full size, cut back on watering or the head will grow too fast and split.
- **Maintenance:** Weed weekly; cut away any extra-large bottom leaves if they are yellow. If large lower leaves are spreading to other squares, cut away any portions that are "over the line." This will not hurt the plant.

HARVESTING

- **How:** Cut off the entire head with a sharp, serrated knife or clippers.
- **When:** Anytime the head starts to develop and feels firm. If you have several plants, don't wait until all the heads are large. They may split in hot weather and go to seed, and then you'll be left with nothing.

PREPARING AND USING

Cabbage is delicious cooked or raw and contains a lot of vitamin C. You can shred it to make cole slaw, sauerkraut, or kimchee.

PROBLEMS

Cabbage worms (their worst enemy), slugs and snails, aphids.

ALL ABOUT CARROTS

Carrots are related to the wildflower Queen Anne's lace. The seeds are so small that planting them can be very tedious; practice dropping a pinch (two or three seeds) on some white paper until you get the hang of it. Carrots can be either long and thin or short and stubby; pick the variety with the shape and size that best suits your garden.

CARROTS

BOTANICAL INFORMATION
Latin Name: *Daucus carata* subsp. *sativus*
Height: 12"
Spacing: 16 per square
EDIBLE SEASON
Spring through fall

Seed to Harvest/Flower: 10 weeks
Seed Storage: 3 to 4 years
Weeks to Maturity: 10 weeks
Indoor Seed Starting: NA
Earliest Outdoor Planting: 3 weeks before last spring frost
Additional Plantings: NA
Last Planting: NA

STARTING

- **Location:** Preferably full sun, but can stand partial shade.
- **Seeds Indoors:** NA
- **Transplanting:** Does not transplant well.
- **Seeds Outdoors:** Sprouts in 2 to 3 weeks outdoors. Seeds are very small; try pelleted seeds if necessary. Plant two or three seeds in each of the 16 spaces in a square. Water the soil and cover the square with a plastic-covered cage. Keep the ground moist at all times, even if it means daily spraying in sunny weather.

GROWING

- **Watering:** Carrots must have constant moisture until they're almost mature to grow quickly and continuously. Then, reduce watering so the carrots don't crack from overly rapid growth.
- **Maintenance:** Weed weekly; otherwise, carrots are relatively work free.

HARVESTING

- **How:** Pull up those with the largest tops. If you're not sure which are biggest, dig around the plant with your fingers to test the size.
- **When:** Pick them early, when they're only half size and at their sweetest and most tender.

PREPARING AND USING

Scrub carrots with a vegetable brush, but don't peel them. Most of the vitamins are in the skin or close to the surface. Rich in vitamin A and thiamine (vitamin B1), carrots also contain calcium. Carrots are delicious fresh and raw—shredded, sliced thinly, or cut into sticks for snacking. They can be cooked by steaming or roasting. They can be served in a variety of dishes or added to soups and stews but seem best when served with dressing, a dab of sour cream, or a sprinkling of parsley and grated cheese. Carrots are so versatile you can even make a wonderfully moist cake with them.

PROBLEMS

Carrot rust fly; rabbits, woodchucks, deer, voles; virtually disease free

ALL ABOUT CAULIFLOWER

Even though cauliflower is a member of the cabbage family, it is not as cold hardy as its fellow cole crops and is more susceptible to the heat. Fall is the best season for planting because the plant will mature in the cool weather. White cauliflower is the most popular variety, but the purple one is considered to be more flavorful and does better in the heat. The white variety needs 14 to 15 weeks to mature, while the purple variety can take up to 19 weeks.

STARTING
- **Location:** Preferably full sun, but will tolerate partial shade.
- **Seeds Indoors:** Will sprout in 5 to 10 days at 70°F. Plant 5 to 10 seeds in a cup of vermiculite—or plant one seed ¼ inch deep in potting soil in each of the individual compartments of a seedling flat—10 weeks before the last spring frost. For a second crop in the fall, repeat the process anytime between June 15 and July 1. Keep warm (70°F) until sprouted; move to full sunlight as soon as first shoots appear.
- **Transplanting:** Set out in the garden 4 weeks before the last spring frost. Place a cutworm collar around the stem, water, and provide a shade cage. Be extra careful when planting; cauliflower suffers more from transplanting than any other cabbage family member.
- **Seeds Outdoors:** Not satisfactory; the season is too short before hot weather arrives.

GROWING
- **Watering:** Never let plants dry out.
- **Maintenance:** Weed weekly; mulch in hot weather.

HARVESTING
- **How:** Cut off the entire head at its base with a sharp knife or clippers.
- **When:** Harvest as soon as the head enlarges, is firm, and has a nice color, before the buds separate or open. Do not delay your harvest, as the head will grow fast and pass the ideal harvest point in just a few days.

CAULIFLOWER

BOTANICAL INFORMATION
Latin Name: *Brassica oleracea* var. *botrytis*
Height: 18 to 24"
Spacing: 1 per square
EDIBLE SEASON
Spring and fall

Seed to Harvest/Flower: 14 weeks
Seed Storage: 5 to 6 years
Weeks to Maturity: 8 weeks
Indoor Seed Starting: 10 weeks before last spring frost
Earliest Outdoor Planting: 4 weeks before last spring frost
Additional Plantings: 8 to 10 weeks before first fall frost
Last Planting: NA

PREPARING AND USING
Serve florets fresh and raw with any salad dressing or dip. Chopped cauliflower is excellent in tossed salads. Cook by steaming, roasting, or stir-frying. Serve hot with cheese sauce, salad dressing, or just a sprinkling of grated cheese. It makes a marvelous addition to any soup or stew; cauliflower soup is superb and quite unusual. Marinate any leftovers for addition to salads or relishes. Many people "rice" cauliflower in a food processer to use it as a healthy and gluten-free substitute for pasta, or rice and potatoes—it makes a great alternative for flour in pizza crust.

COMMON PROBLEMS
Cutworms, root maggots, occasionally cabbage worms, cabbage loopers; club root

ALL ABOUT CELERY

Celery is a long-season vegetable that can be a little tricky to grow. Some people, in fact, grow it for the challenge. It can take as long as 90 days for indoor seeds to reach transplant size, And it does not like transplanting, so considerable care is needed if you are starting it indoors 8 to 10 weeks before last spring frost for late-summer harvest. Or, you can sow seeds directly into the garden in late summer for fall production.

STARTING
- **Location:** Full sun.
- **Seeds Indoors:** In the north, sow seeds in a warm, well-lighted area 10 to 12 weeks before the last frost date in spring, ¼ inch deep in seed-starting mix. Southern gardeners can sow directly in the garden.
- **Transplanting:** Move seedlings to the garden when they have at least three pairs of leaves and are about 6 inches tall, and when the danger of frost has passed.
- **Seeds Outdoors:** Not recommended except in the South, where you can sow outdoors from spring to late summer.

GROWING
- **Watering:** Keep constantly moist.
- **Maintenance:** Keep well weeded. Shade the plants for 2 weeks before harvesting stalks to make them sweeter.

CELERY

BOTANICAL INFORMATION
Latin Name: *Apium graveolens*
Height: 12 to 16"
Spacing: 4 per square
EDIBLE SEASON
Spring to fall
Seed to Harvest/ Flower: 12 to 14 weeks

Seed Storage: 2 to 5 years
Weeks to Maturity: 115 days after setting transplants in garden
Indoor Seed Starting: 8 to 12 weeks before last frost
Earliest Outdoor Planting: 4 weeks before last spring frost
Additional Plantings: NA
Last Planting: NA

HARVESTING
- **How:** Cut off stalks 2 inches above ground level with a sharp knife.
- **When:** Harvest when stalks reach 8 to 12 inches in length.

PREPARING AND USING
Celery is great as a snack or when chopped as an ingredient in salads and stir-fry dishes. After harvest, wash, pat dry, and store in the refrigerator.

COMMON PROBLEMS
Earwigs, leafminers, aphids; downy mildew, celery mosaic

ALL ABOUT CHIVES

CHIVES

BOTANICAL INFORMATION
Latin Name: *Allium schoeneprasum*
Height: 6 to 12"
Spacing: 16 per square
EDIBLE SEASON
Late spring and summer
Seed to Harvest/ Flower: 16 weeks

Seed Storage: 2 years
Weeks to Maturity: 10 weeks
Indoor Seed Starting: 10 weeks before last frost
Earliest Outdoor Planting: Late spring
Additional Plantings: NA
Last Planting: NA

This is a fun little plant with a spiky hairdo. The slim, round leaves are hollow and have a mild onion scent when cut. The pinkish-purple flowers are edible, appear in late spring, and make a pretty garnish for salads. Chives are a member of the onion family, and oddly enough, it is one of the few herbs that hasn't really been used for medicinal purposes during its long history. It is simply a unique garden plant that has enhanced the flavor of savory foods for centuries. If left to send up seed pods, the bright purple flowers are very attractive.

STARTING
- **Location:** Full sun.
- **Seeds Indoors:** Plant seeds indoors in late winter. Seeds can take up to 21 days to germinate.
- **Transplanting:** Set plants out in spring. Although chives are cold hardy, it is best to set new plants out after all danger of frost has passed.
- **Seeds Outdoors:** Seeds sprout in late spring to early summer.

GROWING
- **Watering:** Keep soil moist.
- **Maintenance:** Plants will spread, so divide clumps every few years to rejuvenate the plants.

HARVESTING
- **How:** Snip the tips of the leaves as needed. Don't cut off more than one-third of the plant at any one time.
- **When:** Chives can be harvested anytime after the new leaves have reached 6 to 8 inches. To enjoy the tasty pink flowers, don't harvest the plant until you can see the flower buds, then clip around them or wait until they bloom. The flowers make a lovely garnish.

PREPARING AND USING
Cut one-third of the tops off all leaves if you like the flat-top look, or cut a few leaves down to one-third of each leaf. Snip the fresh hollow leaves to garnish baked potatoes, fresh fish, and creamed soups or add them into salads, sauces, or dips.

COMMON PROBLEMS
Thrips, mildew, rust; insufficient water can cause leaf tips to turn brown

ALL ABOUT CILANTRO

The fresh leaf of the cilantro plant is probably the most widely used of all flavoring herbs throughout the world, used in Middle Eastern, Indian, Southeast Asian, and South American cuisines. Cilantro is a pretty plant that looks somewhat like parsley. Use it like parsley in smaller quantities for a unique tang. When cilantro goes to seed, it becomes another herb altogether—coriander. Ancient peoples used to chew coriander seeds to combat heartburn (probably after weeding their long single-row gardens). The seeds are sweet when they're ripe but terribly bitter when immature.

STARTING
- **Location:** Full sun to partial shade.
- **Seeds Indoors:** NA
- **Transplanting:** Does not transplant well.
- **Seeds Outdoors:** Plant seeds outdoors after the last frost in spring.

GROWING
- **Watering:** Water weekly.
- **Maintenance:** Shelter the plants from wind. Otherwise, cilantro needs little care besides watering.

CILANTRO

BOTANICAL INFORMATION	
Latin Name: *Coriandrum sativum*	**Seed to Harvest/Flower:** 5 weeks (leaves), 12 weeks (coriander seeds)
Height: 1 to 2'	**Seed Storage:** NA
Spacing: 1 per square	**Weeks to Maturity:** 5 weeks
EDIBLE SEASON	**Indoor Seed Starting:** NA
Late spring and summer	**Earliest Outdoor Planting:** After last frost
	Additional Plantings: 2-week intervals until early summer for continuous harvest
	Last Planting: NA

HARVESTING
- **How:** Pick cilantro leaves as you need them, even if the plant is only 6 inches tall. For coriander seeds, cut whole plants and hang to dry, then shake the dried seeds into a paper bag.
- **When:** Harvest the cilantro leaves anytime after the plant has reached 6 to 8 inches. Harvest the seeds after the plants have turned brown but before the seeds start to fall. Cilantro self-sows with abandon.

PREPARING AND USING
Cilantro leaves and coriander seeds are both used in curries and pickling The strong, spicy leaves can be added to salads, fish, or beans, and it is found as an ingredient in recipes from many cultures around the world. The milder, sweeter seeds can be ground and used in breads or cakes.

COMMON PROBLEMS
Usually pest and disease free but suffers in humid, rainy weather

ALL ABOUT COLLARD GREENS

COLLARD GREENS

BOTANICAL INFORMATION
Latin Name: *Brassica oleracea* cultivar
Height: 24 to 36"
Spacing: 1 per square
EDIBLE SEASON
All year in the South; fall in the North

Seed to Harvest/Flower: 60 to 75 days
Seed Storage: Up to 6 years
Weeks to Maturity: 60 days
Indoor Seed Starting: NA
Earliest Outdoor Planting: 4 weeks before last spring frost
Additional Plantings: 6 to 8 weeks before first fall frost
Last Planting: 6 to 8 weeks before first fall frost

This cool-season vegetable is a Southern tradition. Like other leafy vegetables, collard greens are a great source of vitamin C and beta carotene. In the South, seeds are often planted in late summer and early autumn for winter harvest. Because it is one of the most cold hardy of all vegetables, northern gardeners can plant it 4 weeks before the last spring frost, or 6 to 8 weeks before first fall frost for late-season harvest.

STARTING
- **Location:** At least 4 to 5 hours of full sun per day.
- **Seeds Indoors:** NA
- **Transplanting:** NA
- **Seeds Outdoors:** Sow in the garden 4 weeks before the last spring frost or 6 to 8 weeks before first fall frost.

GROWING
- **Watering:** Collard greens require moist soil—1½ inches of water per week.
- **Maintenance:** Mulch thickly to keep the soil cool.

HARVESTING
- **How:** Cut off leaves near the base of the stem.
- **When:** Harvest when leaves are young—less than 10 inches in length. Longer leaves will be tough and bitter.

PREPARING AND USING
Wash carefully after harvest and remove tough stems and central veins. Refrigerate. Greens may be used in salads or chopped for use in soups, stews, and broths.

COMMON PROBLEMS
Aphids, cabbage worms

ALL ABOUT CORN

Corn is a longtime favorite of most gardeners. The taste of store-bought corn can't compete with home-grown corn, so many plant a whole 4 × 4 Square Foot Garden box of just corn. Most of the varieties for home use are planted four per square foot; only one crop can be grown per season because it needs a long time to mature and lots of hot weather.

There are many colors and varieties of corn. The later-season types taste better than the earlier-season varieties; the "extra sweet" variety is unusually good and keeps its sweetness even after picking. The most common color of corn is yellow, but the best tasting are the bicolor and white varieties. As new varieties of corn are developed, check with the seed companies for the latest recommendations on how far apart to plant various types of corn so they don't cross-pollinate.

STARTING
- **Location:** Full sun; locate corn where it won't shade other crops with its height.
- **Seeds Indoors:** NA
- **Transplanting:** Does not transplant well.
- **Seeds Outdoors:** Sprouts in 5 to 10 days outdoors. Plant your presoaked seeds 1 to 2 inches deep, at the proper spacing. Water the soil and cover with a chicken-wire cage to keep out birds. To get a continuous harvest, plant a new crop every 2 weeks with several varieties of different maturation dates.

GROWING
- **Watering:** Weekly; more often in hot weather.
- **Maintenance:** Weed weekly; remove the chicken wire cage when the corn is 6 inches tall. Place a raccoon-proof fence around your squares when the ears are starting to form.

CORN

BOTANICAL INFORMATION
Latin Name: *Zea mays*
Height: 5 to 6'
Spacing: 4 per square
EDIBLE SEASON
Summer
Seed to Harvest/ Flower: 9 to 13 weeks

Seed Storage: 1 to 2 years
Weeks to Maturity: 9 weeks
Indoor Seed Starting: NA
Earliest Outdoor Planting: Immediately after last spring frost
Additional Plantings: Every 2 weeks
Last Planting: Midsummer

HARVESTING
- **How:** Use two hands to harvest, one to hold the stalk and the other to pull down and break off the ear—otherwise you may break the stalk. If there are no other ears left on a particular stalk, it's best to cut it down to the ground. Don't pull it out or you may disturb the roots of the surrounding stalks.
- **When:** Check the ears daily when the silk first browns and the ears feel full and slightly bumpy. The final test of each ear before harvesting is to peel away a small strip of the husk to expose the kernels. They should be plump and full. To see if the ear is ready, puncture a kernel with your thumbnail. If milky juice squirts out, it's ready; if the juice is clear, the corn is not quite ready to pick.

PREPARING AND USING
Corn loses its sweet taste very quickly after being picked, so try to cook and eat it as soon as possible. If you can't use it immediately, husk and refrigerate it. Up to 50 percent of the flavor is lost in the first 12 hours of storage—more if it's not refrigerated. If you harvest more than you eat, cut the kernels off the cob and freeze them, add to a relish dish, or serve warm with butter and parsley. Of course, corn is excellent added to any kind of soup or stew.

COMMON PROBLEMS
Corn has more pest problems than any other garden crop, including corn borer, ear worm, birds, raccoons, and squirrels; however, there are relatively few diseases that affect corn

ALL ABOUT CUCUMBER

CUCUMBER

BOTANICAL INFORMATION
Latin Name: *Cucumis savinus*
Height: NA (vine)
Spacing: 2 per square
EDIBLE SEASON
Summer

Seed to Harvest/Flower: 9 weeks
Seed Storage: 5 to 6 years
Weeks to Maturity: 7 weeks
Indoor Seed Starting: NA
Earliest Outdoor Planting: 1 week after last spring frost
Additional Plantings: NA
Last Planting: NA

The cucumber is a garden favorite and very easy to grow in warm weather. Although both vine and bush varieties are available, bush cucumbers take a lot of room and don't produce like the vine types. Use the vertical method to grow your vine cucumbers.

There are many varieties, ranging in size, shape, and use, including ones for pickling or serving raw. The pickling varieties are picked much earlier, when they are smaller—just the right size for the pickle jar—but they can also be eaten as cucumbers. The slicing types are grown larger and are more commonly used for salads or sandwiches. Don't let the fruit get too large; pick early and often. Try some of the long, thin varieties for a fun crop.

STARTING
- **Location:** Full sun, although the vine types will tolerate some shade.
- **Seeds Indoors:** Plant one seed each in individual paper cups filled with Mel's Mix. Punch holes in the cup bottoms for drainage. Keep warm (at least 70°F) until sprouted; move to full sunlight as soon as the first shoots appear. Seeds sprout in 4 to 8 days at 70°F and even faster at 80°F.
- **Transplanting:** Plant seeds, still in their cups, in the ground at the proper plant spacing. If the cup is waxed cardboard or a heavy paper, tear away the bottom carefully; avoid disturbing the roots. Water and cover with a shade cage.
- **Seeds Outdoors:** Cucumber sprouts in 5 to 10 days; place presoaked seeds at proper spacing, water, and keep the soil moist until seeds sprout.

GROWING
- **Watering:** Weekly; twice weekly in hot weather. Never let the soil dry out. Avoid wetting the leaves, as this spreads any fungal disease that may be present. Cucumbers have the highest water content of any vegetable, so plenty of moisture is required for proper growth.
- **Maintenance:** Weed weekly. Keep vines on the trellis, watch out for beetles, and mulch in hot weather.

HARVESTING
- **How:** Cut (don't pull) the stem connecting the fruit to the vine.
- **When:** Harvest continually! Never allow any cucumbers to become yellow or overly large, or the plant will stop producing.

PREPARING AND USING
Wash and scrub with a vegetable brush. Serve long, slender burpless varieties with the skins left on. Peel the fatter varieties before slicing, cubing, or cutting into long sticks. Serve fresh slices on sandwiches with onions, or marinate for relish. Many gardeners like cucumbers simply soaked in vinegar overnight and served with lots of pepper. They also go well in any salad or arranged around a spoonful of cottage cheese.

COMMON PROBLEMS
Cucumber beetles; mildew, wilt, mosaic

ALL ABOUT DILL

DILL

BOTANICAL INFORMATION
Latin Name: *Anethum graveolens*
Height: 36"
Spacing: 1 per square
EDIBLE SEASON
Summer
Seed to Harvest/ Flower: 5 weeks

Seed Storage: 4 to 5 years
Weeks to Maturity: 6 to 9 weeks
Indoor Seed Starting: NA
Earliest Outdoor Planting: As soon as danger of frost has passed
Additional Plantings: NA
Last Planting: NA

Dill is a tall herb with airy, fern-like foliage that is popular as a seasoning for soups and pickling recipes. Gardeners quickly learn that the fresh herb is much tastier than the commercial dried product. Dill is very easy to grow from seed and, in fact, will readily self-seed in the garden. You may well have to pick out seedlings that have strayed from their squares in following years. Dill has the virtue of attracting beneficial insects to your garden.

Both leaves and seeds of dill are edible.

STARTING
- **Location:** Full sun.
- **Seeds Indoors:** NA
- **Transplants:** Dill sprouts so readily from seed that there is no need to start seeds indoors or plant from transplants.
- **Seeds Outdoors:** Sow seed outdoors when the danger of frost has passed. Dill does not like to be planted near carrots.

GROWING
- **Watering:** Weekly waterings are sufficient.
- **Maintenance:** Dill requires very little maintenance. Harvest seedheads frequently to prevent rampant self-seeding. Keep weeded, and mulch soil to maintain even soil temperatures. Remove flowers as they appear to prevent seeds from forming prematurely.

HARVESTING
- **How:** Pinch or cut off leaves and seedheads.
- **When:** Begin harvesting as soon as the plant has 4 or 5 leaves, then continuously until frost.

PREPARING AND USING
Many people enjoy making dill pickles from their own homegrown cucumbers and dill. Dried dill leaves and seeds also can be used as flavoring for countless soups, stews, and other recipes.

COMMON PROBLEMS
Free of most problems but may suffer from leaf spot and root diseases

ALL ABOUT EGGPLANT

Eggplant is an attractive plant with fruit that comes in a wide variety of colors and shapes; most types yield a rather large, egg-shaped fruit that is black to purple. However, some of the newer varieties are yellow, brown, or white and smaller and rounder. Eggplant yields a very large harvest and is used in many different styles of cooking. It is easily grown but takes a long time to mature—so you need to start plants indoors in early spring or buy transplants locally.

STARTING
- **Location:** Full sun and lots of heat; pick your sunniest spot for eggplant.
- **Seeds Indoors:** Sprouts in 12 days at 70°F but only requires 6 days at 85°F; it won't sprout below 65°F. Sprinkle 5 to 10 seeds ¼ inch deep in a cup filled with vermiculite 7 weeks before your last spring frost. Keep warm (at least 70°F) until sprouted, move to full sunlight as soon as first
  shoots appear, then pot up in seedling trays as soon as plants are large enough (usually 1 to 3 weeks). Keep a careful watch over the plants, especially after transplanting them into seedling trays, because any pause or stoppage of the growth will affect the ultimate bearing capacity of the plant.
- **Transplanting:** Plant into the garden 2 weeks after the last spring frost, disturbing the roots as little as possible. Water and cover with a shade cage. Because eggplant is so vulnerable to cold weather, cover the wire cage with a clear plastic cover as well as a sun shade to provide a greenhouse atmosphere if it is at all chilly. In a few days, the sun shade can be removed.
- **Seeds Outdoors:** Not satisfactory, as the season is too short before hot weather arrives.

EGGPLANT

BOTANICAL INFORMATION	
Latin Name: *Solanum melongena*	**Seed to Harvest/Flower:** 19 weeks
Height: 24 to 30"	**Seed Storage:** 5 to 6 years
Spacing: 1 per square	**Weeks to Maturity:** 10 weeks
EDIBLE SEASON	**Indoor Seed Starting:** 7 weeks before last spring frost
Summer	**Earliest Outdoor Planting:** 2 weeks after last spring frost
	Additional Plantings: NA
	Last Planting: NA

GROWING
- **Watering:** Eggplant needs constant moisture, especially when fruits are forming and enlarging.
- **Maintenance:** Weed weekly and lay down a thick mulch when hot weather sets in. Provide a wide mesh, open-wire cage support when the eggplant is half grown; the plants will grow right through it and will be supported without staking.

HARVESTING
- **How:** Always cut the fruit from the bush with clippers; watch out for sharp spines on the stems and fruits.
- **When:** Edible almost anytime after the fruit turns dark and glossy (when it's about 6 inches). Don't let them get too large. If they turn a dull color, they are overripe, and the seeds will be large and hard.

PREPARING AND USING
Peel and slice or dice, then stew, fry, stir-fry, or bake; add to casseroles; or bread and fry by itself. Eggplant mixes especially well with tomatoes and onions. If you're not going to use the eggplant right away, don't refrigerate it—instead, store it on the kitchen counter and enjoy its good looks! Handle carefully or the fruit will bruise.

COMMON PROBLEMS
Cutworms, flea beetles; verticillium wilt.

ALL ABOUT FENNEL

Fennel is an herb with a very old history, used by the Egyptians and Chinese for medicinal purposes before being adopted by Europeans during medieval times, when it was thought to ward away evil spirits. Today, its anise-like flavor makes it a favorite for recipes, especially egg and fish dishes.

Fennel has a long taproot that doesn't transplant well, so planting is done by seed. It can be sown directly in the garden as soon as the soil warms in the spring and is an easy grower. It can grow up to 6 feet in height, so it is best to plant it in the back of the garden.

A bulb form of fennel is sown in midsummer for fall harvest.

STARTING
- **Location:** Full sun.
- **Seeds Indoors:** Not recommended.
- **Transplants:** Not recommended.
- **Seeds Outdoors:** Sow directly in the garden as soon as the soil warms in the spring. Moisten the soil well, then sow. Cover the seeds with ⅛ to ½ inch of soil, and keep moist until they sprout. Presoaking the seeds may help them sprout faster; normally it takes 7 to 10 days.

GROWING
- **Watering:** Apply 1 inch of water weekly; more in very dry weather.
- **Maintenance:** Fennel requires little maintenance. You can cut it back early in the season to prompt bushier growth.

FENNEL

BOTANICAL INFORMATION	
Latin Name: *Foeniculum vulgare*	Seed to Harvest/Flower: 6 weeks
Height: 30 to 72"	Seed Storage: 5 to 6 years
Spacing: 1 per square	Weeks to Maturity: 8 to 12 weeks
EDIBLE SEASON	Indoor Seed Starting: NA
Spring, summer, fall	Earliest Outdoor Planting: When soil temps reach 60°F
	Additional Plantings: NA
	Last Planting: NA

HARVESTING
- **How:** Snip green growth with scissors. Seedheads can be harvested and dried.
- **When:** Leaves can be harvested constantly. Bulbs can be harvested in the fall until after frost.

PREPARING AND USING
Enjoy the sweet anise-like flavor of the leaves and seeds in salads, coleslaw, and soups and stews. Bulbs can be sliced for use in salads.

COMMON PROBLEMS
Parsleyworm, slugs; root rot; aphids may appear but rarely seriously harm the plants

ALL ABOUT GARLIC

Garlic is a relative of the onion and, like fennel, has an ancient history. It is very easy to grow and is planted from individual cloves broken off a bulb. It needs well-drained soil and doesn't tolerate a lot of moisture. It is best to avoid planting garlic in the same spot where onion or another garlic plant was grown the year before.

Garlic cloves can be planted early in the spring as soon as the soil can be worked, but it is best to plant them during the fall about 6 to 8 weeks before the ground freezes to develop growth before overwintering in the soil for harvest the next summer.

STARTING
- **Location:** Full sun
- **Seeds Indoors:** NA
- **Transplanting:** NA
- **Seeds Outside:** Cloves are best planted in the fall about 6 to 8 weeks before first frost. Break the bulbs into cloves and push individual cloves 1 to 2 inches into the ground. Water well, and in regions with freezing winters, cover with about 4 inches of protective mulch. Garlic can also be planted in the early spring, using the same techniques; harvest time will be later in the fall.

GROWING
- **Watering:** Keep moist while new leaves are growing. Keep soil mulched to retain moisture. Once leaves stop growing, restrict watering to prevent bulb rot.
- **Maintenance:** Cut off flower stalks if they appear. When new leaves stop appearing, remove the mulch, as the bulbs have now begun to grow.

GARLIC

BOTANICAL INFORMATION	**Seed Storage:** NA
Latin Name: *Allium sativum*	**Weeks to Maturity:** 13 to 34 weeks
Height: 18 to 24"	**Indoor Seed Starting:** NA
Spacing: 9 per square	**Earliest Outdoor Planting:** As soon as soil can be worked; best planted in fall
EDIBLE SEASON Summer, fall	**Additional Plantings:** NA
Seed to Harvest/ Flower: 90 days	**Last Planting:** NA

HARVESTING
- **How:** Dig up bulbs with a garden fork or trowel.
- **When:** Garlic is ready to harvest when all leaves have turned brown and dry, usually in mid-July or August.

PREPARING AND USING
Lay the garlic out to dry for 2 to 3 weeks, then store in a cool, dark place. Garlic cloves have many recipe uses and can be chopped, grated, or used whole in soups, stews, and main dishes.

COMMON PROBLEMS
Fungal problems, root rot, nematodes, mites; problems are usually related to excess soil moisture

ALL ABOUT KALE

Kale has become an enormously popular plant in recent years due to its healthful properties. This member of the cabbage family is a cool-season plant that grows best in the spring and fall. Seeds can be planted outside 3 to 5 weeks before the last frost in the spring for late- spring and early-summer harvest, then again in midsummer for a harvest that will last well through the first frosts of fall. Kale develops a woody taste in hot months, so gardeners often replace it with a warm-season crop in summer and then replant for the fall. Kale will not grow well during most of the year in warmer climates but may be an excellent winter crop there.

STARTING
- **Seeds Indoors:** NA
- **Transplants:** Purchased transplants can be placed in the garden as soon as soil can be worked in the spring; they may need protection from hard frosts but will tolerate light frost. Plant in late summer and early fall for fall harvests.
- **Seeds Outdoors:** Sow seeds 3 to 5 weeks before last frost in spring, or in midsummer for fall harvest. Cover seeds with ¼ inch of soil and keep moist until they sprout.

GROWING
- **Watering:** Keep well watered during dry periods—1 to 1½ inch of water per week.
- **Maintenance:** Control weeds, and avoid disturbing soil around the base of the plants. Mulch around the base to keep the soil cool.

KALE

BOTANICAL INFORMATION
Latin Name: *Brassica oleracea* var. *sabellica*
Height: 10 to 24"
Spacing: 1 per square
EDIBLE SEASON
Spring, Fall

Seed to Harvest/Flower: 6 weeks
Seed Storage: 4 years
Weeks to Maturity: 7 to 9 weeks
Indoor Seed Starting: No
Earliest Outdoor Planting: 3 to 5 weeks before last spring frost
Additional Plantings: Midsummer for fall harvest
Last Planting: Midsummer

HARVESTING
- **How:** Pick or cut off outer leaves, leaving the inner stem to produce new growth.
- **When:** Harvest when leaves are 6 to 8 inches long. The taste will be sweeter after the first frost in fall.

PREPARING AND USING
Refrigerate kale leaves unwashed in a plastic bag, then wash before use. Use kale as a substitute wherever you might use lettuce, cabbage, or other greens. Try making kale chips by tossing the leaves in olive oil and salt, then baking them at a low temperature until crisp—it's a great alternative to potato chips.

COMMON PROBLEMS
Cabbage worms, harlequin bugs, aphids

ALL ABOUT KOHLRABI

Kohlrabi is another member of the cabbage family but a most unusual one. A cool-season vegetable, kohlrabi has a tuberous stem that produces a bulbous section with a flavor similar to broccoli or turnips. The stems are harvested when they are young, up to 3 inches in diameter. After that, the stem becomes tough and bitter. The plant is fast growing, with the stems ready to harvest within only a few weeks of seedlings appearing. Kohlrabi is generally planted early for a late spring harvest, then planted again in the late summer for a fall harvest.

STARTING
- **Location:** At least 6 hours of sun daily.
- **Seeds Indoors:** NA
- **Transplants:** If purchasing transplants, put out in the garden about 4 weeks before the last spring frost. For fall harvest, plant transplants about 6 weeks before the first fall frost.
- **Seeds Outdoors:** Sow in the garden as soon as the danger of frost has passed. Cover seeds with ¼ inch of soil, press the soil firmly, and keep them evenly moist until they sprout, in 14 to 21 days.

GROWING
- **Watering:** Apply about 1 inch of water per week. Avoid overhead watering.
- **Maintenance:** Keep mulched to preserve soil moisture and keep the soil cool. Control weeds.

KOHLRABI

BOTANICAL INFORMATION
Latin Name: *Brassioca oleracea* var. *gongylodes*
Height: 12 to 18"
Spacing: 9 per square
EDIBLE SEASON
Spring and fall

Seed to Harvest/Flower: 4 to 5 weeks
Seed Storage: 3 years
Weeks to Maturity: 6 to 7 weeks
Indoor Seed Starting: NA
Earliest Outdoor Planting: When danger of frost has passed
Additional Plantings: 6 weeks before first fall frost
Last Planting: NA

HARVESTING
- **How:** Pull the plant from ground and cut away the bulbous section for consumption. Leaves can also be cut for use in recipes.
- **When:** Harvest when the bulbous portion of the stem is 1½ to 3 inches in diameter.

PREPARING AND USING
Cut and save the bulbous portions of stems for up to 3 weeks in the refrigerator. The tubers can be sliced raw to be eaten with dips or in salads, similar to radishes. Leaves can be used in recipes in the same way as cabbage or other greens.

COMMON PROBLEMS
Aphids, root maggots, caterpillars; club root and black rot disease are common

ALL ABOUT LEAF LETTUCE

Lettuce is so easy to grow, very gratifying, and extremely well suited for Square Foot Gardening—it grows quickly and prolifically, and it looks great. While it does grow best in the cool seasons and withstands cold weather, it tolerates some heat and can be grown nearly year-round.

There are several types of lettuce: the solid head usually found in grocery stores; the loosehead, or Bibb, a faster growing, and smaller variety of head lettuce; and romaine, or cos, which is a loosehead with a rougher texture than the leaf types. The romaine leaf is composed of many tight, upright leaves and is probably the best pick for home gardeners—but there are also so many great types of leaf and Bibb lettuces that every gardener should try to grow at least four varieties at all times! They do best as a spring or fall crop, but with care and protection, they can be grown in summer and even in winter in many parts of the country. Look for the types that are suitable for summer or winter seasons.

LETTUCE (LEAF)

BOTANICAL INFORMATION
Latin Name: *Latuca sativa*
Height: 6 to 12"
Spacing: 4 per square
EDIBLE SEASON
Spring, fall, and winter

Seed to Harvest/Flower: 7 weeks
Seed Storage: 5 to 6 years
Weeks to Maturity: 4 to 7 weeks
Indoor Seed Starting: 7 weeks before last spring frost
Earliest Outdoor Planting: 4 weeks before last spring frost
Additional Plantings: Every other week
Last Planting: Early summer

STARTING

- **Location:** Full sun to partial shade; lettuce welcomes shade in the hot summer. As with all leafy vegetables, the stronger the light, the higher the vitamin C content will be.
- **Seeds Indoors:** Sprouts in 2 to 3 days at 70°F. Start 5 to 10 seeds of several different varieties in cups filled with vermiculite 7 weeks before your last spring frost date. Keep warm (70°F) until sprouted; move to full sunlight as soon as first shoots appear, then pot up in seedling trays as soon as plants are large enough (usually 1 to 3 weeks).

- **Transplanting:** Move plants into the garden anytime until they are half grown. Plant a new square or two of lettuce every other week until early summer. The hot weather, long days, warm nights, and dry soil of summer cause lettuce to bolt; plant special varieties sold as heat or bolt resistant. After summer is over you can start planting the same varieties you did in the spring.
- **Seeds Outdoors:** Seeds sprout in 5 to 10 days outdoors and grow fairly rapidly; however, this method is time saving but space consuming. If space is your concern, start all seeds indoors or off to the side of the garden and move plants into the garden when they're half grown. Transplants bolt to seed more easily than direct-seeded plants, so plant the summer crop directly in the garden. Plant one or two seeds in each hole; water daily until they sprout.

GROWING
- **Watering:** Try not to wet the leaves, as you may spread fungal diseases. Don't water at night; morning is the best, followed by noon or late afternoon.
- **Maintenance:** Weed weekly; don't let any weeds grow. Lettuce has such a shallow root system that it can't compete with weeds. Provide shade covers for plants in summer.

HARVESTING
- **How:** You can cut individual outer leaves or the entire plant. If you're going to cut outer leaves, you can start when the plant is half grown. This makes a surprisingly large harvest when combined with a few leaves of beet, spinach, and swiss chard. If you take just one leaf from each plant, you can still harvest a lot and hardly notice what has been harvested.

- **When:** Harvest leaf varieties at 7 weeks and Bibb varieties at 9 weeks, or harvest outer leaves from either one when the plant is half grown. You can also cut the entire plant at any time; it doesn't have to grow to full size to be edible. If you wait until all your plants reach full size, you will have to harvest almost all of them at once or they will go to seed.

PREPARING AND USING
Rinse lettuce under cool water, spin or pat dry, and store in the refrigerator in a plastic bag until you're ready to use it. Lettuce will stay fresh and crisp for several days, although it's even better to harvest almost daily for maximum nutritional value. Lettuce contains vitamins A and B, calcium, and iron (especially the dark-green outer leaves).

COMMON PROBLEMS
Slugs, cutworms, sow bugs, wire worms; rabbits, deer, woodchucks; not many diseases to be concerned about unless the lettuce is quite wet at ground level

ALL ABOUT LEEKS

Closely related to onions, leeks have a milder taste. Rather than producing edible bulbs, they store their energy in thick, edible stalks that can be steamed and eaten by themselves or used in soups and stews.

Leeks tolerate frost and in warmer climates can be left in the ground through the winter. In colder climates, they can be planted as soon as the ground can be worked in the spring. Leeks can be started from seed indoors but are more often planted from purchased transplant sets, similar to onions. Leeks have a fairly long growing period, so plant as early as possible for fall harvest.

STARTING
- **Location:** Full sun.
- **Seeds Indoors:** In cold climates, start seeds indoors 8 to 12 weeks before the last spring frost.
- **Transplants:** In early spring, as soon as the soil can be worked, work the seedlings into the soil, 6 to 8 inches deep–up to where the stem begins to turn green.
- **Seeds Outdoors:** Sow in late spring when the danger of frost has passed. Cover with ¼ inch of soil.

GROWING
- **Watering:** Provide about 1 inch of water per week.
- **Maintenance:** As leeks grow, mound soil around the plants so that the white bases remained covered. Soil and grit can become trapped in the leaf folds, and protecting the base of the plant with a cardboard or plastic tube may prevent this.

LEEKS

BOTANICAL INFORMATION
Latin Name: *Allium ampeloprasum porrum*
Height: 24"
Spacing: 9 per square
EDIBLE SEASON
Fall

Seed to Harvest/Flower: 14 weeks
Seed Storage: 2 years
Weeks to Maturity: 14 weeks
Indoor Seed Starting: NA
Earliest Outdoor Planting: As soon as soil can be worked
Additional Plantings: NA
Last Planting: NA

HARVESTING
- **How:** Pull them straight out of the ground if the soil is moist enough. A garden fork may sometimes be necessary.
- **When:** Leeks can be harvested nearly anytime after they stalks are 1 inch or more in diameter.

PREPARING AND USING
Leeks tend to be gritty, so thorough cleaning is essential. This requires that you open the leaves and carefully wash the folds to remove all traces of dirt, or first chop them and then rinse thoroughly with cold water. Leeks are perfect in soup stocks or can be used chopped as an addition to salads and baked recipes.

COMMON PROBLEMS
Slugs are the biggest problem; leeks may also experience leaf rot during wet weather

ALL ABOUT MELONS

All melons need about 3 months of hot weather to grow, but they are a fun and exciting crop. Even though the yield isn't large, when the harvest finally comes, it all seems very worthwhile. Melons should be grown on vertical frames, as they will mature sooner and save space as compared to growing on the ground. Of course, one of the biggest rewards is seeing melons hanging 4 to 5 feet off the ground on your vertical frame—that's not something you're used to seeing in your old single-row gardens!

Although smaller melons, such as cantaloupes and muskmelons, are the most common choices for a Square Foot Garden, the information here will also apply to large watermelons. Make sure, though, that your vertical frame or trellis is strong.

STARTING

- **Location:** Full sun; grow on a vertical frame.
- **Seeds Indoors:** Seeds sprout in 5 to 10 days at 70°F; the hotter the better, even up to 90°F. Plant single seeds in individual paper cups. Melons do not transplant well, so don't start them until 2 weeks before planting outside.
- **Transplanting:** Plant outdoors 2 weeks after the last frost date. Sink the entire cup into the ground after tearing off the bottom.
- **Seeds Outdoors:** Melon seeds won't sprout in soil colder than 65°F; sprouting takes 5 days in 70°F soil. Plant a presoaked seed in each square foot 1 week after last frost. Cover with a plastic-covered cage.

MELONS

BOTANICAL INFORMATION	
Latin Name: *Cucumis melo*	**Seed to Harvest/Flower:** 12 weeks
Height: NA (vine)	**Seed Storage:** 5 to 6 years
Spacing: 1 per 2 squares if trained vertically	**Weeks to Maturity:** 12 weeks
EDIBLE SEASON	**Indoor Seed Starting:** 2 weeks before transplanting
Summer	**Earliest Outdoor Planting:** 2 weeks after last spring frost
	Additional Plantings: NA
	Last Planting: NA

GROWING

- **Watering:** Mulch heavily in hot weather. Reduce water when melons are almost ripe to develop their sweetness. Keep the leaves dry to avoid fungal diseases and mildew.
- **Maintenance:** Weed weekly. Support the half-grown melons in slings and pinch out all new, small melons near the end of the edible season so that all the plant's strength goes into ripening the larger melons that are already set.

HARVESTING

- **How:** Twist the melon with one hand while holding the stem with the other. If it resists parting, the melon is not ripe.
- **When:** Harvest whenever the fruit has a strong melon scent and, if it's a cantaloupe, when the netting pattern on the rind becomes very prominent. The stem will slip off easily when the melon is rotated. If each melon is held in a sling, it won't roll around and accidentally twist itself off when it's ripe.

PREPARING AND USING

Some people like melons served warm; others, chilled. Cut muskmelons or cantaloupes in half, scoop out the seeds, and cut into wedges or serve an entire half filled with ice cream, blueberries, or custard. The flesh of all melons can also be scooped out using a melon baller or cut into cubes and added to a fresh fruit salad. They're excellent for breakfast or served as an after-dinner dessert.

COMMON PROBLEMS

Cutworms; mildew, wilt disease

ALL ABOUT MINT

NOTE: Mint grows very well in a Square Foot Garden; perhaps too well. It is a voracious spreader and can overtake other squares even in one season. You can still grow it, but it is a good idea to line the mint square with landscape fabric to keep the plant from spreading.

Mint has the distinguishing characteristic of square stems. Mint plants come in many flavors, such as spearmint, peppermint, apple, lemon, and chocolate, and they all give off a pleasant aroma when the leaves are crushed. But beware—mint is invasive. It sends out tough runners that grow roots and leaves every few inches and will crop up anywhere it can.

To keep mint plants inbounds, plant it inside a 12-inch clay pot or bucket with holes in the bottom and embed the pot in the Square Foot Garden grid square. This will confine the growth of the plant. Pull the entire pot up in the fall and take it inside as a houseplant.

STARTING
- **Location:** Sun to partial shade.
- **Seeds Indoors:** NA
- **Transplanting:** Plant divisions anytime from spring through fall.
- **Seeds Outdoors:** NA

GROWING
- **Watering:** Water weekly.
- **Maintenance:** Cut back to promote bushiness.

MINT

BOTANICAL INFORMATION	
Latin Name: *Mentha* spp.	**Seed to Harvest/Flower:** NA (perennial)
Height: 1 to 3'	**Seed Storage:** NA
Spacing: 1 per square	**Weeks to Maturity:** NA
EDIBLE SEASON	**Indoor Seed Starting:** NA
Summer	**Earliest Outdoor Planting:** Early spring
	Additional Plantings: Anytime throughout edible season
	Last Planting: NA

HARVESTING
- **How:** Cut mint stems back to a pair of leaves; this is where new branches will form. Use the leaves as flavoring and sprigs as a garnish.
- **When:** Harvest mint anytime after the plant has reached 6 inches tall.

PREPARING AND USING
Use fresh mint leaves in sauces, jelly, salads, or herb teas. Float a sprig of mint in your favorite summer drink, bruising the bottom leaves a little to impart that refreshing flavor. Tuck a sprig of mint into a fruit cup for color and scent.

COMMON PROBLEMS
Basically disease and pest free; plants may wilt and turn brown without sufficient water but should spring right back after a good soaking

ALL ABOUT MUSTARD GREENS

This new favorite is extremely nutritious. A cool-season plant that is perfect for spring and fall, mustard greens can be grown from transplants, but because seeds are so easy to grow, sowing seeds directly in the garden is the preferred method. They grow quickly, with edible greens appearing within 4 weeks of planting, so succession planting of seeds every 3 weeks starting about 3 weeks before first frost date will give you fresh greens from spring up until early or midsummer. Mustard greens do not do well in the heat of midsummer, but fresh seeds can be planted at that time for more greens in the fall.

MUSTARD GREENS

BOTANICAL INFORMATION
Latin Name: *Brassica juncea*
Height: 20 to 24"
Spacing: 1 per square
EDIBLE SEASON
Spring and fall

Seed to Harvest/Flower: 4 weeks
Seed Storage: 4 years
Weeks to Maturity: 7 to 10 weeks
Indoor Seed Starting: NA
Earliest Outdoor Planting: 3 weeks before last frost date
Additional Plantings: Midsummer for fall harvest
Last Planting: Midsummer

STARTING
- **Location:** Mustard greens do best with at least 6 hours of sun, but like many leafy vegetables they will tolerate some shade.
- **Seeds Indoors:** NA
- **Transplants:** Transplant seedlings 3 weeks before first frost date.
- **Seeds Outdoors:** Plant seeds in the garden 3 weeks before first spring frost date. Place seeds just under the surface, covered with about ¼ inch of soil. Plant again 6 weeks before the first fall frost for a fall crop.

GROWING
- **Watering:** Give mustard greens plenty of water—2 inches per week.
- **Maintenance:** Mulch to keep the soil moist, and keep weeded to limit competition for nutrients and water.

HARVESTING
- **How:** Pick or cut individual leaves or pull the entire plant and cut the leaves.
- **When:** Mustard greens are best harvested when the leaves are young and tender, when they're about 6 to 8 inches long—beginning about 4 weeks after seeds are planted. Plants should be pulled and discarded once the leaves become large and bitter.

PREPARING AND USING
Mustard greens can be used in much the same way as kale and collard greens and as a replacement for or addition to any recipes calling for those greens. They have a lively, peppery taste but can get bitter unless picked when the leaves are young. Use them in salads or as an ingredient in any recipe calling for greens. They are delicious when sautéed with soy sauce or sesame oil.

COMMON PROBLEMS
Cabbage loopers, cabbage worms, flea beetles

ALL ABOUT OKRA

Okra is a tall warm-season annual vegetable. It is a pretty plant with large hibiscus-like yellow flowers, heart-shaped leaves, and a thick, woody stem. The edible part is a long, ribbed, fuzzy pod that can be yellow, red, or green. Once the flowers have bloomed, the pods grow very quickly, so check the plant daily for young pods, as these have the best flavor and texture. Okra loves hot weather and may not get a long enough period of heat to grow well in areas with a short edible season, but try it anyway, as it does grow very quickly during the hottest days of summer. You might also look for smaller, short-season varieties.

STARTING
- **Location:** Full sun.
- **Seeds Indoors:** 6 to 8 weeks before the last spring frost. Soak seeds overnight and plant at a depth of 1 inch.
- **Transplanting:** Set seedlings out after the soil has warmed, 7 to 10 days after the last frost.
- **Seeds Outdoors:** Soak seeds overnight, then plant them 1 inch deep, 2 weeks after the last frost and at least 3 months before the first fall frost.

GROWING
- **Watering:** Keep soil fairly moist, and mulch in very hot weather.
- **Maintenance:** Remove old, hard pods from the plant unless you are saving them for seed or dried arrangements.

OKRA

BOTANICAL INFORMATION	
Latin Name: *Abelmoschus esculentus*	**Seed to Harvest/Flower:** 12 weeks
Height: 18 to 24"	**Seed Storage:** 2 years
Spacing: 1 per square	**Weeks to Maturity:** 10 weeks
EDIBLE SEASON Summer	**Indoor Seed Starting:** 6 to 8 weeks before last spring frost
	Earliest Outdoor Planting: After soil has warmed, 7 to 10 days after last frost
	Additional Plantings: NA
	Last Planting: NA

HARVESTING
- **How:** Cut pods from plants with a pruner or knife. Breaking or pulling the pods can damage the plant.
- **When:** Harvest pods daily when they are young—no more than 4 inches long. Older pods can be too tough to eat.

PREPARING AND USING
Okra can be stored in the refrigerator in a paper bag or wrapped in a paper towel in a perforated plastic bag for 2 to 3 days; it may be frozen for up to 12 months after blanching whole for 2 minutes. Cooked okra can be stored in the refrigerator for 3 to 4 days. Okra can be served raw, marinated in salads, or cooked on its own and goes well with tomatoes, onions, corn, peppers, and eggplant. Whole, fresh okra pods also make excellent pickles.

COMMON PROBLEMS
Aphids cabbage worms; verticillium, *Fusarium* wilt

ALL ABOUT ONIONS

The onion is a biennial member of the allium family of bulb plants. They can be planted from seed, from bundles of seedling plants, or from small bulb "sets" (plants that are at the start of their second year of growth). Large table onions are plants that are at the end of their second year of growth, and when this is the desired harvest, they are normally planted from bulb sets in the spring.

Onions planted from seeds or seedling bundles can be harvested when very young, at which point they are known as scallions. There are also specific onion varieties that are sold as scallions and intended to be harvested before they form large bulbs.

Onions are very easy to grow, but they become a little unsightly near the end of the season when the tops turn brown and fall over. This is a good sign, though, because it's the indication they are ready to harvest. Trim off the brown, dead tops to keep the garden looking good.

The size of the bulb is determined by the length of the edible season before the summer solstice (on or around June 21). If you have a short edible season, don't bother with seeds—get the seedling bundles or bulb sets, which look like miniature onions. If you live in a milder climate, though, you could try the seed method.

There are many types of onions, from large, fat ones to small, golfball-sized varieties. Some need to be used soon after harvest, while others are fine for storing. Check the seed-catalog descriptions and pick your favorites.

STARTING
- **Location:** Onions like a sunny spot but will tolerate some shade.
- **Seeds Indoors:** Seeds sprout in 5 days at 70°F. Sprinkle about 20 seeds of each variety desired into cups filled with vermiculite 8 to 12 weeks before your last spring frost. Keep warm (70°F) until sprouted; move to full sunlight as soon as first shoots appear, then pot up in seedling trays as soon as plants are large enough (usually 1 to 3 weeks).
- **Transplanting:** At 4 weeks before the last spring frost, shake most of the vermiculite from your young plants and gather them together in small bunches. With scissors, cut off both the tops and the roots so the plant is balanced with about 2 inches of each. Make a hole at each space in your planting square with a pencil and slip in a plant, firm the soil, and water.
- **Seeds Outdoors:** If the season is not long enough for seeds, use sets. Push the tiny onion sets into the ground, pointed side up at the proper spacing, with their tops just showing above the soil. Water, and that's all there is to it.

GROWING
- **Watering:** Withhold water when the tops start to fall over.
- **Maintenance:** Weed weekly. When bulbs start expanding, use your finger to remove some of the soil around each bulb and partially uncover it; this makes it easier for the bulb to expand.

continued on following page

continued from the previous page

HARVESTING

- **How:** Pull the onions out of the ground and place on chicken wire or a window screen laid out in the sun for several days. The tops, roots, and outer skin of each onion will then dry thoroughly. Brush them off and clean off any loose skins, dried tops, or roots by rubbing them between your palms, then store for later use. Any onions with green or thick tops should not be stored but used immediately.

- **When:** About the middle of the summer, you'll see the tops of the onion foliage turning brown and falling over. When the majority of the leaves have fallen, bend over the remaining ones with your hand. In a short while, the tops will dry up while the bulbs attain their maximum size.

ONIONS

BOTANICAL INFORMATION
Latin Name: *Allium cepa*
Height: 12"
Spacing: 9 to 16 per square depending on variety
EDIBLE SEASON
Summer and fall
Seed to Harvest/

Flower: 20 weeks
Seed Storage: 1 to 2 years
Weeks to Maturity: 14 weeks
Indoor Seed Starting: 8 to 12 weeks before last spring frost
Earliest Outdoor Planting: 4 weeks before last spring frost
Additional Plantings: NA
Last Planting: NA

PREPARING AND USING

You'll find homegrown onions much milder and sweeter than store-bought ones. This makes them more useful, especially for those folks who must be careful not to eat too many onions. For a real treat, try an onion sandwich—thin slices of onion and lots of pepper on your favorite bread. Or add fresh, crisp cucumber slices to the sandwich for a delightful combination. Hang dried onions in a mesh bag or braid the tops together and hang in a cool, dry area for storage all winter.

COMMON PROBLEMS

Onion-fly maggots; onions are resistant to most diseases

ALL ABOUT OREGANO

What would Italian food be without a sprinkling of oregano to give it flavor and color? Oregano is a native of the Mediterranean area and enjoys lots of sunshine. It is a pretty plant with round leaves tightly covering the stems. Variegated oregano is particularly lovely with the leaves edged in white or gold, but the variegated plants are not quite as hardy as the green ones and are used mostly as ornamental plants. Give oregano frequent trimmings to keep it neat and so you can dry the leaves. It is one of few herbs whose flavor is stronger dried than fresh. When the leaves have dried, crumble them lightly and store in an airtight container.

STARTING
- **Location:** Full sun.
- **Seeds Indoors:** Start seeds indoors 4 to 6 weeks before the last spring frost.
- **Transplanting:** Plant divisions anytime after the temperatures reach 45°F.
- **Seeds Outdoors:** Plant outdoors in spring, after the last frost; seeds need light to germinate.

GROWING
- **Watering:** Water weekly, but sparingly; too much water will cause root rot.
- **Maintenance:** Harvest or trim mature plants often to keep them inbounds. Divide every 2 to 3 years.

OREGANO

BOTANICAL INFORMATION
Latin Name: *Origanum vulgare*
Height: 1 to 2'
Spacing: 1 per square
EDIBLE SEASON
Spring, summer, and fall

Seed to Harvest/Flower: 16 weeks; this is a hardy perennial
Seed Storage: NA
Weeks to Maturity: 8 to 10 weeks
Indoor Seed Starting: 6 weeks before last spring frost
Earliest Outdoor Planting: After last frost
Additional Plantings: Anytime throughout edible season
Last Planting: NA

HARVESTING
- **How:** Cut stems back to a pair of leaves; this is where new branches will form.
- **When:** Oregano can be harvested anytime during the summer months, but the flavor is best after the buds have formed but just before the flowers open.

PREPARING AND USING
Oregano loses its distinctive flavor during cooking, so always add it in the last few minutes. Use oregano in salads, casseroles, soups, sauces, poultry dishes, and, of course, pizza. Dried oregano has a stronger flavor than fresh and goes especially well with tomato or rice dishes.

COMMON PROBLEMS
Oregano is usually pest and disease free; too much water can cause root rot

ALL ABOUT PARSLEY

Parsley is a wonderful herb that looks great in the garden, yields a big, continuous harvest, is extremely nutritious, and doesn't need a great deal of care. Pests don't seem to bother this member of the carrot family, and it is disease resistant too. All in all, parsley is a very easy addition to your Square Foot Garden. There are many varieties, but they can be divided into two basic kinds: flat-leaved parsley and curly parsley. It's said the flat-leaf varieties taste better, but the curly-leaf types are better looking and more commonly grown.

STARTING
- **Location:** Full sun to partial shade.
- **Seeds Indoors:** Sprouts in 10 to 15 days at 70°F. Seeds are very slow to germinate and should be soaked in lukewarm water for 24 hours before planting. Sprinkle 10 presoaked seeds in a cup filled with vermiculite 12 weeks before the last spring frost. Keep warm (70°F) until sprouted; move to full sunlight as soon as first shoots appear, then pot up in seedling trays as soon as plants are large enough (usually 1 to 3 weeks).
- **Transplanting:** Move outdoors 5 weeks before the last spring frost or anytime once plants are large enough; plant them at the same depth they grew in the pot.
- **Seeds Outdoors:** It is better to start parsley indoors because seeds are slow and difficult to germinate.

GROWING
- **Watering:** Never let parsley dry out completely because it becomes tough and bitter and may bolt to seed in the first year.

PARSLEY

BOTANICAL INFORMATION	
Latin Name: *Petroselinum crispum*	**Seed to Harvest/Flower:** 14 week
Height: 6 to 12"	**Seed Storage:** 2 to 3 years
Spacing: 4 per square	**Weeks to Maturity:** 7 weeks
EDIBLE SEASON	**Indoor Seed Starting:** 12 weeks before last spring frost
Year-round	**Earliest Outdoor Planting:** 5 weeks before last spring frost
	Additional Plantings: NA
	Last Planting: NA

- **Maintenance:** Weed weekly. Mulch heavily for continual harvest in winter and for early-spring growing the following year.

HARVESTING
- **How:** Cut outer leaves as needed; for a large harvest, cut off the entire plant slightly above the tiny middle shoots. Either way, the plant will continue to grow with no harm.
- **When:** Harvest as soon as the plant gets to be 3 to 4 inches tall and anytime thereafter.

PREPARING AND USING
Parsley is good in soups, casseroles, and stews and with fish or any kind of meat; it's also excellent over steamed vegetables, particularly potatoes. Parsley is loaded with vitamins A and C. Cut up leaves with scissors and sprinkle on food for that decorative gourmet-chef look!

COMMON PROBLEMS
Relatively free from pests and diseases

ALL ABOUT PARSNIPS

Parsnips are regarded as a little difficult to start from seed, but they are quite sturdy and easy to tend once they get established. They will do best if you wait to sow in the garden until the soil is at least 54°F—and even then, don't be surprised if they take 3 or 4 weeks to germinate and poke up. Parsnips have quite a long root, up to 12 inches, so this may be best suited to an extra-deep Square Foot Garden box.

Parsnips will have the best flavor when harvested after a light frost; this is a vegetable that will occupy a grid square from spring until late fall.

Parsnips can be roasted, sautéed, or mashed and have a taste similar to carrots, though less sweet. Unlike most vegetables, whose leftover seeds can be stored at least 2 or 3 years, parsnips really require fresh seeds for each planting.

STARTING
- **Location:** Full sun.
- **Seeds Indoors:** NA
- **Transplants:** Parsnips are not normally planted from transplant.
- **Seeds Outdoors:** Cover with ½ inch of soil, and be patient; seeds may take a full 4 weeks to sprout. Space about 6 inches apart, or 4 per grid square. Because they are slow growing, parsnips are sometimes planted with fast-growing radishes around them.

PARSNIPS

BOTANICAL INFORMATION	
Latin Name: *Pastinaca sativa*	**Seed to Harvest/Flower:** 15 to 17 weeks
Height: 10 to 15"	**Seed Storage:** NA
Spacing: 4 per square	**Weeks to Maturity:** 14 weeks
EDIBLE SEASON	**Indoor Seed Starting:** NA
Plant in spring for fall harvest	**Earliest Outdoor Planting:** After last frost in spring
	Additional Plantings: NA
	Last Planting: NA

GROWING
- **Watering:** Parsnips need about 1 inch of water weekly; watch carefully to make sure they are getting enough water during dry spells.
- **Maintenance:** Keep weeds under control, and be careful not to disturb roots while tending the plants. Mulch can be used to keep weeds from sprouting.

HARVESTING
- **How:** Pull or dig entire the root out of the soil.
- **When:** Parsnips can be harvested as soon as aboveground foliage begins to turn brown and dry, but they will be sweetest if harvested after the first light frost.

PREPARING AND USING
Parsnips can used in much the same way as carrots—roasted, steamed, sautéed, or mashed.

COMMON PROBLEMS
Aphids, leaf miners, carrot rust flies

ALL ABOUT PEAS (SUGAR SNAP)

PEAS

BOTANICAL INFORMATION	
Latin Name: *Pisum sativum*	**Seed to Harvest/Flower:** 10 weeks
Height: NA (vine)	**Seed Storage:** 3 to 4 years
Spacing: 8 per square	**Weeks to Maturity:** 10 weeks
EDIBLE SEASON	**Indoor Seed Starting:** no
Spring (pods) and fall (peas)	**Earliest Outdoor Planting:** 5 weeks before last spring frost
	Additional Plantings: NA
	Last Planting: NA

Fresh peas are a family favorite, but until the advent of sugar snap peas, it was hard to grow enough for much more than a few meals—peas used to take time, space, and effort to harvest, not to mention the shelling. Even when you're all finished, it didn't seem to add up to much!

The sugar snap peas, or edible-pod varieties, have changed all of that. They are extremely high yielding, and you can eat the entire pod, either raw or cooked. They produce about five times the harvest of conventional peas. Sugar snap peas are juicy, sweet, crisp, and absolutely wonderful.

STARTING
- **Location:** Full sun in spring, shaded toward summer if possible.
- **Seeds Indoors:** NA
- **Transplanting:** Does not transplant well.
- **Seeds Outdoors:** Sprouts in 10 to 15 days outdoors. Mix presoaked seeds with legume inoculant powder for an added boost, then plant 1 inch deep about 5 weeks before the last spring frost. Water and cover with a plastic-covered tunnel.

GROWING
- **Watering:** Never let the peas dry out.
- **Maintenance:** Weed weekly, keep water off the vines, and mulch as the weather gets warm. Keep the vines trained up the vertical frame.

HARVESTING
- **How:** Using two hands, carefully pick or cut pods off their stems.
- **When:** The beauty of these peas is that you can eat them at any stage of growth. They're just as tasty (raw or cooked) whether their pods are fully mature and bulging with peas or still thin and barely starting to show the peas inside. If the pods start to lose their nice pea-green color and turn brown on the vine, they are overripe. Pick them immediately and add them to the compost pile, because if you don't harvest them, they will cause the vine to stop producing new peas.

PREPARING AND USING
Just wash, and your peas are ready to cook or eat as-is. Try to use them when they're as fresh as possible; store what you can't use right away in the refrigerator. Sugar snaps are rich in vitamins A, B1, and C and contain phosphorus and iron. As the pods get close to full size, some develop a string along each edge, but it's easy to remove: just snap off the stem end and pull down, and both strings will easily peel off. The pod is still very crisp and tasty even at full size.

The versatility of these tasty peas stretches the imagination. Try them raw in salads, with a dip, plain, or mixed with other fresh vegetables in vinegar or dressing . . . or cook them by steaming or stir-frying.

COMMON PROBLEMS
No pests to speak of, but peas are sometimes prone to powdery mildew, especially during warm weather when the leaves get wet

ALL ABOUT PEPPERS

Most gardeners love to grow peppers; they're easy to grow, they're pest and disease free, and they produce a lot for the space allotted. You can buy transplants locally or start seeds yourself. They look great in the garden, and some people grow several types for their ornamental virtues. If all you've grown are green bell peppers, give the sweet yellow banana varieties a try. Peppers come in several different shapes, from the bell varieties to the skinny, curved hot chili peppers. They range in color from green and red to orange and yellow.

PEPPERS

BOTANICAL INFORMATION
Latin Name: *Capsicum* spp.
Height: 12 to 24"
Spacing: 1 per square
EDIBLE SEASON
Summer

Seed to Harvest/Flower: 19 weeks
Seed Storage: 4 to 5 years
Weeks to Maturity: 10 weeks
Indoor Seed Starting: 7 weeks before last spring frost
Earliest Outdoor Planting: 2 weeks after last spring frost
Additional Plantings: NA
Last Planting: NA

STARTING
- **Location:** Full sun.
- **Seeds Indoors:** Seed sprouts in 10 to 15 days at 70°F. Sprinkle 5 to 10 seeds in a cup of vermiculite approximately 7 weeks before the last spring frost and cover with ¼ inch more vermiculite. Keep warm (70°F) until sprouted; move to full sunlight as soon as first shoots appear, then pot up in seedling trays as soon as plants are large enough (usually 1 to 3 weeks).
- **Transplanting:** Peppers need warm soil, so don't transplant until 2 weeks after the last spring frost.
- **Seeds Outdoors:** The season is too short to start outdoors except in the warmest climates.

GROWING
- **Watering:** Don't wet the leaves; this causes fungal and wilt infections.
- **Maintenance:** Weed weekly, mulch in hot weather, and cover half-grown plants with an open-mesh wire cage to support plants without staking. The stems and branches of pepper plants are brittle and break easily, so work carefully among them when harvesting.

HARVESTING
- **How:** Carefully cut the fruit from the bush (don't pull or you'll accidentally break other branches). Leave about 1 inch of stem on each pepper for a longer storage life.
- **When:** Harvest at almost any stage of development–as soon as they are big enough for your use. You can leave them on the vine and they will turn red or yellow once they are full grown. Bell peppers can still be eaten when red or yellow; in fact, many people prefer them, as their taste becomes sweeter and less spicy when they lose their green color. Of course, the hot chili peppers should turn color before you use them.

PREPARING AND USING
Use peppers raw or cooked. They are excellent as a salad or casserole garnish. Cut them into strips, cubes, or thin slices as you would a tomato. Peppers stuffed with a meat, rice, or vegetable mixture and then baked make a great summer supper. Peppers are high in vitamins A and C.

COMMON PROBLEMS
Cutworms, flea beetles; no diseases to speak of except an occasional wilt or fungus problem

ALL ABOUT POTATOES

POTATOES

BOTANICAL INFORMATION	
Latin Name: *Solanum tuberosum*	**Seed Storage:** NA; plant from last year's potatoes
Height: 12 to 24"	**Weeks to Maturity:** 12 weeks
Spacing: 4 per square	**Indoor Seed Starting:** NA
EDIBLE SEASON Spring through fall	**Earliest Outdoor Planting:** In spring when soil has reached 45°F
Seed to Harvest/ Flower: 12 weeks	**Additional Plantings:** Late spring for a second crop to store over the winter
	Last Planting: Late spring

Potatoes are perhaps the most common vegetable of all, but growing your own potatoes is the best way to sample the large variety of potato shapes, sizes, and colors. Harvest them early for small, tasty nuggets or dig them up later for large tubers to store over the winter. The potato plant itself is bushy and pretty, doing double duty as an ornamental and an edible. The white flowers are the indicator that the small, new potatoes are ready to harvest out of the ground and onto the table.

Potatoes will grow in a standard 6-inch-deep box, but for best results, plant them in an extra-deep garden box to give the roots plenty of room.

STARTING
- **Location:** Full sun.
- **Seeds Indoors:** NA
- **Transplanting:** NA
- **Planting Outdoors:** Plant in the spring when the soil has reached 45°F. Use only certified disease-free seed potatoes. Don't plant seeds; 1 week before planting time, cut up potatoes into small pieces and place them in a tray where they will receive light (not sun) and temperatures of about 65°F. A day or two before planting, cut potatoes into "seed pieces" about 1½ inch square with at least one "sprouted eye" per section. Remove about 5 inches of your soil in that square foot, place four seed pieces at the proper spacing with eyes up, and just barely cover them. When sprouts appear, add enough Mel's Mix to again cover the green leafy sprouts. Keep doing this until the hole is filled back to the top

GROWING
- **Watering:** Increase watering during flowering.
- **Maintenance:** Protect from frost.

HARVESTING
- **How:** Gently loosen the soil around early potatoes and remove the largest tubers, leaving the smaller ones to continue growing. For later potatoes, gently dig outside the plant and remove the potatoes as you find them. Take care not to stab or cut the potatoes as you dig. If the weather is dry, leave the potatoes on top of the soil for 2 to 3 days to dry. If the weather is wet, bring the potatoes into a garage or basement to dry. This will toughen the skin for storage. Store potatoes in a cool (40°F), dark location for 3 to 6 months. Do not store potatoes near apples, which give off a chemical that will damage the potatoes.
- **When:** Small early potatoes can be harvested as needed in early summer after the plants finish flowering. Later potatoes can be left in the soil until 2 to 3 weeks after the foliage has died back in fall and lifted all at once for storing.

PREPARING AND USING
Potatoes can be boiled, fried, steamed, grilled, or baked. All potatoes should be cooked or placed in water immediately after peeling to prevent discoloration. To peel or not to peel is generally a question of your preparation method or personal preference. The exception is thin-skinned new potatoes, which should not be peeled.

New potatoes are moist and waxy and are best for steaming and boiling. Oblong, mature white potatoes are the most popular type to use for french fries, and they are also great for baking and mashing. Round red potatoes have a rather waxy texture, meaning they too are ideal for boiling and mashing. Round white potatoes are thin skinned and hold their shape in salads as well as through boiling and roasting. Yellow-fleshed potatoes are good for steaming, roasting, and mashing.

COMMON PROBLEMS
Flea beetles, leaf hoppers, slugs; blight, scab, root-knot nematode; tubers exposed to sunlight while growing will turn green and are mildly toxic

ALL ABOUT PUMPKINS AND WINTER SQUASH

PUMPKINS & WINTER SQUASH

BOTANICAL INFORMATION
Latin Name: *Cucurbita* spp. (pumpkins are *Curcurbita pepo*)
Height: NA (vine)
Spacing: 1 per 2 square feet when trained vertically

EDIBLE SEASON
Summer to fall

Seed to Harvest/Flower: 12 weeks
Seed Storage: 5 to 6 years
Weeks to Maturity: 12 weeks
Indoor Seed Starting: NA
Earliest Outdoor Planting: 2 weeks after last spring frost
Additional Plantings: NA
Last Planting: NA

The term "winter squash" is applied to those types of squash that keep well into the winter months after harvesting in the fall. Among the most recognized is the pumpkin used for Halloween decoration, but the group also includes acorn squash, hubbard squash, and butternut squash.

All winter squash have thick skins that harden in the fall, and they are generally picked after the vines have been killed by frost. These are space hogs in a Square Foot Garden, so many gardeners train them up a vertical trellis (yes, even pumpkins) or grow them on outside grid squares and allow the rambling vines to explore surrounding territory.

STARTING
- **Location:** Full sun is preferable, but squash tolerates a little shade.
- **Seeds Indoors:** NA
- **Transplanting:** Does not transplant well because of long taproot.
- **Seeds Outdoors:** This is the best method because seeds sprout quickly. Plant two presoaked seeds in the center of a double grid space (2 square feet), leaving a 2-inch depression around the seeds to hold water. Cover the bed with a plastic-covered cage to warm the soil and hasten sprouting. Cut off the weakest plant if both seeds sprout.

GROWING
- **Watering:** Keep soil moist.
- **Maintenance:** Weed weekly; keep vines trained up a vertical trellis or frame.

HARVESTING
- **How:** Cut the pumpkin or squash from the vine, leaving as long a stem as possible—at least 2 inches. Then, set the fruit out in the sun to cure for a few days, protecting it against nighttime frost.
- **When:** Harvest after the first light frost (which kills the leaves and vines) but before a hard frost.

PREPARING AND USING
Peel, cut in half, scoop out seeds, and prepare for steaming, roasting, or baking. Excellent served mashed or in chunks with butter and parsley. Store winter squash in a cool, dry place (40°F to 50°F).

COMMON PROBLEMS
A few beetles; powdery mildew

ALL ABOUT RADISHES

Radishes are a great crop for all gardeners, whether you're an expert or a beginner. They come in a multitude of shapes, from small and round to long, carrot-like shapes. They vary in color, including red, pink, white, and even some black varieties. Radishes planted in the spring are normally red or white and will mature in 3 to 4 weeks. Fall radishes take 6 to 8 weeks and store very well; they're referred to as winter radishes.

It's easy to plant too many radishes. Decide how many you can use each week and then plant no more than double that number every other week for a continuous, but controlled, harvest.

STARTING
- **Location:** Full sun to partial shade.
- **Seeds Indoors:** NA
- **Transplanting:** Radishes do not transplant well.
- **Seeds Outdoors:** Seeds sprout in 5 to 10 days outdoors depending on temperature. Plant a grid square every other week for a staggered but continuous harvest. Plant ½ inch deep in spring, 1 inch deep in summer. If you really like radishes a lot, plant some every week of the growing year, even through the hot weather. The plants will still do fairly well then if you give them some shade, lots of water, and a thick mulch. Winter and long-keeping varieties need 2 months to mature, so start them at least that long before the first fall frost.

GROWING
- **Watering:** Don't let plants stop growing or dry out; lack of water causes hot-tasting and pithy radishes.
- **Maintenance:** Weed weekly, and mulch in hot weather. Keep covered with a screen-covered cage if root maggots are a problem.

RADISHES

BOTANICAL INFORMATION	
Latin Name: *Raphanus raphanisturm* subsp. *sativus*	**Seed to Harvest/Flower:** 4 weeks
Height: 6 to 12"	**Seed Storage:** 5 to 6 years
Spacing: 16 per square	**Weeks to Maturity:** 3 weeks
EDIBLE SEASON Spring through fall	**Indoor Seed Starting:** NA
	Earliest Outdoor Planting: 3 weeks before last spring frost
	Additional Plantings: Every other week
	Last Planting: 4 weeks before first fall frost

HARVESTING
- **How:** Pull up the entire plant and trim off the top. Refrigerate the edible portions if they're not used immediately.
- **When:** Harvest anytime when radishes are between the size of a marble and that of a Ping-Pong ball—the smaller they are when you pull them, the sweeter they taste. The long fall varieties can be left in the ground until frost, then either mulched to keep the ground from freezing or pulled and stored in damp peat moss or sand after the tops are removed.

PREPARING AND USING
Slice, dice, or cut into fancy shapes for eating out of hand, add to salads, or use as garnish. If you have too many all at once, twist or cut off the tops and store in a plastic bag in the refrigerator. Radishes will keep for up to 1 week before getting soft.

COMMON PROBLEMS
None to speak of, except possibly root maggots

ALL ABOUT SPINACH

Spinach is somewhat difficult to grow but very popular. It usually does well if it stays cool in the spring. A rapid grower, it can be grown in a fairly small space and looks great in the garden. It will quickly bolt to seed in the summer heat but grows very well in the early spring and then again in the fall. Spinach is very cold hardy, and in many areas of the country it will winter over; in warmer climates, it can be grown all winter.

There are two types of spinach—the smooth-leaved kind and a crinkly-leaf type called savoy, which is more popular and more attractive. Neither will endure heat, so both should be grown in cool weather. Some varieties are more resistant to frost than others and are particularly adaptable for growing in the fall and possibly into the winter season. Check your seed catalog for appropriate varieties.

STARTING

- **Location:** Any location in full sun to partial shade is suitable.
- **Seeds Indoors:** NA
- **Transplanting:** Does not transplant well.
- **Seeds Outdoors:** Spinach sprouts outdoors in 1 to 2 weeks. Plant seeds ½ inch deep, water, and cover with a plastic-covered cage. Plants can withstand any temperature between 25°F and 75°F, so judge your spring and fall planting accordingly.

GROWING

- **Watering:** Being a leaf crop, spinach needs constant moist soil.
- **Maintenance:** Weed weekly; mulch in warm weather. Don't work in the spinach square if the leaves are very wet–they are brittle and break easily.

SPINACH

BOTANICAL INFORMATION	
Latin Name: *Spinacia oleracea*	**Seed to Harvest/Flower:** 7 weeks
Height: 6 to 12"	**Seed Storage:** 5 to 6 years
Spacing: 9 per square	**Weeks to Maturity:** 7 weeks
EDIBLE SEASON	**Indoor Seed Starting:** NA
Spring and fall; winter in some climates.	**Earliest Outdoor Planting:** 5 weeks before last spring frost
	Additional Plantings: Every 2 weeks until late spring
	Last Planting: 8 weeks before first fall frost

HARVESTING

- **How:** Cut outer leaves as needed; small inner leaves will continue to grow rapidly.
- **When:** Harvest as soon as the plants look like they won't miss an outer leaf or two. Keep picking and the plant will keep growing right up until hot weather. If it's a spring crop and you think the plants are going to bolt soon, cut off the entire plant for a little extra harvest.

PREPARING AND USING

Wash carefully; soil tends to cling to the undersides, especially on varieties with crinkled leaves. Spin or pat dry and store in the refrigerator just like lettuce. Better yet, eat spinach right away. Serve fresh in salads, cook slightly for a wilted-spinach salad, or steam lightly. Spinach goes great with any meal, especially when garnished with a chopped hard-boiled egg. It's high in vitamins A, B1, and C and is a valuable source of iron.

COMMON PROBLEMS

Leaf miner insects, flea beetles; white rust, downy mildew

ALL ABOUT STRAWBERRIES

Growing your own strawberries is fun and rewarding. Because strawberries are so popular, most families like to plant an entire 4 × 4 box with them—it's easy to protect and harvest. You might also like to build a pyramid box and plant it in all strawberries. Strawberry plants bear fruit for at least 3 or 4 years, then yields will decrease, and eventually the plant will die. Each plant sends out runners that produce new plants, which can be used as the next generation of strawberries in the garden. However, cutting away the runners will keep the energy fueling the parent plant.

There are three main types of strawberries:

- June bearing, which sets fruit in June
- Ever bearing, which sets fruit twice during the edible season
- Day neutral, which is not affected by the length of the day as the others are

And don't overlook the alpine strawberry, which will reward you with tiny but incredibly tasty fruit over a long period!

STARTING

- **Location:** Full sun.
- **Seeds Indoors:** NA
- **Transplanting:** Transplant in early spring as soon as the soil is no longer frozen. Be sure the soil is not wet. Most gardeners buy strawberry plants in packets of a dozen or so. Soak first, then trim off the roots slightly, and plant 4 per square foot. Leave a saucer-shaped depression around each plant for effective watering.
- **Seeds Outdoors:** NA

GROWING

- **Watering:** Water weekly; more during dry periods. Keep the soil moist, and increase water when strawberries are fruiting.
- **Maintenance:** Cut off all the runners as soon as you see them; that way, all the energy will stay in the parent plant for an increased harvest each year. After 3 or 4 years,

STRAWBERRIES

BOTANICAL INFORMATION	
Latin Name: *Fragaria × ananassa*	**Seed to Harvest/Flower:** NA
Height: 6 to 12"	**Seed Storage:** NA
Spacing: 4 per square	**Weeks to Maturity:** NA
EDIBLE SEASON	**Indoor Seed Starting:** NA
Spring, fall	**Earliest Outdoor Planting:** 4 weeks before last spring frost
	Additional Plantings: NA
	Last Planting: NA

when the harvest starts to diminish, it is best to pull out those plants and replant, perhaps in a different square with brand-new certified disease-free plants from the nursery. It's true that those runners will produce baby plants and it seems a waste not to use them; some people like to let them grow. However, the problem comes from too many runners producing too many baby plants (because the gardener forgets to cut them off); they take all the energy from the parent, reducing the harvest. Cover plants with bird netting to preserve the harvest.

HARVESTING

- **How:** Pick the fruit, leaving a short piece of stem attached; use scissors for a clean cut.
- **When:** Harvest as fruit ripens, for 2 to 3 weeks.

PREPARING AND USING

Use strawberries as soon as possible after picking; pop a few right in your mouth. They can be used in fruit salads, on cakes, and in pies. Freeze whole strawberries for use in smoothies—they will be soft when they defrost and still flavorful.

COMMON PROBLEMS

Slugs; birds; *Verticillium* wilt

ALL ABOUT SUMMER SQUASH AND ZUCCHINI

Summer squash refers to the type of squash that ripens in summer and must be eaten quickly because it does not keep well. (By contrast, see the entry for winter squash on page 247.) The most popular summer squash is the prolific zucchini, although there are several other types:

• **Yellow squash** are buttery yellow and elongated; some types have crooked necks. Overripe fruits turn into warted gourds.

• **Pattypan squash** are an old type of summer squash that produces fruits shaped like plump flying saucers with scalloped edges. Varieties range from dark green to bright yellow to white.

• **Zucchetta squash** produce large, curvaceous fruits with light-green skins. Naturally resistant to insect pests, these rowdy vining plants grow best on a trellis.

Summer squash need a lot of room to grow and hot weather to do well, but they are unbelievably prolific and easy and fast to grow. There are many colors and shapes—round, straight, crookneck, and flat—each with its particular taste.

Most of the varieties sold are the bush types (especially zucchini), so you'll have to assign a larger space to just one plant—a 3 × 3 area rather than a single square foot. However, these plants can produce a vast amount of fruit, so most gardeners think it's worthwhile, at least for one or two plants.

An alternative solution is to grow the vining types on vertical frames, which is quite a space saver. (Zucchini can be trained to grow vertically, but it still takes a lot of room because of those huge leaves and prickly stems.) Check the seed packet or catalog to make sure you are getting a vine type; if the seed packet or catalog doesn't say so, call the seed company's toll-free number and ask.

STARTING

• **Location:** Full sun.
• **Seeds Indoors:** Squash doesn't transplant well because of the long taproot, so it's best to start seeds outdoors. If you do want to start indoors, plant one seed in a paper cup of Mel's Mix 1 inch deep. Plant 2 weeks before your last frost date.
• **Transplanting:** Plant outdoors on your last spring frost date.
• **Seeds Outdoors:** Seeds sprout in 5 to 10 days outdoors. For bush types, plant two presoaked seeds in the center space of a nine-square grid. For vine types, plant two presoaked seeds in the middle of a 2-square-foot space under your vertical frame. Make sure you hollow out a dish shape around the planted seeds to hold plenty of water. Place a plastic-covered cage over the seeds to warm the soil. After sprouting, cut off the weakest plant if both seeds sprout.

continued on following page

continued from the previous page

GROWING

- **Watering:** Keep the leaves dry to prevent powdery mildew.
- **Maintenance:** Weed weekly; keep vines trained up vertical frames or within the bounds of the square.

HARVESTING

- **How:** Carefully cut through the fruit stem, but do not cut the main vine or leaf stems. Handle the squash gently, as their skins are very soft and easily damaged if scratched by fingernails or dropped.
- **When:** You can harvest as soon as the blossoms wilt and as late as when the fruits are 6 to 9 inches long. Don't let them grow any longer. Sometimes you have to harvest at least three times a week; they grow that fast. Squash loses flavor as the seeds inside mature.

SUMMER SQUASH AND ZUCCHINI

BOTANICAL INFORMATION
Latin Name: *Cucurbita pepo* (zucchini is *Cucurbita pepo* var. *cylindrica*)
Height: 30" (bush) or vine
Spacing: 1 per 9 square feet (bush); 1 per 2 square feet (vine)

EDIBLE SEASON
Summer

Seed to Harvest/Flower: 8 weeks
Seed Storage: 5 to 6 years
Weeks to Maturity: 6 to 8 weeks
Indoor Seed Starting: 2 weeks before last spring frost
Earliest Outdoor Planting: Immediately following last spring frost
Additional Plantings: NA
Last Planting: NA

PREPARING AND USING

Rinse lightly and serve sliced or cut into sticks, with a dip, or just as an appetizer anytime. Cook lightly by steaming or stir-frying and use in any number of dishes or combinations. Serve squash by itself or with other vegetables, seasoned with a little dressing, grated cheese, or chopped parsley. Squash is high in vitamins A, B1, and C.

COMMON PROBLEMS

Squash vine borer, squash bug; powdery mildew

ALL ABOUT SWISS CHARD

SWISS CHARD

BOTANICAL INFORMATION
Latin Name: *Beta vulgaris* subsp. *vulgaris*
Height: 12 to 18"
Spacing: 4 per square
EDIBLE SEASON
Spring through winter

Seed to Harvest/Flower: 8 weeks
Seed Storage: 4 to 5 years
Weeks to Maturity: 8 weeks
Indoor Seed Starting: 7 weeks before last spring frost
Earliest Outdoor Planting: 3 weeks before last spring frost
Additional Plantings: NA
Last Planting: NA

Swiss chard is known best for its vitamin-rich leaves and its succulent stems. It is essentially a beet plant that does not form a bulbous root. It's one of the easiest vegetables to grow in any part of the country—it can grow in the sun or shade all spring, summer, and fall for a continuous harvest. In most climates, it can even be carried over the winter. Chard is available in white- or red-stemmed varieties and is also available in many rainbow colors. It can have either smooth or crinkled leaves, whichever you like; try both! It is also virtually pest and disease free.

STARTING
- **Location:** Swiss chard does best in full sun but can grow in partial shade.
- **Seeds Indoors:** Plant 10 seeds in a cup of vermiculite, or place one seed ½ inch deep in potting soil in each compartment of a seedling tray, 7 weeks before your last spring frost. Seeds will sprout in 5 to 10 days at 70°F. Keep warm (70°F) until sprouted; move to full sunlight as soon as first shoots appear.
- **Transplanting:** Plant into the garden 3 weeks before the last spring frost. Water and cover with a plastic-covered cage.
- **Seeds Outdoors:** Plant presoaked seeds ½ inch deep in each square 3 weeks before your last spring frost. Seeds sprout outdoors in 2 to 3 weeks. Water and cover with a plastic-covered cage.

GROWING
- **Watering:** Water twice weekly in hot weather. Like all leaf crops, swiss chard needs lots of water for luxurious leaf growth.
- **Maintenance:** Weed weekly and cut off any yellow or overgrown outer leaves.

HARVESTING
- **How:** Carefully cut off each outer stem at the plant base with a sharp knife when the leaves are 6 to 9 inches tall. The smaller inner leaves will continue to grow.
- **When:** Start harvesting when the outer leaves are about 6 to 9 inches tall (approximately 8 weeks after planting seeds), and continue harvesting the outer leaves (stalk and all) every week or so. Don't let outer leaves get too large before harvesting.

PREPARING AND USING
Both the leaves and the stems are edible, and the leaves are very rich in vitamins A and C, calcium, and iron. The stalks can be cooked and served like asparagus; the leaves can be used fresh or cooked and are similar to, but milder in taste than, spinach.

After harvest, rinse and pat dry like lettuce or spinach; refrigerate if not using immediately. Cut out the central stalk and use the leaves as fresh greens for salads, or steam as you would spinach. Add freshly chopped greens to any appropriate soup for a garden-fresh taste. Chop the central stem or stalk into convenient-size pieces and steam like asparagus or celery. Serve with your favorite salad dressing, covered with bread crumbs, or with grated cheese. Marinate leftover stalks overnight for a salad or appetizers.

COMMON PROBLEMS
Slugs and snails, cutworms, leaf miners; occasionally rabbits, woodchucks, and deer; free of most diseases.

ALL ABOUT TOMATOES

If you don't plant anything else, you should plant tomatoes—a few different varieties at the very least. There is a huge selection available, some specifically suited to eating, juicing, cooking, or canning. They're available in early, midseason, and late types in different colors ranging from red and pink to orange and yellow. Size also varies from the small cherry tomato to the extra-large 4-pound types that win awards at the county fair.

When choosing varieties, it's very important to consider whether they are pest and disease resistant. Resistant varieties are labeled VFN—V indicates the plant is resistant to *Verticillium* wilt; F is for *Fusarium* wilt; and N is for nematodes, which are tiny, tiny worms that infect roots. There are some very good nonresistant traditional varieties, but when growing these you do run the risk of losing your plants virtually overnight if a disease problem strikes.

The resistant varieties taste great and also mature in early season, midseason, or late season. Usually the early-season fruits are best suited to the colder climates in the north. If you live in a longer-season climate, you can grow a few different varieties that will produce all season long.

Tomatoes have two different growth habits: determinate and indeterminate. Determinate types produce their crop in one short period, while indeterminate

TOMATOES

BOTANICAL INFORMATION
Latin Name: *Solanum lycopersicum*
Height: 3' (bush); 6' (vine)
Spacing: 1 per 4 square feet (bush); 1 per square foot (vine)
EDIBLE SEASON
Summer

Seed to Harvest/Flower: 17 weeks
Seed Storage: 4 to 5 years
Weeks to Maturity: 11 weeks
Indoor Seed Starting: 6 weeks before last spring frost
Earliest Outdoor Planting: NA
Earliest Outdoor Planting: immediately after last spring frost
Additional Plantings: NA
Last Planting: NA

types will continue producing in a gradual manner over many weeks. Most determinate tomatoes are bush types with plants no more than about 3 feet tall. Most indeterminate tomatoes are vining types that will put out prodigious amounts of growth and require substantial staking or support by sturdy cages. Indeterminate types grow the biggest tomatoes, take the longest to mature, and will last until frost kills them.

STARTING

- **Location:** Full sun.
- **Seeds Indoors:** Seeds sprout in 1 week at 70°F. Sprinkle five or so of each variety you want to grow in individual cups filled with vermiculite 6 weeks before your last spring frost. Just barely cover with vermiculite and water; move to full sunlight as soon as the first shoots appear, then pot up in seedling trays or individual pots as soon as the plants are large enough (usually 1 to 3 weeks). Keep a careful watch over the plants, especially after transplanting them into seedling trays, because any check or stoppage of the growth will affect the ultimate bearing capacity of the plant.

- **Transplanting:** Harden off transplants for 1 to 2 weeks, and plant outside on or after your frost-free date. Plant one vine-type plant per square foot. Bush types are planted in the center of 9-square-foot area; they take up so much room that many gardeners grow only vine-type varieties. Water and cover with a plastic-covered wire cage for protection from the cold and wind. Leave the cage on until the plants are at least 18 inches tall and pushing at the top.
- **Seeds Outdoors:** The season is too short in most regions to start tomatoes from seeds outdoors.

GROWING

- **Watering:** Keep water off the plant leaves.
- **Maintenance:** Prune off side branches (suckers) weekly for vine types and guide plant tops up through netting. Prune off dead or yellow lower leaves. Keep adding mulch as the season gets hotter.

HARVESTING

- **How:** Gently twist and pull ripe tomatoes so the stem breaks (if it's ripe it should easily break away) or, even better, cut the stem so as not to disturb the rest of the remaining fruit.
- **When:** Harvest fruit as soon as it's fully red on the vine or pick them 1 or 2 days before full redness and allow to ripen completely indoors on the countertop. If you leave them on the vine too long, they will turn soft and mushy, so inspect daily.

PREPARING AND USING

Tomatoes can be used in a multitude of ways. You can enjoy plate after plate of sliced tomatoes seasoned with lots of pepper, or with freshly harvested basil, some olive oil, and balsamic vinegar. Try pouring your favorite salad dressing over that same dish of sliced tomatoes. Soak a plate full in vinegar overnight for the next day's treat. Add thick slices of fresh tomatoes to any casserole and enjoy a flavor not experienced the rest of the year. If you have a lot of tomatoes, use them fresh in cooking instead of canned tomatoes.

COMMON PROBLEMS

Cutworm, whitefly, and the big, bad but beautiful tomato horn worm; various wilt diseases

VEGETABLES

Name	Family	Height	Spacing per Square Foot	Growing Season	Weeks from Seed to Harvest	Years You Can Store Seeds
Asparagus	Lily	4-6 feet	1 or 4	spring, summer	3 years	3
Bean, Bush	Pulse	12-18 inches	9	summer	8	3-4
Bean, Pole	Pulse	4-7 feet	8	summer	10	3-4
Beet	Goosefoot	12 inches	large-9 small-16	spring, summer, fall	8	4-5
Broccoli	Mustard	18-24 inches	1	spring, fall	16	5-6
Cabbage	Mustard	12-18 inches	1	spring, fall	16	5-6
Carrot	Carrot	12 inches	16	spring, summer, fall, winter*	10	3-4
Cauliflower	Mustard	18-24 inches	1	spring, fall	14	5-6
Chard, Swiss	Goosefoot	12-18 inches	4	spring, summer, fall, winter*	8	4-5
Corn	Grass	5-6 feet	4	summer	9-13	1-2
Cucumber	Gourd	vine	2	summer	9	5-6
Eggplant	Nightshade	24-30 inches	1	summer	19	5-6
Lettuce	Composite	6-12 inches	4	spring, summer*, fall, winter*	7	5-6
Melon	Gourd	vine	1 per 2 sq. ft.	summer	12	5-6
Okra	Lily	18-24 inches	1	summer	12	2
Onion	Lily	12 inches	16	spring, summer	20	1-2
Parsley	Carrot	6-12 inches	4	spring, summer, fall, winter*	14	2-3
Pea, Sugar Snap	Pulse	vine	8	spring, fall	10	3-4
Pepper	Nightshade	12-24 inches	1	summer	19	4-5
Potato	Nightshade	12-24 inches	4	spring, summer, fall	12	Plant last year's potatoes
Radish	Mustard	6-12 inches	16	spring, summer*, fall	4	5-6
Spinach	Goosefoot	6-12 inches	9	spring, fall, winter*	7	5-6
Strawberry	Rose	6-12 inches	4	spring, fall	perennial	Use plants

VEGETABLES (continued)

Name	Family	Height	Spacing per Square Foot	Growing Season	Weeks from Seed to Harvest	Years You Can Store Seeds
Summer Squash	Gourd	bush vine	1 per 9 sq. ft. 1 per 2 sq. ft.	summer	8	5-6
Winter Squash	Gourd	vine	1 per 2 sq. ft.	summer	12	5-6
Tomato	Nightshade	bush vine	1 per 9 sq. ft. 1 per 1 sq. ft.	summer	17	4-5

HERBS

Name	Family	Height	Spacing per Square Foot	Growing Season	Weeks from Seed to Harvest	Years You Can Store Seeds
Basil	Mint	1-2 feet	small-4 large-1	summer	12	5
Chive	Lily	6-12 inches	16	late spring, summer	16	2
Cilantro	Umbellifer	1-2 feet	1	late spring, summer	5 (leaves) 12 (seeds)	N/A
Mint	Mint	1-3 feet	1	spring, summer, fall	N/A	N/A
Oregano	Mint	1-2 feet	1	spring, summer, fall	16	N/A

FLOWERS

Name	Family	Height	Spacing per Square Foot	Growing Season	Weeks from Seed to Harvest	Years You Can Store Seeds
Dahlia	Daisy	1-3 feet	small-4 medium-1	summer, fall	10-12	2-3
Dusty Miller	Daisy	12-18 inches	4	late spring, summer, fall	15	N/A
Marigold	Daisy	6-12 inches 1½-3 feet	dwarf-4, large-1	summer, fall	10	2-3
Pansy	Viola	6-9 inches	4	spring, summer (if cool), fall	20	N/A
Petunia	Nightshade	6-18 inches	4	late spring, summer, early fall	14	N/A
Salvia	Mint	1-2 feet	4	late spring, summer, early fall	14	1 (use fresh seed)

*In some parts of the country and under certain weather conditions, these can be grown in this season.
N/A = Not advised to store seed.

APPENDIX 1

EDIBLES AT A GLANCE

NAME	HEIGHT	SPACING PER SQUARE FOOT	EDIBLE SEASON	WEEKS FROM SEED TO HARVEST	SEED STORAGE
Asparagus (*Asparagus officinalis*)	To 5'	1	Spring, early summer	2 to 3 yrs.	NA
Basil (*Ocimum basilicum*)	1 to 2'	1 or 4	Summer	12	2 yrs.
Beans (*Phaseolus vulgaris*)	12 to 18" (bush); to 7' (pole) 9	8 to 10	Summer	3 to 4 yrs.	2 yrs.
Beets (*Beta vulgaris*)	12"	9 or 16	Spring to fall	8	4 to 5 yrs.
Bok Choy (*Brassica rapa* subsp. *Chinensis*)	1 to 2'	4	Fall	6 to 7	4 yrs.
Broccoli (*Brassica oleracea* var. *italica*)	18 to 24"	1	Spring, fall	16	5 to 6 yrs.
Brussels Sprouts (*Brassica oleracea* var. *gemmifera*)	2½'	1	Spring to fall	20	4 yrs.
Cabbage (*Brassica oleracea* var. *capitata*)	12 to 18"	1	Spring, fall	16	5 to 6 yrs.
Carrots (*Daucus carata* subsp. *sativus*)	12"	16	Spring to fall	10	3 to 4 yrs.
Cauliflower (*Brassica oleracea* var. *botrytis*)	18 to 24"	1	Spring, fall	14	5 to 6 yrs.
Celery (*Apium graveolens*)	12 to 16"	4	Spring to fall	12 to 14	4 to 5 yrs.
Chives (*Allium schoeneprasum*)	6 to 12"	16	Late spring, summer	16	2 yrs.
Cilantro (*Coriandrum sativum*)	1 to 2'	1	Late spring, summer	5 (leaves)	12 (seeds)
Collard Greens (*Brassica oleracea*)	2 to 3'	1	Spring to winter	8 to 10	6 yrs.
Corn (*Zea mays*)	5 to 6'	4	Summer	9 to 13	1 to 2 yrs.
Cucumber (*Cucumis savinus*)	Vine	2	Summer	9	5 to 6 yrs.
Dill (*Anethum graveolens*)	3'	1	Summer	5	4 to 5 yrs.
Eggplant (*Solanum melongena*)	24 to 30"	1	Summer	19	5 to 6 yrs.
Fennel Herb (*Foeniculum vulgare*)	30 to 72"	1	Spring to fall	6	5 to 6 yrs.
Garlic (*Allium sativum*)	18 to 24"	9	Summer, fall	12	No
Kale (*Brassica oleracea* var. *sabellica*)	10 to 24"	2	Spring, fall	6	4 yrs.

NAME	HEIGHT	SPACING PER SQUARE FOOT	EDIBLE SEASON	WEEKS FROM SEED TO HARVEST	SEED STORAGE
Kohlrabi (*Brassioca oleracea* var. *gongylodes*)	12 to 18"	9	Spring, fall	4 to 5	3 yrs.
Leaf Lettuce (*Latuca sativa*)	6 to 12"	4	Spring, fall, winter	7	5 to 6 yrs.
Leeks (*Allium ampeloprasum porrum*)	24"	9	Fall	14	2 yrs.
Melons (*Cucumis melo*)	Vine	1 per 2 squares	Summer	12	5 to 6 yrs.
Mint (*Mentha* spp.)	1 to 3'	1	Summer	NA	NA
Mustard Greens (*Brassica juncea*)	20 to 24"	16	Spring, fall	4	4 yrs.
Okra (*Abelmoschus esculentus*)	18 to 24"	1	Summer	12	2 yrs.
Onions (*Allium cepa*)	12"	16	Summer, fall	20	1 to 2 yrs.
Oregano (*Origanum vulgare*)	1 to 2'	1	Spring to fall	16	NA
Parsley (*Petroselinum crispum*)	6 to 12"	4	Spring to winter	14	2 to 3 yrs.
Parsnips (*Pastinaca sativa*)	10 to 15"	4	Fall	15 to 17	No
Peas (Sugar Snap) (*Pisum sativum*)	Vine	8	Spring, fall	10	3 to 4 yrs.
Peppers (*Capiscum* spp.)	12 to 24"	1	Summer	19	4 to 5 yrs.
Potatoes (*Solanum tuberosum*)	12 to 24"	4	Spring to fall	12	NA
Pumpkins, Winter Squash (*Cucurbita* spp.; pumpkins are *Curcurbita pepo*)	Vine	1 per 2 squares	Summer to fall	12	5 to 6 yrs.
Radishes (*Raphanus raphanisturm* subsp. *sativus*)	6 to 12"	16	Spring to fall	4	5 to 6 yrs.
Spinach (*Spinacia oleracea*)	6 to 12"	9	Spring, fall, winter	7	5 to 6 yrs.
Strawberries (*Fragaria* × *ananassa*)	6 to 12"	4	Spring, fall	NA	NA
Squash/Zucchini (*Cucurbita pepo*; zucchini is *Cucurbita pepo* var. *cylindrica*)	Bush or Vine	1 (bush), 1 per 2 (vine)	Summer	8	5 to 6 yrs.
Swiss Chard (*Beta vulgaris* subsp. *vulgaris*)	12 to 18"	4	Spring to winter	8	4 to 5 yrs.
Tomatoes (*Solanum lycopersicum*)	3' (bush); 6' (vine)	1 per 4 squares (bush)	Summer	17	4 to 5 yrs.

PLANTING CHARTS

GERMINATION TIMES AND SOIL TEMPERATURES

This chart shows the number of days required for vegetable seeds to sprout at different soil temperatures.

CROP	32°F	41°F	50°F	59°F	68°F	77°F	86°F	95°F
Beans	0	0	0	16	11	8	6	6
Beets	—	42	17	10	6	5	5	5
Cabbage	—	—	15	9	6	5	4	—
Carrots	0	51	17	10	7	6	6	9
Cauliflower	—	—	20	10	6	5	5	—
Corn	0	0	22	12	7	4	4	3
Cucumbers	0	0	0	13	6	4	3	3
Eggplant	—	—	—	—	13	8	5	—
Lettuce	49	15	7	4	3	2	3	0
Muskmelons	—	—	—	—	8	4	3	—
Onions	136	31	13	7	5	4	4	13
Parsley	—	—	29	17	14	13	12	—
Peas	—	36	14	9	8	6	6	—
Peppers	0	0	0	25	13	8	6	9
Radishes	0	29	11	6	4	4	3	—
Spinach	63	23	12	7	6	5	6	0
Tomatoes	0	0	43	14	8	6	6	9

0 = Little or no germination   — = Not tested

Adapted from J. F. Harrington Agricultural Extension Leaflet, 1954.

PERCENTAGE OF GERMINATION

This chart indicates the percentage of normal vegetable seedlings produced at different temperatures.

CROP	32°F	41°F	50°F	59°F	68°F	77°F	86°F	95°F
Beans	0	0	1	97	90	97	47	39
Cabbage	0	27	78	93	—	99	—	—
Carrots	0	48	93	95	96	96	95	74
Corn	0	0	47	97	97	98	91	88
Cucumbers	0	0	0	95	99	99	99	99
Eggplant	—	—	—	—	21	53	60	—
Lettuce	98	98	98	99	99	99	12	0
Muskmelons	—	—	—	—	38	94	90	—
Onions	90	98	98	98	99	97	91	73
Parsley	—	—	63	—	69	64	50	—
Peas	—	89	94	93	93	94	86	0
Peppers	0	0	1	70	96	98	95	70
Radishes	0	42	76	97	95	97	95	—
Spinach	83	96	91	82	52	28	32	0
Tomatoes	0	0	82	98	98	97	83	46

0 = Little or no germination   **—** = Not tested

Adapted from J. F. Harrington Agricultural Extension Leaflet, 1954.

SPRING INDOOR SEED-STARTING SCHEDULE

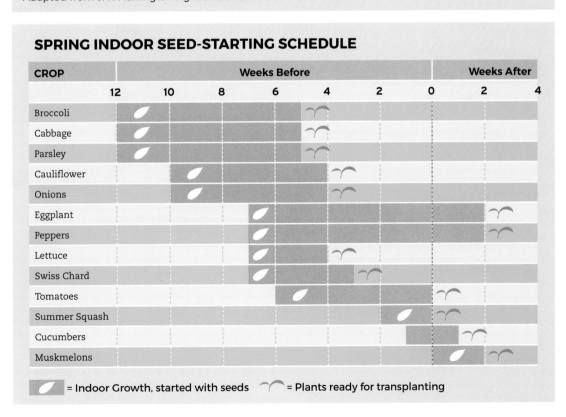

CROP	Weeks Before						Weeks After		
	12	10	8	6	4	2	0	2	4

Broccoli, Cabbage, Parsley, Cauliflower, Onions, Eggplant, Peppers, Lettuce, Swiss Chard, Tomatoes, Summer Squash, Cucumbers, Muskmelons

🌱 = Indoor Growth, started with seeds   〜 = Plants ready for transplanting

OUTDOOR PLANTING SCHEDULE FOR SPRING AND SUMMER CROPS

CROP	Weeks Before					Weeks After							
	8	6	4	2	0	2	4	6	8	10	12	14	16
VERY EARLY SPRING (4-6 weeks before last spring frost)													
Broccoli													
Cabbage													
Parsley													
Peas													
Spinach													
Cauliflower													
Lettuce (leaf)													
Lettuce (leaf)													
Onions													
EARLY SPRING (2-4 weeks before last spring frost)													
Beets													
Bok Choy													
Carrots													
Mustard Greens													
Radishes													
Swiss Chard													
Swiss Chard													
SPRING (on last frost day)													
Beans (bush)													
Beans (pole)													
Corn													
Kohlrabi													
Leeks													
Squash (summer)													
Squash (summer)													
Tomatoes													

OUTDOOR PLANTING SCHEDULE FOR SPRING AND SUMMER CROPS

CROP	Weeks Before					Weeks After							
	8	6	4	2	0	2	4	6	8	10	12	14	16
LATE SPRING (after last spring frost)													
Cucumbers						🌱(transplant)				🪣(harvest)			
Cucumbers						🌿(seed)					🪣(harvest)		
Eggplant							🌱(transplant)					🪣(harvest)	
Muskmelons							🌱(transplant)					🪣(harvest)	
Muskmelons							🌿(seed)						🪣(harvest)
Peppers							🌱(transplant)					🪣(harvest)	
Squash (winter)							🌿(seed)						🪣(harvest)

🌿 = Growth Period, started with seeds 🌱 = Growth Period, started with transplants

🪣 = Harvest Period

PLANTING SCHEDULE FOR CONTINUOUS HARVEST CROPS

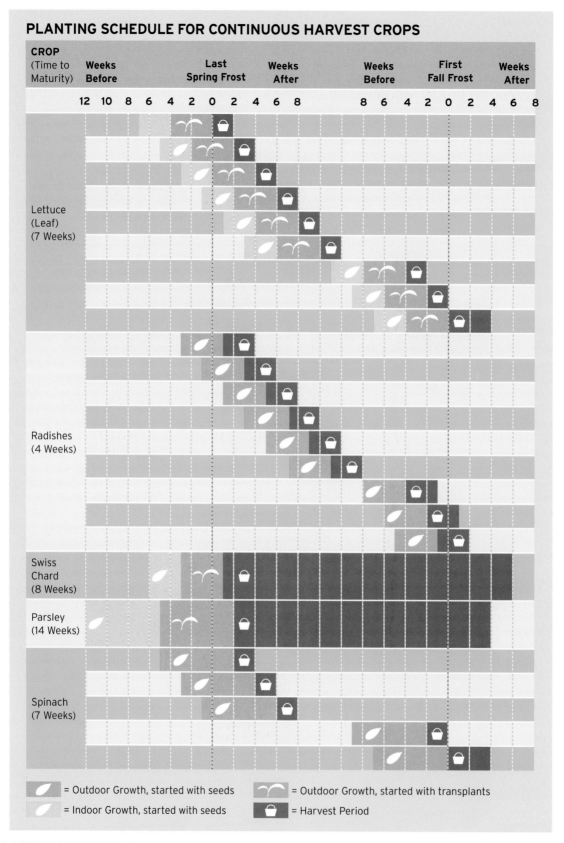

| = Outdoor Growth, started with seeds | = Outdoor Growth, started with transplants |
| = Indoor Growth, started with seeds | = Harvest Period |

PLANTING SCHEDULE FOR CONTINUOUS HARVEST CROPS

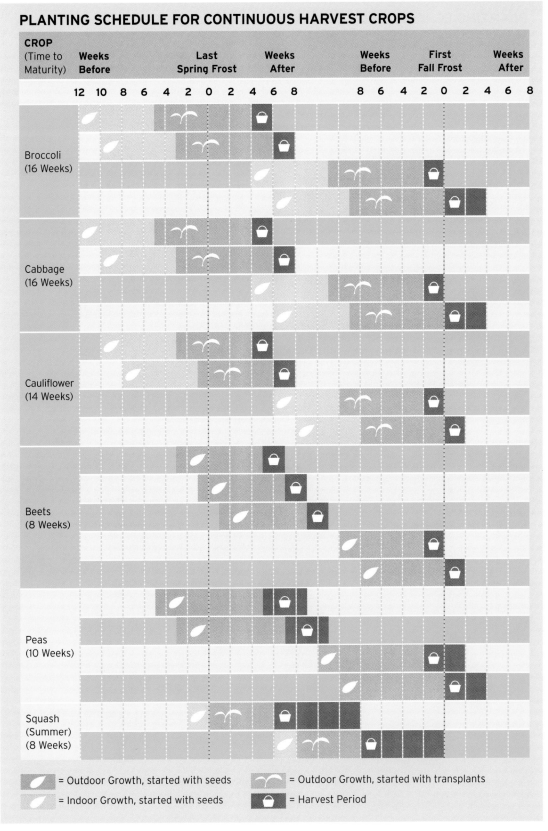

CROP (Time to Maturity)	Weeks Before					Last Spring Frost		Weeks After				Weeks Before			First Fall Frost		Weeks After		
	12	10	8	6	4	2	0	2	4	6	8	8	6	4	2	0	2	4	6	8

Broccoli (16 Weeks)

Cabbage (16 Weeks)

Cauliflower (14 Weeks)

Beets (8 Weeks)

Peas (10 Weeks)

Squash (Summer) (8 Weeks)

= Outdoor Growth, started with seeds
= Outdoor Growth, started with transplants
= Indoor Growth, started with seeds
= Harvest Period

PLANTING SCHEDULE FOR CONTINUOUS HARVEST CROPS

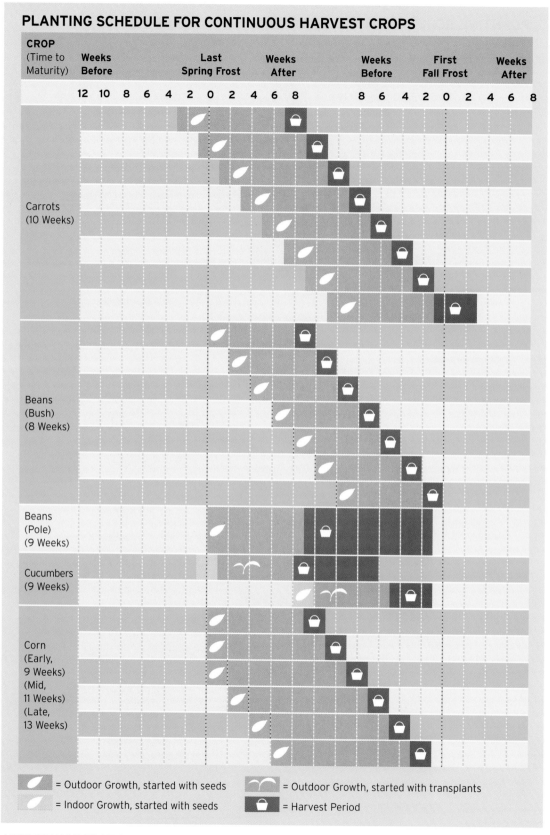

= Outdoor Growth, started with seeds

= Outdoor Growth, started with transplants

= Indoor Growth, started with seeds

= Harvest Period

PLANTING SCHEDULE FOR CONTINUOUS HARVEST CROPS

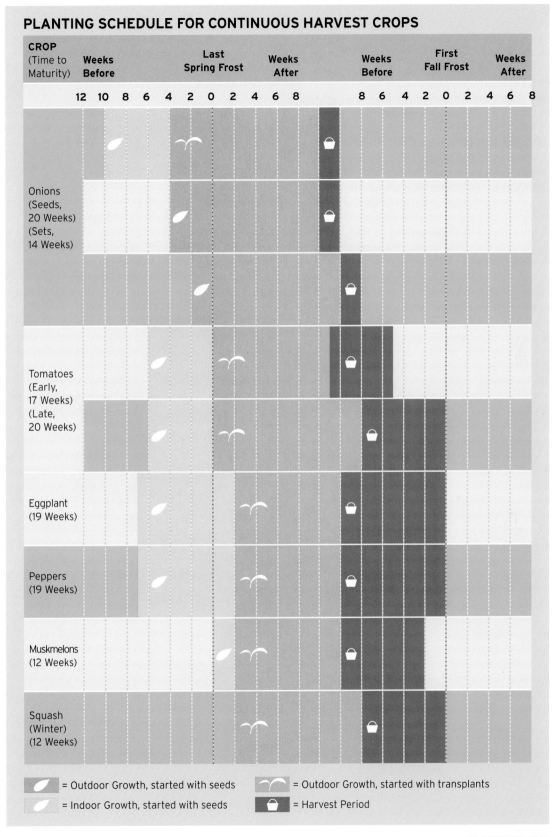

CROP (Time to Maturity)

| Weeks Before | Last Spring Frost | Weeks After | Weeks Before | First Fall Frost | Weeks After |

12 10 8 6 4 2 0 2 4 6 8   8 6 4 2 0 2 4 6 8

Onions (Seeds, 20 Weeks) (Sets, 14 Weeks)

Tomatoes (Early, 17 Weeks) (Late, 20 Weeks)

Eggplant (19 Weeks)

Peppers (19 Weeks)

Muskmelons (12 Weeks)

Squash (Winter) (12 Weeks)

= Outdoor Growth, started with seeds

= Outdoor Growth, started with transplants

= Indoor Growth, started with seeds

= Harvest Period

PLANTING SCHEDULE FOR FALL CROPS

CROP	Weeks to Maturity	Weeks Before								First Fall Frost	Weeks After		
		16	14	12	10	8	6	4	2	0	2	4	6
Broccoli	16												
Brussels Sprouts	5												
Cabbage	16												
Cauliflower	14												
Carrots	11												
Kale	10												
Mustard Greens	6												
Parsnips	16												
Peas	10												
Beets	8												
Lettuce	7												
Spinach	7												
Radishes	4												

= Outdoor Growth, started with seeds
= Outdoor Growth, started with transplants
= Indoor Growth, started with seeds
= Harvest Period

PHOTO CREDITS

Alachua County (Flickr): 20 (top left)

Andy Walker (Flickr): 20 (top right)

Bill Kersey: 35, 36, 37, 38, 39, 41, 42, 43, 62, 63 (all), 64 (all), 65 (all), 86 (both)

Bob Markey: 68, 204

GAP Photos: 2

Greg Jensen: 200

iStock: 212

J. Paul Moore: 8, 28, 34 (bottom left), 52, 99, 100 (top left), 101 (bottom right), 109 (bottom left), 113 (all), 115 (all), 145 (all), 154 (all), 168 (left), 178 (top right), 187 (top left)

LDI: 129, 156, 195, 213, 215, 218, 236, 246, 247, 249, 252, 253

Melanie Powell: 47, 89, 96, 123

Neil Soderstrom: 153

Paul Markert: 18 (bottom), 24, 31, 34 (top left), 61, 74 (bottom right), 82-85, 87 (both), 88 (both), 90, 92 (top), 93 (all), 100 (middle and bottom left, right), 101 (top, bottom left), 102-105, 111 (all), 112, 114, 116, 117 (all), 119 (all), 122 (top right), 124, 127, 128, 134, 135, 137, 139, 140 (all), 141 (bottom), 159, 160, 161, 162, 167, 172, 173 (all), 175 (all), 178 (bottom left and right), 179 (all), 180, 181 (both)

pdbreen (Flickr): 20 (bottom right), 33 (top)

Shutterstock: 17, 19 (both), 20 (bottom left), 27, 33 (bottom), 56 (all), 57 (all), 74 (bottom left), 121, 164, 168 (right), 176, 182, 187 (bottom left), 189, 191, 198, 208, 210, 211, 214, 216, 217, 219, 220, 221, 222, 223, 224, 225, 226, 227, 228, 229, 230, 231, 232, 234, 235, 237, 238, 240, 241, 242, 243, 244, 245, 248, 250, 254

Square Foot Gardening Foundation: 12, 44

Tracy Walsh: 122 (bottom left, both)

INDEX

A

accessories, 38, 118
air temperatures
  for cold storage, 194
  frost, 147–148, 193, 195
  and germination rate, 148, 152
aisles
  in community gardens, 202
  options for covering, 123
  width, 33, 66
animals. *See* pests
annual output, 22
archways, 110–111, 112
asbestos, 135
Ashoka's Youth Venture, 203
asparagus, 146, 210

B

balconies, 66
Bartholomew, Mel, 13, 14, 24–27, 28
Basic Sampler Garden, 53
basil, 211
beans, 161, 212
beets, 57, 213
beginners, 14, 46, 147
bok choy, 214
boxes, 37. *See also* grid system
  accessibility, 18, 19, 64, 67
  bottoms, 77
  configurations, 64, 65, 75, 86–87
  construction, 71, 74, 78–79
  depth, 33, 76–77, 87
  drainage, 61, 77
  elevated, 19, 82–85
  finishings, 77
  joinery, 74
  location in yard, 31, 60–62
  materials, 73, 88
  positioning, 66
  yield by square feet, 46
bricks, 61, 73, 88, 123
broccoli, 56, 215
brussels sprouts, 56, 216
bush beans, 161, 212
butt joints, 71

C

cabbage, 217
Canning Garden, 54
Captain Planet Foundation, 203
carrots, 57, 161, 195, 218
cauliflower, 219
celery, 220
Certified Instructors, 204

cherry tomatoes, 160–161
children
  best plants for, 160–161
  boxes for, 18, 75, 160
  gardening with, 67, 158–159
  teaching through gardening, 68,
    163, 204–205, 207
chives, 221
Christmas ideas, 197
churches, 200, 205
cilantro, 222
climate, 22, 147, 192, 195
coconut coir, 134
cold air drainage, 195
cold storage, 194
collard greens, 57, 223
community gardens
  conventional types, 26, 205
  dos and don'ts, 202–203
  features, 68
  garden layouts, 68, 201
  grants for, 203
  liability insurance, 203
  locations for, 67, 200, 201
  return on investment, 200
  setting guidelines, 68, 202
  success story, 205
  vandalism, 202
composite materials, 73, 88
compost
  buying, 127, 132–133
  characteristics of, 127, 129, 132
  decomposition processes, 128
  ideal conditions for, 130
  ingredients, 128, 130, 131
  making your own, 128–129
  municipal supplies, 133
  replenishing, 39, 169
  turning, 132
  volume, 129
compost bins, 120–121, 122
concrete blocks, 73, 88
corn, 161, 224
county extension agents, 176
covers, 38, 192
  commercial types, 193
  covered-wagon supports,
    114–115
  crop cages, 116–117
  domes, 112–113
  as pest barriers, 106, 113, 116,
    178
  wire cages, 106–109
crops. *See* vegetables

cucumber, 225
Culinary Herb Garden, 54

D

deck gardens, 65, 66, 87
decorative archways, 112
designs. *See* garden layouts
digging, 126, 166
dill, 226
diseases
  in compost, 128, 181
  and crop rotation, 189
  fungal, 181
  and plant diversity, 34, 49, 144,
    180
  removal of diseased plants,
    180–181
  transmission, 181, 186
domes, 112–113, 193
drainage
  bottom of boxes, 67, 77
  of growing medium, 126, 127,
    171
  yards, 61

E

Easy-to-Grow Garden, 53
eggplant, 227
electrical conduit, 98, 99, 118
elevated gardens, 19, 67
  assembly, 84–85
  materials, 82
  preparation, 83

F

fall crops, 148, 193, 195, 196
fennel, 228
fertilizers, 14, 68, 168–169
flowers, 49, 168, 257
food banks, 200, 205
frost, 147–148, 193, 195

G

garden layouts, 36. *See also* yards
  community gardens, 68, 201
  mapping squares, 23, 47, 49,
    50–51
  practical setups, 16–21
  sample designs, 53–55
garden tools, 165, 166, 167
garlic, 229
greenhouses, 89, 192
green methods, 42
grid system